The Assault on Diversity

The Assault on Diversity

*An Organized Challenge to Racial
and Gender Justice*

LEE COKORINOS

With a Foreword by Hon. Harold R. Tyler, Jr. and
an Introduction by Theodore M. Shaw

ROWMAN & LITTLEFIELD PUBLISHERS, INC.
Lanham • Boulder • New York • Oxford

ROWMAN & LITTLEFIELD PUBLISHERS, INC.

Published in the United States of America
by Rowman & Littlefield Publishers, Inc.
A Member of the Rowman & Littlefield Publishing Group
4501 Forbes Boulevard, Suite 200, Lanham, Maryland 20706
www.rowmanlittlefield.com

P.O. Box 317, Oxford OX2 9RU, United Kingdom

Copyright © 2003 by the Institute for Democracy Studies

British Library Cataloguing in Publication Information Available

Library of Congress Cataloging-in-Publication Data Available

ISBN 0-7425-2475-2 (cloth : alk. paper)
ISBN 0-7425-2476-0 (pbk. : alk. paper)

Printed in the United States of America

♾™ The paper used in this publication meets the minimum requirements of American National Standard for Information Sciences—Permanence of Paper for Printed Library Materials, ANSI/NISO Z39.48-1992.

Contents

Foreword

As a founding board member of the Institute for Democracy Studies, I believe this volume represents an important milestone.

Some forty years ago I had the privilege of serving as assistant attorney general in charge of the Civil Rights Division of the Department of Justice under President Eisenhower. After serving for almost twelve years as United States district judge for the Southern District of New York, I returned to the Justice Department under President Ford as deputy attorney general. Whatever role I played, whatever administration I served, I was always keenly aware that ours was a great nation that could only be made greater by healing our wounds from within.

The strides in civil rights over these past forty years are a matter of national record, and a source of national pride. Legally, socially, even spiritually we have traveled a great way from those earlier years of racial conflict and division. As with any great cause, the gains were hard-won, with enormous sacrifices from men and women of every color. But we prevailed—as a nation, as a people.

Today, even as we celebrate the triumph of justice over injustice, tolerance over intolerance, we hear troubling new voices that threaten all that we have gained and all that we hold dear. As one who has lived and worked through the decades of turmoil and struggle, these voices trouble me deeply.

The Assault on Diversity reminds us that the battle for equality in America is never finally and permanently won; that it must be fought time and time again by each succeeding generation. The form and manner of the assault on our democratic system are different from those of forty years ago. The burning crosses and angry mobs are gone. In their stead are high-profile attorneys and well-financed organizations. But the intent is very much the same: to deny the full benefits of America to some segments of our society.

I am proud to have been associated with the legacy that we know as the civil rights movement, and I am proud of the Institute for Democracy Studies for publishing this very important study.

Hon. Harold R. Tyler, Jr.

Introduction

In 1980, when Ronald Reagan was elected president of the United States, I was a young lawyer in the Civil Rights Division of the Justice Department. In the months to come the Reagan administration considered a series of individuals for assistant attorney general for civil rights before settling on William Bradford Reynolds. Reynolds, a tax lawyer, had served a stint in the Solicitor General's office during which he had argued a civil rights case or two, but otherwise had no experience that qualified him for the job.

One day, between his nomination and confirmation, Reynolds visited the various sections of the Civil Rights Division to introduce himself. When I questioned him about his reasons for taking the job, he responded that he had had a lifetime commitment to civil rights. If so, it was not apparent before his tenure in the Civil Rights Division, and it has not been apparent since. During his tenure Reynolds became the Reagan administration's point person for the assault on school desegregation, affirmative action, and other pet targets of the far right. Under his wing he developed a cadre of assistant attorneys general and others who worked tirelessly to turn civil rights enforcement on its head. In time these individuals would go on to establish right-wing policy institutes and legal defense funds that sustained the attack on affirmative action; one, with almost no litigation experience, was successfully nominated to a federal circuit court. He is now the chief judge and the court is perceived to be the most conservative in the nation.

In the early days of the Reagan Justice Department, I was among a group of career lawyers who were in conflict with Reynolds and his associates on the division's attempt to withdraw from school desegregation cases and on the department's reversal, in *Bob Jones University v. IRS,* of a well-established governmental policy of denying tax-exempt status to private schools that practiced racial discrimination. It became clear that my days at the Justice Department were numbered.

My deliverer came in the person of Jack Greenberg, then director-counsel of the NAACP Legal Defense and Educational Fund, who hired me in early 1982. During the last twenty years I have witnessed the growth of an ultraconservative network of lawyers, judges, and organizations committed to reversing what they perceived to be the wrongheaded policies and practices of the civil rights era, especially school desegregation and affirmative action in employment and higher education.

I have always been puzzled by individuals who were missing in action during the struggles against discrimination directed at racial minorities, and who later became zealous opponents of affirmative action, arguing passionately that white people—who continue to occupy the overwhelming majority of positions of privilege in the United States—are now the victims of the most insidious forms of racial discrimination. Taken at their word, which some of these anti-affirmative action crusaders surely must be, they are truly offended by any measure that is race conscious because they believe that race consciousness is inherently offensive and dangerous. But why now, when the race-conscious measures they oppose are aimed at finally including those who have been excluded because of race? Why devote so much of one's time, money, resources, indeed life's energy to fighting so passionately against affirmative action when so much racial inequality, as a consequence of our nation's long history of white supremacy, remains intact?

And then there are the others: those who actually believe in the stuff of racism. They have learned to cloak what they believe and what they do in the language of nondiscrimination and color blindness. They have appropriated the vision and the language of the civil rights movement and have turned fact and history on their heads. And they have found shelter and sanctuary among those who oppose affirmative action in good faith. Try as I might, I have never with certainty been able to separate the intellectual and ideological descendants of white supremacy proponents from the good faith affirmative action opponents. Even David Duke claims not to be a racist, and I am not capable of peering into anyone's heart or of reading minds. I can only judge individuals by their deeds.

Whatever their intent, those who have been leading the assault on affirmative action have been more organized, better funded, and more deliberate than we knew twenty years ago. In *The Assault on Diversity: An Organized Challenge to Racial and Gender Justice*, the Institute for Democracy Studies has exposed this part of the far-right matrix in a manner that boggles the mind. The result is the illumination of a network of anti-affirmative action activists who have been fighting effectively in the courts of law and of public opinion, with the goal of reversing much of what constitutes the corpus of civil rights law and ending the practices that have opened the doors of opportunity to women and to people of color.

One does not have to master every intricacy of this exquisitely detailed matrix to conclude that the anti-affirmative action forces are formidable. Affirmative action opponents will inevitably take issue with their portrait in this book, but the sheer weight of the research presented shifts the terrain of the affirmative action battle. This is a book that cannot be ignored. The extensive proportions of the anti-diversity movement serve as a wake-up call to the naive, the uninformed, and the willfully blind. If the civil rights movement was a revolution that transformed the United States into a more inclusive society, the counterrevolution is here. Here is its road map.

Theodore M. Shaw
Associate Director-Counsel
NAACP Legal Defense and Educational Fund, Inc.
New York, NY

Acknowledgments

The work of many people went into the making of this book. First and foremost, I want to thank IDS President Alfred F. Ross for striving indefatigably to create a unique institution where high caliber research can be brought together with a passionate commitment to social justice. Alfred's steady faith in the importance of this project reflects his long-standing personal commitment to the values of the civil rights movement.

I express my gratitude to Julie R. F. Gerchik, for her contribution to the book in preparing sections on Pacific Legal Foundation and Southeastern Legal Foundation, as well as her other suggestions on the manuscript. Yvonne Nix helped enormously with the initial research on Southeastern Legal Foundation.

Communications Director John Tessitore heroically assumed stewardship of the manuscript in midstream with a skill, grace, and warmth that makes his legendary status at the United Nations Association, from where he joined us, all the more understandable.

Special thanks go to René Redwood, Barbara Arnwine, and Diane Gross, who have been a source of great encouragement from the outset of this project.

Thanks also to the wonderful team of hardworking interns who contributed their time and talent, including Anurima Bhargava, Grace Bonilla, Linda Cho, Allison Feder, Natalie Hwang, Jason Heller, Loren Jacobson, Connie Montoya, Yvonne Nix, David Roseth, Marco Roth, and David Yocis. Thanks also to Laura Flanders for her important contribution, to Tanya Melich for some acute suggestions, and to IDS's Martina Pomeroy for providing research support.

A debt of gratitude is owed to Lee Mickle and her team of copyeditors at EEI, and to our colleagues at Rowman & Littlefield Publishers for their consummate professionalism, in particular Executive Editor Jennifer Knerr.

Thanks also to my wife, Sarah Murison, and daughter, Erica, for their long-suffering patience as this book neared its completion.

Finally, many thanks to those more senior hands who, while fighting for freedom many years ago, also gave our country the gift of the civil rights movement. In countless ways researching and writing this book has been a work of intergenerational collaboration—yet another inspiring example of diversity at work. I hope that in some small way it will be considered partial repayment from a grateful generation determined to carry on their work in spite of the challenges ahead.

Lee Cokorinos

Chapter 1

The New Threat to Diversity

> The court believes that the attainment of a racially diverse student body is not a compelling state interest.
> —Hon. Bernard A. Friedman, U.S. District Court (Mich.)[1]

> Demands for affirmative action, redistributive taxation, expansion of social welfare, and other transfers of wealth and influence are all rooted, we should not forget, in the dogma that poverty is due to exploitation of the poor by the less poor, and the non-white "minorities" by the white "majority"—never in any significant part to cultural deficiencies or lower IQ.
> —Roger Pearson, *Race, Intelligence, and Bias in Academe*[2]

> This country is going so far to the right you won't recognize it.
> —John N. Mitchell, Attorney General to President Richard M. Nixon[3]

This is a book about one of the most audacious, sustained attempts to turn back the clock on social justice in recent American history. As we begin the twenty-first century, the historic efforts by American institutions to implement racial and gender diversity policies are in danger of succumbing to what the far right has called a "permanent revolution."[4]

While there is broad national consensus that practical steps are necessary to achieve a fair and diverse society, people always have held differences of opin-

1

ion about how best to achieve those ends. Today those differences are being exploited by a political movement that can oppose not only the means, but also the very goal of diversity itself.[5] With the coming to power of the George W. Bush administration, those who have built up the organizational and political capacities of this movement for over a generation have gained newfound leverage over government enforcement of civil rights policies while maintaining control of the private organizations filing the constitutional litigation challenging them.[6]

It was not by chance that Theodore Olson was appointed solicitor general of the United States by Bush after Olson won the *Bush v. Gore* electoral case in the Supreme Court.[7] Olson, the former president of the Washington, D.C., chapter of the Federalist Society, boasted the best of "movement credentials" for the job. Olson while in California chaired California Lawyers for Reagan, and then went on to serve as President Reagan's first assistant attorney general in charge of the strategically central Office of Legal Counsel in the Department of Justice. He argued the landmark *Hopwood* (University of Texas) case that ended affirmative action throughout the Fifth Circuit, represented one of the Los Angeles police officers in the racial beating of Rodney King, and argued the *Virginia Military Institute* case in the Supreme Court in defense of the right to discriminate against women. Indeed the legal battles around the contested Florida results of the 2000 election were fought and won by Federalist Society-affiliated attorneys, such as Olson, Michael Carvin (chair, Civil Rights Practice Group), Douglas R. Cox and Alex Azar (Federalism Practice Group), Timothy Flanigan (a recipient of Federalist Society funds for research and a former member of the Program Committee under Ted Olson), Ted Cruz (Religious Liberties Practice Group), and James Bopp, Jr. (Free Speech and Election Law Practice Group).

The purpose of this volume is to illustrate in a precise way the enormous scope of the social, political, and monetary network that is moving a national anti-civil rights agenda. This network consists of foundations, organizations, and individuals who share the common belief that government either should have no role in effecting social justice, or that its role should be circumscribed severely. Rather than a comprehensive study of the history and agendas of the anti-civil rights movement, this volume is far more modest in scope. Given the urgency of these issues brought about by a confluence of court decisions, aggressive administrative actions, and a plethora of institutions actively seeking to roll back civil rights, this book is intended to serve as a reference volume to identify and explain the backgrounds and interconnections of the key individuals and organizations involved in that effort; indeed, the index alone will serve as an invaluable tool. It therefore should be immediately useful to all those working on, or covering in the media, civil rights issues, and those who have a need to understand the vast array of players on the Right who are organized in opposition to civil rights. It also is assumed that this book will serve as a platform from which further work will spring to deepen the historical understanding of the development of the personalities, ideas, and policies that underlie the anti-civil rights movement and its very close ties to the larger right-wing political movement in the United States. Woven within this volume, for instance, the reader will find footprints of individuals such as William Bradford Reynolds, Charles Cooper, Michael Carvin, Michael McDonald, Michael Greve, and Clint Bolick, who later emerged as key strategists and activists.

Of course, it is understood that the Right will respond to this volume with cries of outrage. They will point out that just as those on the Left and in the Center are every bit as likely to work cooperatively to advance their respective agendas, they are equally entitled to promote their own political and ideological ends. And, of course, they are correct. Most important, however, is that we critically understand what the people and organizations active in public affairs stand for, why they support the positions and organizations they do, and what the realization of their vision would mean for the future of our country. On this score, the organizations of the Center and Left certainly should be willing, even proud, to bear scrutiny, and to welcome open comparison with the Right.[8]

More than competing values are at play, however. As the Right itself has taught us over recent decades, resources and access to power are critically important and the light of day should be cast upon the Right's achievements in this area. Seldom does one read or hear of the tens of millions of dollars that have gone into supporting organizations opposed to diversity policies, or of the elaborate overlapping boards of directors that guide them in a politically focused direction. Even the twenty-year-old Federalist Society, with its high-profile leadership and 25,000 members, existed in virtual anonymity until the Bush administration catapulted it to national attention.[9] Indeed, leading members of the Bush administration have been reluctant to have the extent of their ties with this movement discussed in public.[10]

Underpinning the political, intellectual, and legal attack on diversity is an agenda that lies beyond the realm of traditional conservatism, though it claims that mantle. It is the work of a relatively small cohort of figures involved in this network who, over the past two decades, have been able to surround themselves with a dense fog of think-tank-backed rhetoric. These organizations and individuals have exploited the inevitable problems of conception and implementation that go with any governmental, educational, or institutional program, and the regulations that govern it, to undermine the idea of a public commitment to diversity. By turning the very language of civil rights against itself, this movement has been able to prevent the adverse public reaction that inevitably would arise were its real agenda to be understood: the elimination of many of the central gains of the civil rights movement over the last half century.

The major institutions of society—notably business, government, and higher education—have given substance to the national consensus to redress two centuries of racial and gender imbalances. These institutions have often led the way in implementing the necessary practical steps to achieve diversity. One of those steps was affirmative action, which arose as a bipartisan, compromise solution.

Opposing those steps are many of the same people who resisted every advance in civil rights over the previous decades. After an initial period of legal uncertainty, the Supreme Court ruled in the 1978 *Bakke* decision that the consideration of race as a factor in university admissions is indeed constitutional. This and other decisions created the legal freedom for universities and businesses to define for themselves the best means for achieving and capitalizing on the benefits of diversity.

Far from conceding defeat, however, opponents of those initiatives have shifted their focus. Using affirmative action as a foil, they now seek to undermine the mainstream policy consensus around diversity programs and the ability of major American institutions to support them. As a result, many of those programs are under severe attack.

The Myth of a Popular Groundswell against Affirmative Action

Affirmative action is typically understood either as a measure adopted to correct or compensate for past or present discrimination (the "remedial" rationale) or to foster values of inclusiveness and diversity (the "diversity" rationale). Whether such measures are constitutionally permissible, for which purposes they may be adopted, and which variants of these measures are acceptable, all have been the subject of decades of litigation in the federal courts.

From a constitutional standpoint, these issues play out under the mandate— expressly applicable to the states via the Fourteenth Amendment's "Equal Protection" clause, and made applicable to the federal government by the Supreme Court via the Fifth Amendment's "Due Process" clause—of equal protection, which requires that governmental entities provide all citizens with equal protection of the laws. Historically applied in the century following the Reconstruction period merely to forbid invidious forms of discrimination intended to harm minorities, these constitutional provisions more recently have been used to support more benign governmental programs intended to assist minorities through either remedial or diversity programs. However, in recent years the Right also has availed itself of these equal protection guarantees by cynically using these provisions to attack the legal and political legitimacy of programs which once rested upon these very protections. Exemplifying this tactic, the Right increasingly has argued that these programs discriminate against white males and thus are unconstitutional.

In the Supreme Court's 1978 *Bakke* decision, the Court held that race may be taken into account in designing university admissions programs. Following the Court's plurality decision in *Bakke* there has been much debate over whether to use the remedial or diversity justification for benign affirmative action programs and which, if either, meet the required compelling state interest standard. The Court appears for the moment to have put that particular debate on hold (until the next case) with its 5-4 decision in *Adarand v. Pena*, 515 U.S. 200 (1995).[11] Writing for the majority, Justice O'Connor held that, with respect to any governmental program that classifies according to race (which necessarily includes all affirmative action programs), such "racial classifications . . . must serve a compelling governmental interest, and must be narrowly tailored to further that interest." It is this "compelling state interest" aspect (along with the narrowly tailored component) of the strict scrutiny test that is now the hot-button issue with respect to the future of affirmative action in the United States. Unless a governmental entity can satisfy the rigorous requirements of demonstrating a compelling state interest in, for example, achieving diversity in higher education, its affirmative action program necessarily will fail to pass constitutional muster.

That we are at a critical historic juncture is clearly illustrated by the fact that two federal appeals courts now stand directly opposed to one another. The Supreme Court also may confront this crucial issue in the near future if it decides whether the pro-affirmative action *Grutter* (University of Michigan) or anti-affirmative action *Hopwood* holdings should govern admissions policy at America's institutions of higher learning.[12] However, the process leading to this judicial reopening of a nation's basic principles and commitments did not occur overnight.

It is important to understand from where the opposition to affirmative action comes. In reading the preponderance of press reports, one might be left with the impression that the passage of such anti-diversity measures as California's Proposition 209 or Washington State's I-200 (described in detail below) were either a mistake—by voters casting ballots for misleadingly labeled "civil rights" initiatives they didn't understand—or a reflection of genuine popular discontent. A decade ago, a *Business Week* cover story explained the roots of that discontent in a way that was typical of the media coverage of the time: "Many whites are resentful—and blacks feel affirmative action has stalled."[13]

From such reporting, superficially it would be easy to attribute opposition to affirmative action to an economic crunch. In financially tight years, the theory goes, when jobs are scarce and average wages low, white workers become increasingly protective of their positions and impatient with morality-driven policies that seem to compromise their chances of self-advancement in the interest of racial fairness. According to this argument, people of color and women who benefited from affirmative action in the years immediately following desegregation find those gains outweighed now by the disadvantages associated with being perceived as "less able" than whites and in need of special government help.

The popular groundswell theory of opposition to affirmative action is appealing to some—and not entirely unjustified. For certain, there is genuine discontent in the country, particularly with the status quo when it comes to access to the best education and most rewarding work. The fight over affirmative action, occurring at the nexus of those two issues, does stir up people's opinions and even passions; and commercial talk radio, the Internet, and increasingly cable television provide a place to air those views in inflammatory ways.

But there are two problems with the "grassroots rebellion" version of the story. First, surveys show that the majority of Americans continue to *support* affirmative action policies for women and people of color[14] and to support government action to ensure that all races have access to schools and health care.[15] Second, it ignores the extent to which organized opposition to affirmative action is a product of coordinated, strategic political action rather than a groundswell at the grassroots level. This coordinated action is designed to affect the commitment to racial and gender diversity of both public and private institutions, and to fundamentally undermine the public support on which this commitment depends.

Key Landmarks

The backdrop to the current challenges to civil rights was forged in the critical 1973-1974 period. The right wing having lost *Brown v. Board of Education, Roe v. Wade,* and *Miranda v. Arizona* launched a number of important strategic initiatives to undermine the mainstream consensus that threatened their vision of America. This concerted effort combined the wealth of key right-wing private foundations and individuals and the talents of political strategists. One of the key historic events in this process, and to that extent an important event in American political history, was the formation of the Heritage Foundation in 1973 by wealthy (and, as important, strategically minded) hard-line conservative funders, in particular Richard Mellon Scaife, Edward Noble, and Joseph Coors.[16]

On the legal front, the Pacific Legal Foundation (PLF; see below) also was formed in 1973, the same year as Heritage, by J. Simon Fluor, the uncle of J. Robert Fluor, who at the time was a member of the Heritage board. Ultra rightist Georgia congressman Benjamin Blackburn (R-GA), who chaired the board of the Heritage Foundation from 1974-1982, founded the Southeastern Legal Foundation (based in Atlanta; see below) in 1976. As a Republican congressman from Georgia from 1967 to 1975, Blackburn strongly opposed the establishment of the Legal Services Corporation[17] and voted against what *Newsweek* magazine referred to as "every major piece of civil-rights legislation, including the 1968 Fair Housing Act."[18] Edward E. Noble, who has been identified by Edwin Feulner as one of the Heritage Foundation's three founding fathers (along with Joseph Coors and Richard M. Scaife),[19] serves on Southeastern Legal's board of trustees (see below).

Following the formation of the Heritage Foundation in 1973, a series of legal groups[20] was formed under the aegis of the Washington, D.C.-based National Legal Center for the Public Interest (NLCPI)—a conservative legal policy organization emphasizing property rights—to attempt to roll back the gains of the environmental, consumer rights, and civil rights movements. Other right-wing legal organizations that eventually came under the umbrella of NLCPI included the Mountain States Legal Foundation (Denver); the Gulf and Great Plains Legal Foundation

(Kansas City, Missouri), since renamed the Landmark Legal Foundation; the Mid-America Legal Foundation (Chicago); the New England Legal Foundation (Boston); and the Capital Legal Foundation (Washington, D.C.).[21]

Beginning in 1980, five key landmark events spanning the next two decades, while not telling the full story, stand out as markers along the path of the Right's twenty-year effort to reverse America's commitment to diversity. Running through all of them is the work of one man, Clint Bolick. Although the overall strategy to implement the assault on diversity was worked out at a higher political level—in the foundations and umbrella institutions of the Right, such as Richard Mellon Scaife's foundations and the Heritage Foundation—the twenty-year career of Clint Bolick illuminates the nature of the challenge to diversity:

- 1980: The staffing of the Reagan administration with veteran opponents of civil rights and the young trainees of the "permanent revolution."
- 1983: The initial outlining by Clint Bolick—in the pages of the far-right *Lincoln Review*—of a new strategy to assault civil rights.
- 1988: Publication of Bolick's *Changing Course: Civil Rights at the Crossroads,* which attacked the civil rights movement for supporting diversity remedies and protections, and condemned governmental action to secure them.
- 1990: The laying of the groundwork for the creation of organizations specifically dedicated to overturning the gains of the civil rights movement through a careful process of consultation and the publication of a blueprint—Bolick's *Unfinished Business: A Civil Rights Strategy for America's Third Century.*
- 1996: The refining of the rhetorical and legal strategy to use affirmative action as a wedge issue to drive the wider agenda of the far right, as crystallized in the guidebook of the anti-diversity movement, Bolick's *The Affirmative Action Fraud.*

Staffing of the Reagan Administration

In the early 1980s, the right-wing network that attacked the gains of the civil rights movement drew on the same talent pool that the white minority regime in South Africa chose to represent itself in the United States. The foremost example was the selection of *Lincoln Review* editor Jay Parker—an African American—to head the EEOC transition team responsible for civil rights in the first Reagan administration. Parker was at the forefront of the defense of the racist regime in South Africa and served as a paid political propagandist for the embassy of South Africa through his company, International Public Affairs Consultants Inc.[22] It was fresh from this position, and his work with the World Anti-Communist League (WACL),[23] that he proceeded to set up a political hatchery of young operatives, many of whom would go on to lead the attack on civil rights over the next two decades. Others built on his work as the Reagan Justice Department took shape over the next few years.

As discussed below in the section concerning the Center for Individual Rights, the Reagan legal strategy within his Justice Department was developed and overseen by a closely knit group of senior Reagan loyalists that began to coalesce during his term as governor of California. This group included Edwin Meese, William French Smith as well as Ted Olson, and was later expanded by the addition of other conservative lawyers such as William Bradford Reynolds and Charles Cooper.

Terry Eastland, who according to former solicitor general Charles Fried, was a key opponent of Brennan-era civil rights decisions in the first Reagan administration, summed up the experience a few years later in what was then the Heritage Foundation's flagship journal, *Policy Review*:

> The Reagan Justice Department benefited from a large cadre of bright conservatives, many of them in their 20s and 30s. At the assistant attorney general level they included John Bolton and Henry Habicht. Below that level, they included James M. Spears, Carolyn Kuhl, Michael McConnell, Roger Clegg, Michael Carvin, Mark Disler, John Harrison, Gregory Walden, Steve Matthews, Gary McDowell, Steven Calabresi, Robert Syncar, Patricia Bryan, Fred Nelson, and Lee Liberman. No department in the administration had such a large number of able, committed young people, and none was as important in the administration-wide effort to implement the president's social and political philosophy.[24]

This list, a "Who's Who" of future Federalist Society stalwarts (Lee Liberman Otis, Steven Calabresi, Michael Carvin), George W. Bush judicial appointees (Carolyn Kuhl, Michael McConnell), leaders in extreme right organizations now attacking affirmative action (Michael Carvin, a cofounder of the Center for Individual Rights, which is responsible for key University of Texas (*Hopwood*) and University of Michigan (*Grutter and Gratz*) anti-affirmative action cases, and veterans of the battle over Florida's electoral votes in the last presidential election (John Bolton, Michael Carvin again), were the kind of bright twenty-somethings who were handpicked by the transition team set up under Edwin Meese and Jay Parker's direction to fill the positions of the Reagan Justice Department. Other names can be added, not least that of Linda Chavez, who became staff director at the U.S. Commission on Civil Rights in the first Reagan term. Another name, of course, is Clarence Thomas, who was selected to chair the Equal Employment Opportunity Commission from 1982 to 1990—where he was aided by a young assistant named Clint Bolick. Their relationship is so close that Thomas is godfather to Bolick's second child.[25] Bolick refers to Thomas as his mentor,[26] and *Newsday* reported that Jay Parker was Thomas's political mentor"[27]

Writing nearly twenty years ago in the pages of the *Lincoln Review*, the flagship journal of Jay Parker's Lincoln Institute for Research and Education, Clint

Bolick outlined an agenda that has since materialized in the form of a half dozen organizations fighting diversity policies.[28] Later expanded into book form, Bolick's argument was that the assault on the gains of the civil rights movement required a "focused, aggressive legal agenda." The problem, according to Bolick, was that such an agenda was being hobbled by "inadequate leadership, risk avoidance, co-optation by special interests, and the lack of a principled, coherent, long range vision."[29]

The venue for Bolick's groundbreaking article is informative. Parker helped shape the assault on the gains of the civil rights movement by mentoring Clarence Thomas, who later served on the advisory board of *Lincoln Review*.[30] It was from this precinct that the first intellectual bugle call for a widespread, aggressive offensive against the legal system issued forth, with affirmative action as the primary wedge issue.

Laying the Groundwork: Changing Course and Unfinished Business

In his 1988 *Changing Course: Civil Rights at the Crossroads*, Bolick cites the importance of the work of political scientist Charles Murray as a framework for the necessary rethinking of America's approach to civil rights.[31] Attracting widespread criticism and condemnation, Murray's views on race and genetics were developed in conjunction with Harvard psychology professor Richard Herrnstein (with whom he collaborated on the controversial *The Bell Curve*). Murray and Herrnstein argue that intelligence is predetermined by genetic factors correlating significantly with race, and that social policy—particularly in the area of education—should be formulated accordingly. Murray and Herrnstein in turn built upon educational psychologist Arthur Jensen's theories on the genetically imposed limitations to intelligence and educability (see below).[32]

In *Changing Course*, Bolick essentially claimed that legal action to redress historic injustices and secure racial inclusivity would produce dysfunctional and slothful minorities.[33] Standing in the way of such "reform," however, was what he viewed as an unfocused array of new right-wing leaders and organizations, including Robert Woodson, Jay Parker, William Bradford Reynolds, Newt Gingrich, Rickie Silberman, the Manhattan Institute, and the Associated General Contractors.[34] A more organized effort was needed.

Having waged war throughout the 1980s on civil rights remedies, Bolick produced a little noted but significant book in 1990 called *Unfinished Business: A Civil Rights Strategy for America's Third Century*. Aside from laying out a breathtaking blueprint for the reversal of a century of civil rights progress, at the heart of *Unfinished Business* was the new strategy of using think tanks and litigating organizations to roll back race and gender inclusiveness in American institutions.

Urging his colleagues to move beyond their preoccupation with judicial restraint, Bolick called for an aggressive form of judicial activism that would reject the national consensus that practical steps were needed to redress racial imbalances in American institutions. The idea that "the judiciary must always defer to the popular will,"[35] is an "intellectual bogeyman" that the right wing must dispose of according to Bolick. Reflecting this concern, Bolick sketched out a legal agenda that included the overturning of long-standing Supreme Court decisions.[36] Dedicated to advancing a radical conception of "natural rights principles," Bolick's book was, as he acknowledges, a collective endeavor. It was the product of a "task force" that included many of those who play prominent roles in the pages that follow, including Jay Parker, who ten years after the Reagan transition was still heavily involved in strategizing to eliminate civil rights gains; Michael Greve, who acknowledged that his Center for Individual Rights received money from the Pioneer Fund, founded in 1937, which has backed research on the connection between race and genetics with the objective of "throw[ing] light upon heredity in man" and "the problems of human race betterment"[37] (see below); Charles Cooper, who went on to head the Federalist Society's Civil Rights Practice Group and to play an important role in the Florida 2000 electoral battle; Manuel Klausner, who played a central role in overturning affirmative action in California; and Chip Mellor, who works with Clint Bolick at the Institute for Justice.[38]

Charles Murray, coauthor of *The Bell Curve*, was chosen to set the proper intellectual tone for this audacious treatise by writing the foreword. Well-known conservative writer and commentator Ann Coulter, who also went on to work with the Center for Individual Rights, provided research assistance. Murray used the foreword to denounce the compromise measures that led to modest affirmative action programs—brought in part by moderate Republicans in the Nixon and Ford administrations—as "latently poisonous." "During the 1970s," Murray writes, "the poison began to set in" with the introduction of affirmative action, integration of higher education, and minority hiring measures.[39] It was around this time that many of the major anti-diversity organizations were established: Center for Individual Rights (1989), Institute for Justice (1991), Campaign for a Color Blind America (1993), and Center for Equal Opportunity (1994)—all heavily funded by the main foundations of the Right. Networking also played an important role. In 1990, for example, the Federalist Society sponsored a weekend-long symposium on civil rights that featured Charles Murray, Federalist Society frequent speaker (and Ninth Circuit Court of Appeals judge) Alex Kozinski, and future 2000 Republican presidential candidate and conservative talk show host Alan Keyes—a glowing report of which was written up for the *Washington Times* by Dawn Weyrich, daughter of New Right leader Paul Weyrich.[40]

While often taking the form of a battle of ideas and principles, the assault on diversity has, from the beginning, also been an effort to create and build up long-term organized capacities on the Right. Such long-term thinking on a range of issues, including affirmative action, continues to characterize the right wing.[41] It has also involved a parallel political assault on the leaders and institutions— both governmental and private—that made the addressing of historical injustices a reality. Out of this battle, which was led by organizations specifically devoted not only to "defunding" these "liberal" institutions[42] but also to marginalizing them politically, grew the armada of right-wing public policy and legal foundations we see today. During the Clinton years, these foundations built up, funded, and refined their legal strategies and organizational models. Now, with the Bush administration's elevation of many of the leading figures of the anti-diversity movement to government positions, these activists are poised to carry the challenge to civil rights to a new level.

Refining the Rhetorical and Legal Strategy

By the mid-1990s the leadership of the right wing was well versed in the arts of spin doctoring the bitter anti-civil rights politics of the 1970s and 1980s with the language of anti-discrimination (against alleged white male victims of affirmative action). Bolick then produced yet another work, *The Affirmative Action Fraud* (1996).

Published by the Cato Institute (see below), *The Affirmative Action Fraud* was clearly designed to appeal to a younger generation seduced by the overly simplistic libertarian idealism of railing against the government, even when it is securing the rights of those discriminated against. "The only state-imposed discrimination my generation has witnessed is *reverse* discrimination," Bolick declares.[43] Compared to his earlier works, this book went into much greater detail about the agenda favored by the extreme right over the long term, such as the overturning of major Supreme Court decisions, and was much more explicit in its denial of what Bolick calls the myth of pervasive racism in America.[44] This somewhat new and harder tone signaled a reworking of traditional right-wing arguments against racial and gender inclusiveness into the language of the burgeoning Law and Economics movement[45] and a resurgent racially conscious libertarianism.[46]

The use of such extreme language as "poisonous" (Murray), "fraud" (Bolick), "vanity" (Greve), and "hoax" (Wiener and Berley)[47] to describe the careful process that the United States has gone through to arrive at a modest consensus whereby the institutions of higher education, government, and business legally can be given space to secure an inclusive and just society, are indications of the venom with which the far right has viewed the progress of the past half century. Furthermore, the opponents of affirmative action have been able to deftly utilize the civil rights vocabulary formulated to oppose discrimination in order to undermine the moral as well as the legal and constitutional underpinnings of institutional remedies.

Opponents of diversity also have manipulated the inevitable shortcomings in design and implementation of some diversity programs, presenting these as symbols of a supposedly failed policy. While the development and implementation of diversity programs took place over a considerable period of time, and has led to some important corrections in racial and gender imbalances throughout American society, in some instances they have been misapplied or too broadly constructed, as with any other public policy. Those anomalies have been seized upon and exploited by the ideological activists of the Right to place the very idea of racial and gender equality on the defensive. Their fortitude and success in mischaracterizing the nature, necessity, and effectiveness of diversity programs should provoke a rethinking of the seriousness with which this challenge must be met if it is to be turned back. Indeed, the scope of their vision (for example, Bolick's "strategy for a new century") demonstrates just how long they are prepared to struggle in order to achieve their ends.

In spite of the important consequences to society were the Right's agenda to be realized, their backgrounds, beliefs, strategies, and leadership are not widely or well understood, and their efforts have benefited from this lack of scrutiny. The defenders of diversity now face a crowded political chessboard on which the pieces of the Right are increasingly occupying the most important strategic squares. The right-wing organizations perceive this hard-fought encounter in three-dimensional terms. These dimensions are the struggle between organized movements for control of political spin in the media, battles in the courts, and a political war that moves beyond the media and the law to win over the hearts and minds of the public.

Any major institution that wishes to promote diversity will likely experience aggressive opposition from these quarters, both in the arena of public opinion and increasingly in the courtroom, no matter how carefully designed its diversity policies may be. Likewise, the success of any campaign to promote public support for racial and gender diversity must be based on a clear understanding of the opposition to this campaign and where it intends to go.

Major Organizations and Key Players Challenging Diversity Initiatives

Several major foundations, notably the Lynde and Harry Bradley Foundation, John M. Olin Foundation, Sarah Scaife Foundation, and Smith Richardson Foundation, are essential to the opposition to diversity. Significant and consistent multiyear funding from those sources ensures that organizations such as those discussed below can carry on long-range planning and sustained campaigns on key issues. Organized opposition to affirmative action falls into two broad categories:

- Groups that concentrate on waging the political and media battle against inclusive practices by public and private institutions.

• Groups that specialize in waging sustained and protracted legal battles in state and federal courts to erode the legal ability of these institutions to practice affirmative action and to promote diversity as a matter of policy.

There are five main national organizations central to the debate over diversity for which a major focus is opposition to affirmative action: American Civil Rights Institute, Center for Equal Opportunity, Center for Individual Rights, Institute for Justice, and the Civil Rights Practice Group of the Federalist Society. Several regionally based organizations, including the Pacific Legal Foundation, Southeastern Legal Foundation, and Mountain States Legal Foundation, have also conducted anti-affirmative action litigation with national implications.

Those organizations are attempting to:

• Overturn some of the fundamental decisions protecting civil rights.
• Precipitate a series of crises and divisions: in the balance of power between different branches of government; between the federal and state governments over competing policies; and between legislatures and the public through ballot initiatives.
• Use the rhetoric of individual liberty to turn a wave of public sentiment for eliminating some government regulation into a broader movement that will fundamentally transform the American public sector by eliminating the regulatory infrastructure.
• Use direct access to the Bush administration to undermine the enforcement of anti-discrimination measures.

The challenges confronting affirmative action at the turn of the new century come about not because of convincing cases brought by aggrieved individuals or even persuasive arguments made by popular politicians. Rather, the attack represents a concerted effort mounted by sophisticated private organizations. Some are legal in focus, others electoral; however, all are ideologically conservative. Now rich in experience and in allies, including corporate backers and friends at the highest levels of government, theirs is a backlash whose time, they believe, has finally come.

Chapter 2

The Historical Background of the Battle against Affirmative Action

More than thirty years ago, after decades of bloodshed and strife, an organized civil rights movement forced the leading institutions of American society to accept integration as a necessary social goal. To rectify past and present injustices (and for practical reasons as well), in the 1960s state and federal governments began to require their agencies and contractors to assemble workforces reflective of our increasingly diverse society, and their educational institutions to diversify student bodies by adopting admissions policies sensitive to gender and race.

By any practical measure, the effort to desegregate has made great progress. After decades of government-enforced desegregation, increasing numbers of women and people of color have been hired and promoted, known greater job stability, and received fairer wages. After years of de jure as well as de facto exclusion, the country's most selective colleges and universities have educated sizable numbers of qualified black, Latino, and female students, many assuming leadership in the professions, business, politics, and civic life.[48]

However, there always has been strong opposition to the desegregation effort. An important group of political players in the United States has always opposed government intervention to enforce civil rights. Outlawing discrimination is one thing, these critics argue; going beyond "anti-discrimination" to mandating integration is another, amounting to an illegitimate incursion of government power into the private realm. For as long as there has been civil rights law, conservatives have been developing the arguments and instruments to reverse it. As the new century begins, they are succeeding. "Almost a half century after the U.S. Supreme Court concluded that Southern school segregation was unconstitutional and 'inherently unequal,'" Harvard professor Gary Orfield reported in a major study in July 2001 that "new statistics from the 1998–99 school year show that segregation continued to intensify throughout the 1990s, a period in which there were three major Supreme Court decisions authorizing a return to segregated neighborhood schools and limiting the reach and duration of desegregation orders."[49] The legal situation is becoming equally troubling.[50]

Between 1989 and 1996 a series of Supreme Court decisions and a ruling by the Fifth Circuit Court of Appeals in *Hopwood v. Texas* radically reduced the government's legal stake in desegregation. In *Hopwood*, the court ruled that the University of Texas Law School could not take race into account in selecting its students.[51] In effect, *Hopwood* rejected the view that the state had any compelling interest in diversity in higher education. Terence Pell, the senior counsel for the Center for Individual Rights (see below), has argued that "Any evidence or any report that shows, or purports to show, that racial diversity has educational value is besides the point," since "racial diversity is not a compelling state interest, even if racial diversity has educational value."[52] Moreover, *Hopwood* barred the university not just from using race as the only determining factor in admissions, but as a factor *at all*, opening the school up to legal challenge for any diversity effort conducted in a conceivably race-related way.[53] A potential landmark affirmative action ruling is also in the offing in the University of Michigan cases, which seem likely to make their way to the Supreme Court after the U.S. Court of Appeals for the Sixth Circuit ruled that the state has a compelling interest in achieving diversity in higher education and that the Constitution permits institutions of higher education to seek a "critical mass" of black and Latino students in their admissions practices, as long as those objectives do not amount to precise quotas.[54]

On the electoral front, in 1995 the California Board of Regents set the antiaffirmative action ball rolling. That year, the regents, led by African American businessman Ward Connerly, passed a resolution to end affirmative action in admissions and hiring throughout the state's university system, despite opposition from the University of California administration, faculty, students, and staff. A statewide referendum in 1996 went further, not only striking down affirmative action policies, but writing into law a "Civil Rights Initiative" (Proposition 209) that explicitly bars the state from using "race, sex, color, ethnicity or national origin" as criteria for consideration in employment, education, or contracting.

Initiative 200, modeled after California's Proposition 209, passed in Washington State in November 1998, and similar legislation is rapidly appearing elsewhere (more on this below), even as African American enrollment at affected institutions, particularly elite undergraduate, medical, and law schools, shrinks.[55] In the first freshman class admitted at Berkeley—the University of California's most elite campus—since the banning of affirmative action in September 1998, the number of black students plummeted by more than half, to the lowest figures since 1981. Hispanic enrollment decreased by 43 percent. Of 3,735 freshmen, 126 (3 percent) were black, and 269 (7 percent) were Chicano or Latino. Asian-American enrollment went up 6 percent and white enrollment rose by 7 percent. Similar conditions prevailed in Los Angeles.[56] Throughout the University of California system, despite increases at second-tier campuses, the numbers of Latino, African American, and American Indian students admitted at the most competitive campuses have declined to 15.9 percent in 2002 from 22 percent in 1997, according to the *Chronicle of Higher Education*.[57] That trend has continued across the country.[58]

A. The Origins of Affirmative Action

Although affirmative action programs had their roots in efforts to bar discrimination by defense contractors during World War II, the term "affirmative action" was first used in a federal document in 1961. Executive Order 10925, issued by President John F. Kennedy,[59] demanded that federal contractors take "affirmative action" to ensure equality of opportunity for all workers regardless of race (gender was added in 1968). In response to the demands of the civil rights movement, Executive Order 10925 created the Committee on Equal Employment Opportunity, which evolved into the Equal Employment Opportunity Commission (EEOC).

As popular protest accelerated and was met by increasing violence (most notably in Birmingham, Alabama), Kennedy went further, and appeared on television in July 1963 to propose a civil rights bill. The measure outlawed discrimination in public accommodations, permitted a cutoff of federal funds from discriminating institutions, gave increased desegregation responsibilities to the Justice Department, prohibited employment discrimination, and expanded the work of the Equal Employment Opportunity Commission. After Kennedy's assassination, the Civil Rights Act of 1964 was enacted.

In evaluating how the country responded to Congress's civil rights legislation, many observers look at that year's presidential election. The 1964 vote is remembered as a triumph for the civil rights cause. By the biggest popular majority in history, voters endorsed the Democratic Party, which had sponsored the Civil Rights Act,[60] and rejected the opposition that had mounted a 534-hour Senate filibuster in an effort to prevent the bill from being passed.[61] In fact, no representative from either party who had voted for the 1964 civil rights bill was defeated, while fully half the northern members who had opposed it lost.

Those who had anticipated anti-civil rights defections from the Democrats' base were disappointed. "White Backlash Doesn't Develop" declared the *New York Times*.[62] Republicans emerged internally fractured, with moderates blaming the radical right for burdening them with the nomination of archconservative Barry Goldwater, and right-wingers blaming the center for abandoning their nominee. However, as historian Taylor Branch points out in his account of the period, "a warning sign was buried beneath election reviews"—the success of segregationist George Wallace's symbolic campaign for the presidential nomination in Wisconsin, Indiana, and Maryland.[63] In Maryland, for example, the Alabama governor won 43 percent in the Democratic primary—and a majority of all votes cast by whites. Following the primaries, historian and friend Lawrence Reddick wrote to Martin Luther King (who was sitting in a Florida jail cell) and reflected on the results. A majority could be mobilized, he wrote, "by the anti-Negro camp on an appeal that is reasonable and correlated with other long-term, deep-seated desires and irritations."[64] Another contemporary commentator wrote that Wallace "gave every hearer a chance to transmute latent hostility toward the Negro into a hostility toward big government."[65]

The technique had been seen to work. In California, the same voters who wanted Johnson for president embraced a ballot initiative that sought to repeal the state's Fair Housing Act of 1963 on the grounds that private citizens had the right to segregate their own neighborhoods.[66] Proposition 14—an early ancestor in the lineage of Proposition 209[67]—carried California by nearly two to one, promoted by the real estate industry and the chair of California Citizens for Goldwater, Ronald Reagan. Dubbed "the Gipper" in pro-Goldwater campaign ads, Reagan had made precisely the appeal King's correspondent suggested could fly. "A perversion has taken place," Reagan declared on television when filling in for Goldwater one night. "Our natural unalienable rights are now presumed to be a dispensation of the government."[68]

The technique of using voter initiatives to drive the anti-civil rights agenda continues to be a key component of the strategy of the Right. For example, Ward Connerly has launched a major ballot initiative—the so-called Racial Privacy Initiative (set to be on the California ballot in November 2004)—that would end the collection of statistical data essential to monitoring diversity in social and institutional settings by any state agency. This would devastate the enforcement of diversity programs, as well as eliminating the collection of information regarding racial and ethnic statistics in education, health care, and other vital areas of public policy.[69]

B. Think Tanks and Foundations: The New Order of Battle against Diversity

The basic outline of the right-wing case against government desegregation has remained substantially the same for a generation, although the vocabulary has shifted from the private right to discriminate to an anti-government libertarian veneer of individual rights and white victimization. However, in their years out of government during the 1970s, "movement conservatives" who had cut their teeth in the Goldwater campaign focused on building national and regional think tanks (such as the Heritage Foundation, the Manhattan Institute, and the Claremont Institute), gaining grassroots allies (within the religious right, the legal community, and on campuses nationwide), and developing a well-oiled media machine to get their message out.[70]

Following the establishment of those think tanks and several of the earlier right-wing litigation organizations such as Pacific Legal and Southeastern Legal (mentioned above), pressure built from more extreme right precincts to move toward a more nationally focused effort to promote radical legal change. Initially using Capital Legal as an organizing base in Washington, D.C., this effort to centralize and coordinate the legal organization of the Right paralleled the creation of the Heritage Foundation a few years before. Heritage, according to Lee Edwards (a senior editor of *World & I* magazine),[71] was spawned by the fury and dissatisfaction of two young congressional aides—Paul Weyrich and Ed Feulner—with the American Enterprise Institute's (AEI's) inability to get its research out in a timely enough fashion to affect legislative action in Congress.[72]

This alternative approach involved personal, ideological, and political ties, with many of the same individuals founding both the legal groups and Heritage. As always, money played an important role. For example, Peter Fluor, a major shareholder of the Fluor Corporation (a dominant force in engineering and construction), served on the board of Capital Legal;[73] J. Simon Fluor was instrumental in the creation and buildup of the Pacific Legal Foundation; and J. Robert Fluor, who assumed control of the Fluor Corporation from J. Simon, served on the Board of Trustees of the Heritage Foundation. But the rupture with the AEI model also involved a sharp organizational and political battle that defined the far right network that was soon to come to power with the Reagan presidency. It was in those battles that the Weyrich faction, fueled by Scaife and Coors money, prevailed.[74]

This dissatisfaction extended to existing right-wing legal organizations as well. As the pioneering political researcher John Saloma (and first president of the liberal Republican Ripon Society) wrote at the time,[75] not all conservatives were content with the Pacific Legal Foundation-National Legal Center for the Public Interest (PLF-NLCPI) model:

> The Scaife Foundation commissioned attorney and writer Michael Horowitz to evaluate the conservative public-interest law firms prior to the 1980 elections. The Horowitz Report, leaked to the *Wall Street Journal* in March 1981, concluded that conservative law firms, for all their funding, had "not generated anything like the organizational and intellectual force of their liberal counterparts." The report faulted the firms for not lobbying in the capital, concentrating instead on resource-consuming case-by-case litigation. Sensing the need for a more politically sophisticated response to the liberal network of public interest lawyers, a group of conservatives turned to the Capital Legal Foundation in the mid-1980s.

Swept into power with the Reagan presidency, these highly politicized activists used their time in the administration to get allies appointed to the courts and in an attempt to upend the federal commitment to civil rights enforcement. In addition, during the crucial period 1978–1982, some of the young right-wing activists who had cut their political teeth in the campus battles of the 1970s (such as Federalist Society founders David McIntosh, Steven G. Calabresi, Peter D. Keisler, and Lee Liberman) began their long march toward recognition, power, and influence in Washington. Calabresi, now national cochair of the Federalist Society Board of Directors, clerked for Robert Bork on the D.C. Circuit Court, and from there became special assistant to Attorney General Edwin Meese in the Justice Department.[76]

These four young activists, who had dislodged liberals from the leadership of the Yale Political Union (YPU) in fall 1978, set an aggressive, reactionary tone of confrontation on race matters. In addition to inviting the ambassador of the white minority regime in South Africa to speak (this in the aftermath of the brutal suppression of the student uprising in Soweto), the YPU under McIntosh's leadership sponsored a debate on the question "Resolved: That Yale should abolish affirmative action."[77] By the beginning of the 1990s a second generation of anti-civil rights activists was hitting its stride, and the movement as a whole was poised to carry the challenge to civil rights to a new level.

C. Institutionalizing the Assault on Affirmative Action— The Three Transitions: 1980, 1990, and 2001

The Reagan-era assault on the gains of the civil rights movement, which was based in the Justice Department, the Equal Employment Opportunity Commission, and the U.S. Commission on Civil Rights, was the work of a core group of appointees and advisors driven by a consistent ideological agenda. While often tactically moderated by more politically minded senior officials, the impact of this agenda on the scope and effectiveness of civil rights law was substantial and lasting.

The current movement to eliminate affirmative action is a legacy of institutional connections and political relationships cemented in the 1980s. In particular, the Reagan and the first Bush administrations' endowment of a core group of lawyers with political and legal credentials is an important part of this legacy. It is this group that went on to create, nurture, and/or offer key support to the American Civil Rights Institute, the Center for Equal Opportunity, the Center for Individual Rights, the Institute for Justice, and the Federalist Society Civil Rights Practice Group. To understand what motivates these activists, it is crucial to comprehend the history of the Reagan administration and its fundamental goal of eliminating affirmative action in all its forms.[78]

Three key historical processes shaped the recent history of the assault on civil rights in general, and affirmative action in particular:

1. The actions of the 1980 Reagan transition team, and in particular the Equal Employment Opportunity Commission (EEOC) transition team, charged with selecting the hard-line cadre to carry through Reagan's anti-civil rights agenda.
2. An intensive outburst of strategic planning at the beginning of the 1990s, leading to the implementation of another, even more destructive phase of right-wing capacity building through the creation of the groups to be examined below. An important turning point here was the *coordination* (often under the auspices of the Pacific Research Institute) of the strategy that now guides them.
3. The coming to power of the second Bush administration, and its elevation of a second generation of activists to positions of critical importance in the area of enforcing and formulating policy on race and gender equity.

Thus, at the beginning of the new century, we are faced with the possibility of yet another key turning point. Largely under the auspices of Edwin Meese at the Heritage Foundation and Roger Clegg at the Center for Equal Opportunity, the capacity of the right wing to coordinate the activities of the numerous groups working to dismantle programs, laws, and policies underpinning racial and gender equality has deepened throughout the 1990s, threatening a yet more openly aggressive assault on affirmative action and civil rights.

D. The Reagan Administration

This isn't merely a Republican regime, but a conservative regime. . . . We're conservatives, not party people.

—Meese counselor T. Kenneth Cribb, Jr.[79]

The Institute for Justice is fighting "foes like the AFL-CIO, the National Education Association, much of the civil rights establishment, and federal, state, and local governments nationwide."

—Institute for Justice website[80]

An inner core of ideological hard-liners characterized the Reagan Justice Department and gained a reputation among civil rights leaders for collaborating to undermine civil rights protection under the guise of legal principle.[81] Long before coming to Washington, Ed Meese was Reagan's legal affairs secretary, then chief of staff during Reagan's tenure as governor of California (1967–1974). After working with Heritage Foundation officials for years, Meese headed the

Reagan transition team, which promptly received a blueprint from a Heritage task force urging the Reagan administration to uproot affirmative action.[82]

Upon being named U.S. attorney general in 1985, Meese attempted to "purify" criminal law of many basic civil liberties and due process provisions, whether on Miranda rights, the death penalty, habeas corpus, or the exclusionary rule blocking illegally seized evidence.[83] While this didn't exactly mirror William Bradford Reynolds's civil rights agenda, the Meese-style "law and order" agenda coincided with his efforts to roll back civil rights.[84]

Meese's downfall in 1988 under an ethical cloud[85] did not diminish his influence on the Right. To the contrary, by 1995 Meese was cochairing the Law and Justice Committee of the Council for National Policy (CNP), along with Texas Court of Appeals judge and Southern Baptist leader Paul Pressler. The CNP, led by right-wing cadre development specialist Morton Blackwell, is an umbrella body for coordinating broad strategy. It brings together some of the country's most conservative funders (such as the Coors, DeVos, Scaife, and Hunt families) with key organizational leaders such as Pat Robertson, Gary Bauer, Reed Larson,[86] and James Dobson.[87]

The key figures linking the Justice Department to the broader legal right in the Reagan administration were William Bradford Reynolds (assistant attorney general for civil rights, 1981–1987), T. Kenneth Cribb, Jr. (Meese's counselor), and Bruce Fein (associate deputy attorney general, 1981–1982). James McClellan, a former aide to Senator Jesse Helms, played an important role in cementing the hard right from his perch as chief counsel and staff director of the Subcommittee on the Separation of Powers of the U.S. Senate Committee on the Judiciary from 1981 to 1983, and as head of the Center for Judicial Studies from 1983 to 1993.[88] Michael Horowitz, author of the influential memorandum calling for the creation of a network of aggressive right-wing legal organizations, also worked closely with Reynolds to root out affirmative action policies in the early years of the Reagan administration.[89]

There were important supporting roles as well. According to Reagan Justice Department official Douglas Kmiec (now dean of Catholic University Law School), Reynolds worked closely with Office of Legal Counsel director Charles Cooper, a subordinate of Meese. Together, they conceptualized and implemented the Reagan administration's civil rights agenda.[90] Even hard-line conservatives bristled at their ideological fanaticism: "I had the first of many run-ins [over a labor case] with Cooper and Reynolds," Reagan Solicitor General Charles Fried writes, "whom I later came to call the 'federalism police' or the 'Holy Office.'"[91]

Bruce Fein also exerted great influence on the Meese Justice Department, having worked for Attorney General William French Smith and for the Federal Communications Commission as general counsel. In the 1980s, Fein was one of the most visible public opponents of affirmative action from his perch at the American Enterprise Institute. He also served as Supreme Court editor for the

Center for Judicial Studies' *Benchmark*,[92] and has continued vigorously to oppose affirmative action in higher education.[93]

Fein has emphasized the role of Justice Department chief spokesman Terry Eastland, characterizing Meese's eventual firing of him in the wake of the Iran–Contra scandal as the "virtual death knell of the philosophical legal agenda of the Meese Justice Department and the Reagan administration."[94] Eastland was Meese's chief speechwriter until his termination in the midst of the Justice Department meltdown in 1988.[95]

After leaving the Reagan Justice Department, Eastland worked for the influential Ethics and Public Policy Center (EPPC) in Washington, D.C. He then left EPPC to become publisher of the Scaife-funded *American Spectator*, before leaving that controversy-mired publication.[96] He remains ubiquitous as the publisher of William Kristol's *Weekly Standard* and as an anti-affirmative action spokesman in the media.[97] His activities at the Ethics and Public Policy Center included introducing Ward Connerly to a December 1997 EPPC press conference to celebrate the passage of Proposition 209. Eastland and Connerly were joined by Michael Greve, at the time with the Center for Individual Rights; Anita Blair of the Independent Women's Forum; Brian Jones of the Center for New Black Leadership, Center for Equal Opportunity, and Federalist Society (see below); Adam Meyerson of *Policy Review*; Larry Stratton of the Institute for Political Economy;[98] and Robert Woodson of the National Center for Neighborhood Enterprise.[99]

One of the key Beltway figures who has been nurturing the assault on diversity for decades is William Bradford ("Brad") Reynolds. Reynolds's history in the Justice Department stretches back to the early 1970s, when he was an assistant to Solicitor General Erwin Griswold, as well as to future Supreme Court nominee Robert Bork. Reynolds, an heir to the Du Pont fortune,[100] left during the Watergate crisis to join a D.C. law firm—Shaw, Pittman, Potts & Trowbridge—as an antitrust and commercial litigation specialist.[101] He rejected an invitation from Griffin Bell[102] to return to the Justice Department under Carter, but became head of the DOJ's civil rights division during Reagan's first term, at the invitation of Attorney General William French Smith.

In 1985, Reynolds's nomination to become associate attorney general was rejected by the Senate Judiciary Committee. Senators voting against Reynolds said he had been less than candid with them, and seemingly put himself above the law by refusing to accept court interpretations of civil rights statutes.[103] To get around this, Meese named Reynolds his counselor, where Reynolds virtually controlled the Meese Justice Department, working as the key link to the White House and running the DOJ's agenda-setting Strategic Planning Board.[104]

T. Kenneth Cribb, Jr., a classic New Right activist in the Department of Justice going back to the Goldwater movement, now serves as counselor and a member of the Board of Directors of the Federalist Society.[105] Cribb is also listed under "advisors and contributors" on the masthead of *Southern Partisan*, a neo-confederate magazine.[106] As a member of the 1980 transition team, Cribb was the unofficial liaison between the new administration and the Heritage Foundation, whose *Mandate for Leadership* was the blueprint for the Reagan revolution.[107] Cribb played a variety of key roles after the transition, including as an aide to Meese (who was presidential counselor during Reagan's first term) and then Department of Justice chief of staff when Meese became attorney general in 1985. Cribb was known for his role in personnel development—pegging movement activists for staff positions—as well as for his ideological influence in consistently staking out the far-right edge of the Reagan administration's domestic policy agenda.[108]

Cribb, who has served on the board of the Sarah Scaife Foundation with Heritage Foundation president Ed Feulner,[109] was attracted by the forceful anti-abortion rights and judicial selection views of Grover Rees, who had worked for Senator John East (R-NC) on the Judiciary Separation of Powers Subcommittee. Rees was responsible for selecting some 150 Reagan-appointed judges, including Alex Kozinski, Daniel Manion, and Sidney Fitzwater, as well as for the unsuccessful nomination of Lino Graglia.[110]

Cribb served on the Board of Directors of James McClellan's Center for Judicial Studies (CJS), possibly the most significant legal influence on the Meese Justice Department. Rees was senior editor of CJS's influential journal, *Benchmark*; and *Benchmark*'s book review editor, Gary McDowell, worked for Meese as a public affairs aide from 1985 to 1987.[111] James McClellan is a constitutional scholar and one of the driving forces behind the "original intent" movement in constitutional legal theory (see below). A former aide to Senator Jesse Helms and Helms protégé Senator John East,[112] McClellan used CJS as a job placement service for the Federalist Society,[113] according to journalist Sidney Blumenthal. He also served as an editorial adviser to racial theorist Roger Pearson.[114]

E. Parker and Bolick at the Equal Employment Opportunity Commission (EEOC)

Like Clint Bolick, now a senior figure with the Institute for Justice, Jay Parker was a close associate of Clarence Thomas long before Thomas was nominated to the Supreme Court. Parker, the much older of the two, holds more extensive ties to the far right than does Bolick, but their joint work in advancing Clarence Thomas's career represents the coming together of two, and even three, generations of activists opposed explicitly to affirmative action and, more generally, to civil rights protections gained over the past forty years.

Parker was head of the 1980 EEOC transition team. His approach to racial politics is amply illustrated by the fact that, as noted earlier, in the late 1970s he served as a paid agent ($10,000 per month) to the South African apartheid regime's puppet Republic of Transkei Bantustan.[115] A member of the board of directors of the American chapter of the World Anti-Communist League,[116] Parker was virtually the only African American involved in the Draft Goldwater campaign of 1959, according to authors Jane Mayer and Jill Abramson. Mayer and Abramson also report that his company was paid more than a million dollars by the Pretoria regime between 1985 and 1988.[117]

At around the same time Parker was serving as an African American fig leaf for Pretoria's propaganda apparatus, he was also cultivating a young attorney who had just arrived in Washington. As recently as 1999 this once young attorney singled out Parker in a roomful of the most prominent conservative leaders in the country for a glowing personal tribute: "When I first came to Washington," Supreme Court Justice Clarence Thomas gushed, "he was one of the few people who would talk to me in 1979, and who would regularly counsel and advise me, as a young and foolish person."[118]

Clarence Thomas was on the 1980 EEOC transition team with, among others, Hugh Joseph Beard, Jr., who became counsel to Linda Chavez's Center for Equal Opportunity (see below), and served in Ashcroft's Justice Department until his death in July 2002. Another member was Andrew W. Lester, who now serves as membership director of the Federalist Society Civil Rights Practice Group (see below). William Keyes, a Reagan White House staffer and Parker's partner in forming Black PAC (a lobbying group that backed Jesse Helms), advised the EEOC transition team on legislative matters.[119]

Clint Bolick worked under Clarence Thomas in the Equal Employment Opportunity Commission, and then moved to the Civil Rights Division under Reynolds,[120] where he played an important role in Thomas's Supreme Court nomination. Bolick approached Lee Liberman and Boyden Gray (two founders of the Federalist Society who were in charge of judicial selections for George H. W. Bush) to push the nomination of Clarence Thomas, reportedly underscoring Thomas's devotion to the libertarian philosophy of author Ayn Rand.[121]

F. Doctrinal and Political Battles in the Reagan Administration

Early in Reagan's first term, Attorney General William French Smith inaugurated a sweeping transformation in civil rights policy, focusing especially on busing and affirmative action.[122] Over time, however, counter pressure was brought to bear by more moderate elements within the Justice Department, by members of Congress, and by the civil rights movement.

Militant opposition to affirmative action defined the position of the administration on civil rights, but the impact of operating in this intense political environment sometimes caused the Reagan Justice Department officials to equivocate where the choice was between total failure due to public backlash and making in-cremental gains.[123] The latter involved a more gradual but still systematic process of challenging the legal and constitutional underpinnings of diversity remedies, facilitated by extensive public relations work aiming to influence public opinion, provide damage control, and build support among conservative constituencies.

With regard to *legal strategy*, it is fairly clear that the top leadership of the Reagan Justice Department and EEOC, particularly in the first term, aimed to limit the scope and enforcement of existing civil rights legislation so as to roll back civil rights protections in a de facto way, even as the principle of protection remained. Rhetorically, the attack on affirmative action in particular was framed as a return to a "color-blind" Constitution—with desegregation efforts cast as racism in reverse. In terms of legal principle, this was a radical position that even gave hard-line conservatives in the Reagan administration pause.[124]

The first stage in this transformation, with regard to busing, was at the level of enforcement rather than law. The basic Justice Department strategy was to shift the enforcement criteria of public school desegregation toward "voluntary" solutions: magnet schools, outreach programs, as well as district rezoning. With regard to affirmative action, the Justice Department built up a significant case history, one mixed with wins and losses, beginning in 1982. It was a campaign given vocal support by Clarence Pendleton, Reagan's first director of the U.S. Commission on Civil Rights (an African American blazing a conservative trail not unlike Clarence Thomas, then at EEOC), and then by Linda Chavez, Bill Bennett's protégé, who was appointed staff director of the U.S. Commission on Civil Rights in a controversial reshuffling of staff at that agency in 1983.[125]

G. "Litigating the Agenda"[126]

In his account of civil rights litigation in the Reagan years,[127] Terry Eastland re-views the behind the scenes battles in some detail, as does Charles Fried from a different perspective.[128] *Williams v. New Orleans* (1982),[129] which concerned an af-firmative action promotion program in the New Orleans police department, saw the Reagan Justice Department present its central anti-affirmative action argument for the first time before a federal court. As Eastland puts it, Justice argued that "the remedial authority of judges under Title VII extends only to making whole the ac-tual victims of discrimination." The Fifth Circuit Court struck down the program.

Between 1984 and 1986, Justice prevailed again in both *Firefighters Local Union No. 1784 v. Stotts* (1984)[130] and *Wygant v. Jackson Board of Education* (1986).[131] The affirmative action policies in question, which prioritized race over seniority in the case of layoffs, were struck down by the Supreme Court on the same grounds as *Williams*, namely that de facto racial "imbalance" was differ-ent from discrimination by intent.

The Supreme Court did not adopt the Justice Department's brief for a "color-blind" Constitution—not in *Wygant*, where Justice argued for the elimination of racial classification as a criterion under the Fourteenth Amendment's Equal Protection Clause, nor in two subsequent cases: *Local 28, Sheet Metal Workers v. EEOC* (1986),[132] and *United States v. Paradise* (1987). In each of those cases, the Court upheld affirmative action policies, the distinction being that both involved documented histories of racial discrimination. Going beyond this, in 1987 the Supreme Court upheld affirmative action in *Johnson v. Transportation Agency*, a case in which a county government had adopted an employment plan reflecting the proportion of minorities and women in the labor market of the area.

Persisting in its attempt to influence the judiciary despite these setbacks, the Justice Department contributed to a set of decisive victories against affirmative action in the last term of the Supreme Court under Reagan. Finally, in *City of Richmond v. Croson,*[133] the Court ruled in a 5-4 decision that a city ordinance setting aside 30 percent of public works funds for construction firms owned by blacks or other minorities violated the Fourteenth Amendment.[134] Roger Clegg, one of the lawyers in the *Croson* set-aside case, hails *Richmond v. Croson* as the founding achievement, after years of struggle, for what he calls the "anti-preference" community. Clegg (now lead counsel at the Center for Equal Opportunity) and his cohorts received just the encouragement they needed from *Croson* to fuel the vast "public-interest" litigation movement they subsequently built.

H. Back to the Future: The Reagan Administration and "Original Intent"

There was powerful ideological opposition to some of the principal gains of the civil rights movement—especially those secured in the courts in the 1970s[135]— at the core of the Reagan administration. Broadly speaking, most conservative elements of the Reagan administration (Meese, Reynolds, and Cribb formed the core, according to then solicitor general Charles Fried[136]) sought to justify their legal agenda by the founders' supposed original intent in the Constitution. This approach reached its peak at the beginning of Reagan's second term, when Attorney General Edwin Meese delivered a highly controversial address to the American Bar Association in July 1985 and declared what he called a "Jurisprudence of Original Intention" to be the bedrock principle of the Reagan legal philosophy.[137] The prepared text of his speech (but left out in Meese's actual remarks) assailed, among other things, the "doctrine of incorporation," which holds that the Bill of Rights was "incorporated" by the Fourteenth Amendment and thus applied to the states.[138]

The text of Meese's speech provoked an outraged response from Supreme Court Justice John Paul Stevens.[139] "In particular," Stevens told the Federal Bar

Association in Chicago, Meese's argument "overlooks the profound importance of the Civil War and the postwar amendments on the structure of our government, and particularly upon the relationship between the federal government and the separate states." Several weeks later, Justice William Brennan, in a widely reported speech at Georgetown University, referred to Meese's brand of originalism as "arrogance cloaked as humility," whose proponents turned "a blind eye to social progress."[140]

The symbolic politics of the Meese speech were clear and the reaction to it was heated. Would the momentum of the civil rights revolution continue or abate? How should legal and social concepts of equality be defined, applied, and reconciled? Writing in the *Washington Post* shortly after the speech, author Sidney Blumenthal traced the lineage of "original intent" back to Confederate president Jefferson Davis, and essentially charged that Meese was identifying with the philosophical heritage of the Confederacy.[141] At its most refined, Blumenthal wrote, the intellectual lineage of Meese's position extended to the philosophical beliefs of twentieth-century "Southern Agrarian" philosophers such as Richard Weaver (1910-1963) and anti-Lincoln ideologues such as Willmoore Kendall (1909-1967).[142]

The issues raised went well beyond narrow legal questions concerning states rights, the meaning of equal protection, or federalism. The bedrock issue of whether society can or should promote equality by governmental action was in play. The classical Confederate view was, of course, that social stratification is simply a reflection of natural (or divinely mandated) inequality between individual human beings, and thus irremediable. The influence within the administration of such figures as Senate Subcommittee on Separation of Powers chief counsel James McClellan (described as a "confederate loyalist" by fellow conservative author Harry V. Jaffa) and Counselor T. Kenneth Cribb, Jr. (a stout defender of neo-confederate author M. E. Bradford) certainly raises some interesting questions, though it is clear that their views were not shared by other hard-line conservatives within the administration.[143]

Writing about social equality, Douglas W. Kmiec, head of the Office of Legal Counsel under Meese, quotes Reconstruction-era Congressman Benjamin Butler:

> I believe that "equal" in the Declaration of Independence is a political word, used in a political sense, and means equality of political rights. All men are not equal. Some are born with good constitutions, good health, strength, high mental power; others are not. Now, we cannot by legislation make them equal. God has not made them equal, with equal endowments. But this is our doctrine: Equality . . . —and I will embody it in a single phrase, as the true touchstone of civil liberty—is not that all men are equal, but that every man has the right to be the equal of every other if he can.[144]

The debate over the Meese speech echoed the warning issued years before by Justice Harry A. Blackmun in his partial dissent in the affirmative action decision, *Regents of University of California v. Bakke*: "We cannot—we dare not—let the Equal Protection Clause perpetuate racial supremacy."[145]

I. A Right-Wing Convergence: Libertarianism and Traditional Segregationism

While important differences in tactics and emphasis exist between the major groups opposing affirmative action, the political implications of their common assault on federal powers of equal protection pose dangers far beyond the potential elimination of affirmative action. The ideological convergence between the anti-government theology of the libertarians and the "states rights," anti-constitutional fundamentalism of the traditional segregationists is now being forged in the crucible of a common funding base, intellectual infrastructure, and political agenda.

Over time, particularly in the intellectual precincts of the Federalist Society and the wider law and economics movement,[146] the legal arguments for rolling back federal oversight on issues ranging from environmental protection to civil rights have become more nuanced and sophisticated, while retaining their virulent force as a threat to both democratically arrived at public policy positions and settled constitutional law.[147] Thus, contrary to the movement's spin doctors—who are laboring to create the impression that affirmative action and civil rights are two entirely different things—it is extremely important to understand this assault as part of a much deeper legacy of right-wing resistance to federal power, not nearly as far removed from America's segregationist past as it construes itself to be. Eliminating a federal role in civil rights enforcement would be one of the greatest historical defeats for racial and gender fairness in American history.

Chapter 3

The Political Battle: Ballot Initiatives, Media Outreach, and Legislative Action

A. American Civil Rights Institute (ACRI) and the American Civil Rights Coalition (ACRC)

> It was like using affirmative action to defeat affirmative action. We were being pretty cynical, I have to admit.
> —Joe C. Gelman, Proposition 209 campaign manager speaking of Ward Connerly's role in the campaign [148]

Opponents of affirmative action have long recognized that their campaign to overturn decades of progress in civil rights would be made easier if the public faces of their operations were African Americans, Latinos, and women. They have also recognized that in order to erode the hard-won but solid support for civil rights among the American people, they have to strike at the very heart of the message of racial and gender equity. They have done this by developing a beguiling and confusing vocabulary in which carefully selected "victims" of the correct race and sex pose as defenders of civil rights, when they are in fact fronting for its deadliest enemies. The success of this strategy, which entirely depends upon the vast amount of money that has been poured into it, can be measured by the victories of anti-affirmative action campaigns in California and Washington State.

The leaders of the campaign against affirmative action also recognize that message spin and tokenism by themselves are not enough. They must be tied to effective political action: the careful integration of a confusing message, the right black and female faces, and a tight organization financially supported by the national networks of the Right. This combination lies behind the substantial political and material support that groups such as the American Civil Rights Institute and the American Civil Rights Coalition have been able to attract.[149] These two closely related groups, headed by a previously obscure African American California state official named Ward Connerly, grew out of the campaign for Proposition 209, the ballot initiative that banned California's state and local governments from taking race and gender into account in employment practices, contracting, and college admissions. As described in their own literature, ACRI is the tax-exempt entity, and ACRC the "political arm," of "Ward Connerly's shop."[150] They are headquartered in Sacramento and share the same address.[151]

ACRI is heavily funded by the Bradley Foundation, which gave Connerly's group $150,000 in 2000[152] and $475,000 in 1998.[153] The John M. Olin Foundation gave ACRI $150,000 in 2000, $125,000 in 1999, and $225,000 in 1998.[154] The Sarah Scaife Foundation, on whose Board of Trustees Federalist Society counsel T. Kenneth Cribb sits, gave Connerly $75,000 in 2000, $175,000 in 1999, and $275,000 in 1998.[155] The Donner Foundation gave ACRI $110,000 in 1998.[156]

This California model, developing well-resourced campaigning groups like "Connerly's shop" and integrating them with a dense infrastructure of national and local political organizations, funding sources, and media resources, is now being spread across the country. Connerly himself actively has explored ballot initiative campaigns to ban affirmative action in Florida, Michigan, Colorado, Nebraska, and Oregon, even against the opposition (apparently for tactical political reasons) of Republican politicians such as Governor Jeb Bush of Florida.[157] Routed by the Florida Supreme Court in 2000, which ruled that his ballot initiative's wording was misleading, Connerly has returned to his roots.

Connerly and his new partner, Edward Blum, are campaigning for the so-called Racial Privacy Initiative, a California ballot initiative that will end the collection of statistics on race that underpin the very possibility of constructing a factual record for the purpose of ensuring racial and gender fairness.[158] The Racial Privacy Initiative, set to be on the California ballot in November 2004, would devastate the enforcement of diversity programs and eliminate the collection of information regarding racial and ethnic statistics in education, health care, and other vital areas of public policy.[159]

Although ACRI and ACRC were formed in the wake of the campaign for Proposition 209, Connerly and the people who came together to form and fund them have a much longer political lineage, and a much wider agenda than turning back the clock on civil rights. The immediate predecessor of Connerly's shop was Californians Against Discrimination and Preferences (CADAP, formed in 1994), which led the fight for the California Civil Rights Initiative, popularly known as Proposition 209. Prop 209 was coauthored by Manuel Klausner, a lawyer, and two California conservative activists, Thomas E. Wood[160] and Glynn Custred.[161] CADAP has continued its activities, and was represented by Michael A. Carvin—a founder of the Center for Individual Rights (see below)—in the 1997 appeal to the Ninth Circuit on the question of whether Prop 209 violated the equal protection clause of the U.S. Constitution.[162]

A Frontal Attack on Diversity

Both professors Wood and Custred are members of the California Association of Scholars, an affiliate of the conservative National Association of Scholars (NAS).[163] The NAS was formed in 1987 by leading right-wing figures such as Irving Kristol and Jeane Kirkpatrick to combat perceived "liberal bias" in institutions of higher education and has been a staunch opponent of university diversity policies in admissions and faculty promotions. It was cofounded by Herbert London[164] who, according to authors Jean Stefancic and Richard Delgado, at the NAS 1988 annual meeting "railed against the inclusion of literature by women and nonwhites in the core curriculum, because 'it does not lead us toward our true humanity.'"[165] At its annual conference in 2001, Ward Connerly implored the NAS to back his initiative to ban the collection of statistics on race, for which he received a standing ovation; Wood followed by presenting research arguing the lack of correlation between educational excellence and campus diversity.[166]

The Bradley, Olin, and Castle Rock (Coors)-funded NAS has conducted a national campaign against diversity and multiculturalism in higher education. According to Ward Connerly, the idea for Prop 209 was born at a caucus of the NAS.[167] On May 14, 2001, NAS filed an *amicus* brief in the crucial *Gratz v. Bollinger* case opposing the University of Michigan's affirmative action program.[168] Under the auspices of NAS, Wood and Malcolm Sherman, vice president of the New York chapter of NAS,[169] issued a report in April 2001 opposing the idea that diversity is an educational benefit.[170] In particular, the report attacked research produced by an expert witness in the Michigan *Gratz* case, Patricia Y. Gurin, chair of the Department of Psychology and interim dean of the College of Literature, Science, and the Arts at the University of Michigan at Ann Arbor;[171] and a doctoral dissertation by Mitchell J. Chang that developed a comprehensive measure of student body diversity. The Wood/Sherman report received the enthusiastic endorsement of Roger Clegg of the Center for Equal Opportunity, which released a report of its own critiquing Gurin (see below).[172]

Another CADAP founder and cochair was Larry P. Arnn, the current vice chairman and former president of the Claremont Institute.[173] Arnn, who studied under neoconservative author Harry V. Jaffa,[174] has played an important role in the California Right, and was the first to urge Connerly to head the Prop 209 drive.[175] Claremont aspires to play the role on the West Coast that the Heritage Foundation does in Washington—as a focus for coordinating key funding, policy, and academic institutions. Edwin Meese, chairman of Heritage's Center for Legal and Judicial Studies, is also chairman of the Board of Advisors of the Claremont Institute Center for Constitutional Jurisprudence. Together with John C. Eastman (a professor of constitutional law at Chapman University School of Law), Meese filed an *amicus* brief on Claremont's behalf in the *Adarand v. Mineta* anti-affirmative action case that was heard by the Supreme Court in October 2001.[176]

Savings and loan tycoon Howard H. Ahmanson, Jr., a member of Claremont's Board of Directors and one of its largest donors, is a vital player in shaping a social conservative agenda for California.[177] Through his Fieldsted & Co., he contributed $350,000 directly to the "Yes on Prop 209" campaign.[178] Ahmanson funds conservative think tanks as well as Christian Right organizations such as the Sacramento-based Capitol Resource Institute, affiliated with Focus on the Family head James Dobson, to organize opposition to abortion rights.[179] Ahmanson is a longtime supporter of the late Christian Right theocratic ideologue Rousas Rushdoony,[180] a self-described "Christian libertarian" who is known for his anti-democratic views.[181] Ahmanson's role in Connerly's rise to prominence has been reported by Joe Gelman, one of Prop 209's original supporters.[182]

Connerly and the California Right Wing

The origins of the American Civil Rights Institute and the American Civil Rights Coalition lie in Ward Connerly's close relationship with former California governor Pete Wilson.[183] Wilson met Connerly in 1968, when the latter was working at the California Department of Housing and Community Development.[184] Connerly's interest in housing had begun in college when he claims to have fought racial discrimination in housing around his campus. Wilson, then a state assemblyman, liked Connerly and hired him in 1969. Well-placed conservative African Americans in California were hard to find, and race issues were vying with the Vietnam War to dominate the news.

Wilson and Connerly worked together off and on until 1991. Wilson went on to become mayor of San Diego, a U.S. senator, then governor in 1991 (Connerly was among his donors[185]). Apparently not eschewing so-called preferences entirely, Connerly founded his own housing management consulting firm in Sacramento and listed it as "minority-owned."[186]

Governor Wilson appears to have made a habit of appointing colleagues to the University of California's Board of Regents. In 1993, immediately following the controversial appointment of one of his closest friends and biggest campaign financiers, Wilson made Ward Connerly—a businessman with no experience in educational administration—a regent, the board's only black member.[187] Together, they pushed a resolution through the board that ended affirmative action in university admissions, employment practices, and contracts.[188] From the regents, Connerly went on in December 1995 to lead the campaign to qualify Proposition 209 for the ballot.

A young Los Angeles politician named Joe Gelman played a key role in seeing that Proposition 209 could undo three decades of affirmative action and scuttle the civil rights agenda with one sentence in the proposition barring "preferential treatment."[189] According to the *LA Weekly*, it was Gelman who got the Wilson team excited about the prospect of a ballot initiative (Wilson had done well at the polls for his sponsorship of the anti-immigrant Proposition 187). And it was Wilson who realized that Connerly was in the wings, perfectly positioned to shift the spotlight in the initiative effort away from Custred and Wood, who some Republican politicos felt were waging an ineffective campaign. With assurances from Wilson that the Civil Rights Initiative would receive the funding needed to win, Connerly came on board as the campaign's chairman in late 1995.[190]

With Connerly as its most prominent advocate, Proposition 209—the California Civil Rights Initiative—passed by a 54 percent margin in an off-year election in November 1996. The following January, Connerly founded the American Civil Rights Institute with Thomas Rhodes as cochair and Jennifer Nelson, a former Pete Wilson aide, as executive director. The organization received $100,000 each from Bradley and Scaife in 1997.[191] ACRI's stated mission is to promote legislation similar to Prop 209 in states across the nation and in Washington, D.C., initially "focusing on states that have ballot initiatives and on the nation's capitol."[192]

Funding the Prop 209 Drive

The campaign for Yes on Proposition 209, the largest of many pro-209 organizations, raised $5,239,287 and spent $4,396,572, according to the office of the California Secretary of State. More than $3 million came from contributions of $10,000 and up. By comparison, the Campaign to Defeat 209, the largest by far of twenty-six registered opposition groups, raised $2,180,491, with $1,589,138 coming from contributions of $10,000 and up.[193] The Prop 209 campaign was flooded with more than $3 million from the state and national Republican parties, the *Los Angeles Times* reported.[194] Bob Dole recognized that such a racially charged wedge issue could help his presidential campaign, and, according to the *Chicago Sun-Times*, his strategists diverted funding from Northeastern states and poured it into California in a bid to win the crucial state.[195]

Rupert Murdoch's $750,000, given in the last weeks, brought his total contribution to the state party to $1 million for 1996.[196] George Joseph, the CEO of Mercury Casualty Insurance in Los Angeles, donated $500,000 to the party during the period the party was backing Prop 209. Cypress Semiconductor of San Jose donated $100,000. It didn't work for Dole, but it certainly helped Connerly.[197] According to official figures, Thomas L. "Dusty" Rhodes, ACRI's cochair with Connerly and president of *National Review* magazine, gave $10,000 to Yes on 209. The Project for the Republican Future, an organization independent of the GOP where Rhodes served as director, donated $25,000. A friend of Rhodes, John Uhlman, a wealthy businessman from Kansas City, gave $100,000.[198] Richard Mellon Scaife, a conservative philanthropist from Pittsburgh, donated $100,000.[199]

Other big contributors were W. Glenn Campbell, the late president of the Hoover Institution; Ron Unz, a backer of the successful Prop 227 anti-bilingual education drive; Edward Allred, a Long Beach physician; and, as noted above, Howard Ahmanson, Jr., heir to the Home Savings of America fortune ($350,000).[200] Yes on 209 also received funding from the Windway Capital Corporation,[201] owned by Terry Kohler of Wisconsin, who once stated that blacks in South Africa should not be given suffrage.[202]

As civil rights veteran René Redwood, then of Americans for a Fair Chance, told *Emerge* magazine, Yes on 209 was "fueled by a few businesspeople with very deep pockets to perpetuate a system where preferential treatment has been business as usual—which has been the business of exclusion of women and minorities."[203] "They already have 97 percent of the prime, huge contracts," said Connie Rice of the NAACP Legal Defense and Education Fund. "[After 209, they] will get the other 3 percent."[204] Without affirmative action mandates, public contractors stood to gain a portion of that small percentage back.

The Leadership of the American Civil Rights Institute

WARD CONNERLY

> Nobody ever gave me any race or sex preferences when I came into the cold world 56 years ago. I made it anyway—high school, college, my own big business, important friends. If I could make it, anybody can, because the playing field is a lot closer to level now. The truth is that preferences at this point are not just reverse discrimination, they're degrading to people who accept them. They've got to go.[205]

Ward Connerly's personal biography is an important part of the story of the battle against affirmative action—not only because of his frequent use of it but because of its political usefulness to the leading individuals and institutions who have unstintingly backed him. Thus the writing of Connerly's autobiography, *Creating Equal*, was funded by the Lynde and Harry Bradley Foundation, whose former president, Michael Joyce, was instrumental in its appearance.[206] In it, Connerly singles out for praise the John William Pope Foundation,[207] the Montgomery Street Foundation, the William H. Donner Foundation, the Randolph Foundation, the John M. Olin Foundation, the Sarah Scaife Foundation, and the Bradley Foundation.[208]

Connerly was born in 1939 in Louisiana, not far from the Texas border. From mixed-race parents—his father, Irish and black; his mother, Choctaw, Irish, and

French—Connerly was raised by his mother's mother and, later, by his sister. His mother died before the boy turned five, and his father, he was led to believe, "ran out on us." In fact, it turns out Connerly's father Roy "zealously" pursued custody of his child, but Ward was sent west to Sacramento to live with his aunt and her husband, according to a *New York Times* profile.[209]

Though he describes his family's life in Sacramento as stereotypically poor and deprived (his grandmother relocated west), relatives have reported that he lived a relatively privileged life, the apple of his aunt's and grandmother's eyes. Moreover, neighbors and relatives of his grandmother, Mary Soniea, remember her as openly scornful of black people[210] and out to keep Ward from his blacker relatives. "Maybe that's why Ward decided to be as much of a white boy as he could," a cousin told the *New York Times*. "That's the way he was," she continues. "We'd play cowboys and Indians. He was always the cowboy and we had to turn up dead."[211]

Connerly graduated from Sacramento State University in 1962, one of about fifty black students on a campus of two thousand. He was elected student vice president, and pledged to an all-white fraternity.[212] A Young Democrat in those days, he was part of a group that sent black testers into white neighborhoods to investigate discrimination. It was soon after that, he says, that he became a "Goldwater conservative." Two months after graduation Connerly married a white woman, Ilene Crews.[213]

From college he joined the State Department of Housing and Community Development, becoming its liaison to the legislature. There he met Pete Wilson and was recruited by him to a staff job on the Assembly's housing committee and, later, the post of University of California regent—an office with a twelve-year term. In 1994, Connerly ordered a review of the admissions data at California's state universities, after two parents complained to him that their white son had been unfairly refused admission to medical school. When the Board of Regents voted 14 to 10 in July 1995 to end the thirty-year-old policy of affirmative action for minorities and women, Governor Wilson attended the meeting to add support to Connerly's motion. According to the *New York Times*, Connerly only agreed to take over the campaign for Proposition 209 when he received assurances from Wilson that the initiative would succeed—which, the *Times* reported, meant to those involved that the California Republican Party would pay the way.[214]

Connerly's contradictions are numerous. For one thing, he aligns himself with conservative opponents of so-called big government and federal power, while his own business, Connerly & Associates, specializes in administering federal Community Development Block Grants, which are awarded under stringent federal affirmative action rules. The sole client of Connerly's company in its early years was the California Builder's Council (now the California Building Industry Association).[215] In 1994, Connerly & Associates, which had about seventeen employees, reported $1.2 million in sales. According to public records, fifteen communities that hired the company in the 1990s told grant regulators that they had hired a minority and woman-owned enterprise to comply with affirmative action laws. Connerly's business is co-owned by his wife.[216]

Connerly told *Newsweek* that being defined as an affirmative action business-man was degrading,[217] but he received two Energy Commission contracts in 1992 and 1994 as a minority businessman and agent for the California Building Officials, a group that, by law, had to be trained in energy conservation. The contracts were legally awarded without competitive bidding. Even as he took the helm of the campaign to eliminate such programs, Energy Commission records show that Connerly enlisted in the minority program again in 1995.[218]

Moreover, he has been known to contradict his own rhetoric. In October 1998 he shocked participants in a discussion organized by the Bay Area Black Journalists' Association by offering support for so-called racial preferences in the selection of clerks at the U.S. Supreme Court. "The term 'preference' and the term 'affirmative action' are different," Connerly reportedly told the press the next day. "I favor a more pure form of affirmative action. I swear to God that has always been my position from the beginning."[219]

Connerly currently sits on the board of the California Chamber of Commerce, and has served as chairman of the tax-exempt California Governor's Foundation.[220] In 1998 he was named the Republican Party's chief California fund-raiser. Connerly also has targeted the ethnic, women's, and gay/lesbian studies programs taught in California's public universities. "I don't want to suggest in any way that we want . . . to tell [the faculty] whether they should have ethnic studies or not," Connerly claimed, acknowledging he was stepping outside of the regents' tradi-tional role. "But I certainly think it's appropriate for the taxpayers and the public . . . to question all of this."[221]

Connerly works closely with the leading conservative legal groups that oppose the gains of the 1960s civil rights movement. He participates in joint national press conferences[222] and projects, such as the Center for Equal Opportunity's Project for All Deliberate Speed,[223] and cosponsors events, for example, with the Institute for Justice,[224] with whom ACRI held a national strategy conference in Washington in late 1997.[225] Connerly has been honored by some of the country's most conserva-tive organizations, including the Independent Women's Forum[226] and the Council for National Policy (see above).[227]

Along with such veteran opponents of diversity and affirmative action poli-cies as Abigail and Stephan Thernstrom, Linda Chavez, Elaine Chao (now secre-tary of labor), Barbara Ledeen (formerly of the Independent Women's Forum), Gerald Reynolds (formerly of the Center for New Black Leadership, appointed by George W. Bush to the Department of Education's civil rights office in March 2002), Clint Bolick, and others, in 1998 Connerly formed the Citizens Initiative on Race and Ethnicity, a conservative alternative to President Clinton's Initiative on Race.[228]

Despite being "snubbed royally" (his words) by George W. Bush for failing to get behind brother Jeb Bush's One Florida plan (designed by the Bush people to head off a Connerly ballot initiative in that complex swing state during an election year), Connerly ruthlessly attacked Al Gore during the presidential election campaign, calling Gore a "hateful man" who "frightens me."[229] In his autobiography, Connerly claims Gore treated him with cold contempt for his opposition to affirmative action at a December 1997 meeting at the White House with some Citizens Initiative participants.[230]

THOMAS L. RHODES

Rhodes, who sits on the Board of Directors of ACRI, is one of the senior figures in the American conservative movement. His political initiative and support for Connerly's fund-raising efforts have enabled ACRI to carve a national role for itself in the battle against affirmative action.[231] Rhodes is on the Board of Directors of the Bradley Foundation, where he served on the committee charged with selecting a successor to its outgoing head, Michael Joyce.[232] After graduating from the University of Pennsylvania in 1963 and receiving an MBA from Wharton in 1965, Rhodes went on to serve on the board of the Manhattan Institute, and to found Change-NY, a right-wing policy group.[233] Rhodes is the president of *National Review*, the flagship journal of the paleoconservative Right.[234] A long-time friend and associate of William F. Buckley, Jr., founder of *National Review*, he joined the *National Review* Board of Directors in 1988 and its executive committee in 1990. In 1991, Rhodes joined the advisory board of the Empire Foundation for Policy Research,[235] and went on to serve as chairman.[236] On December 1, 1992, Rhodes left the investment house of Goldman Sachs to replace Buckley as president of *National Review*.[237]

National Review opposed the civil rights movement at its inception. Reacting to the 1954 Supreme Court decision in *Brown v. Board of Education* ruling compulsory segregation in public schools unconstitutional, it declared:

> The central question that emerges—and it is not a parliamentary question or a question that is answered by merely consulting a catalogue of rights of American citizens, born Equal—is whether the White community in the South is entitled to take such measures as are necessary to prevail, politically and culturally, in areas where it does not predominate numerically? The sobering answer is Yes—the White community is so entitled because, for the time being, it is the advanced race....
>
> National Review believes that the South's premises are correct. If the majority wills what is socially atavistic, then to thwart the majority may be, though undemocratic, enlightened.... Universal suffrage is not the beginning of wisdom or the beginning of freedom.[238]

National Review has continued under Rhodes's leadership to publish views strenuously opposing diversity initiatives.[239]

WILLIAM J. LEHRFELD

ACRI was incorporated in Washington, D.C. Its incorporation papers name William J. Lehrfeld, Amber Wong, and Tomas Taylor as incorporators. Lehrfeld heads the Fund for a Living Government (FLAG), a D.C. based tax-exempt foundation, which contributed $50,000 to the Paula Jones Legal Fund. At the time of that contribution, Lehrfeld was also counsel to the Arkansas Project, a $2.4 million campaign funded by Richard Mellon Scaife to seek derogatory information about President Clinton.

EDWARD BLUM

In October 2000 the American Civil Rights Institute acquired Edward Blum's Texas-based Campaign for a Color Blind America, creating a new division called American Civil Rights Institute, Legal Defense Fund.[240] Blum, a former Paine Webber trader who resigned after being asked by the company to stop publishing anti-affirmative action views in 1997,[241] has opened a Washington office of ACRI, while Connerly is continuing to operate from Sacramento.[242] Blum, who led the charge against affirmative action in Houston, has assumed the position of director of legal affairs at ACRI.[243] On November 5, 2001, ACRI announced the filing of a federal lawsuit in Miami on behalf of two white children, challenging "accelerated/gifted school programs that racially discriminate in the admissions process."[244]

B. Center for Equal Opportunity and Equal Opportunity Foundation

> We make these decisions based on our idea of fairness, but what we don't realize is that the market is probably a better regulator of fairness. . . . Our attempts to force employers to do things that don't add to productivity can upset the balance and ultimately mean less prosperity for all.[245]
>
> —Linda Chavez

Linda Chavez founded the Center for Equal Opportunity (CEO), a project of the Equal Opportunity Foundation, in 1985 to "counter the divisive impact of race conscious public policies."[246] Of the organizations driving the assault on affirmative action, CEO is the group that most closely reflects the neoconservative ideological strain that so influenced the perspective of senior Reagan administration officials. Secular, pro-business, and with a passion for deregulation, the Center for Equal Opportunity works in strategic ways from inside and outside government to reverse civil rights programs.

Drawing on the success of Reagan's appeal, CEO's representatives cloak their anti-civil rights agenda in talk of "economic justice." They emphasize unfairness: "The truly disadvantaged do not benefit from affirmative action. Many of the beneficiaries of these programs are middle class or affluent members of preferred racial and ethnic groups." They claim civil rights regulations corrupt the economy. Speaking of affirmative action in federal contracting, CEO president Chavez has charged, "This program provides vast incentives for inefficiency and fraud."[247]

Chavez's solution is to do away with government programs in line with what CEO calls "true equality." Ignoring the history of forced segregation and the discrimination that still persists, CEO declares, "The time has come to abandon double standards and to promote true equality before the law."[248] Although CEO does not chiefly conduct litigation, instead preferring to focus on the political, media, and policy research battles around diversity issues, it does weigh in occasionally with *amicus* briefs in cases it considers especially important. For example, CEO filed an *amicus* brief—together with Ward Connerly's ACRI and the Pacific Legal Foundation—supporting the plaintiff in the October 31, 2001, Supreme Court case in *Adarand v. Mineta*, and held a national press conference one day earlier to urge the court to end affirmative action in contracting.[249] Although the court dismissed the case for procedural reasons, CEO general counsel Roger Clegg declared this was "not much of a setback," clearly setting the stage for further legal challenges to measures designed to give minorities greater access to federal contracts.[250] CEO also filed an *amicus* brief in the University of Michigan *Grutter* case (together with ACRI and the Independent Women's Forum),[251] and its chief counsel Roger Clegg coauthored an *amicus* brief in the important *Hi-Voltage* affirmative action case (see section below on Pacific Legal Foundation) on behalf of Glynn Custred and Thomas Wood, two of the originators of the Proposition 209 drive to end affirmative action in California.[252]

Chavez, a former staff director of the U.S. Commission on Civil Rights (1983–1986), was one of the leaders of the Reagan administration's crusade to reverse the government's position on civil rights programs such as school integration (mandatory busing), affirmative action, bilingual education, and pay equity. At the end of the 1980s she chaired an obscure conservative think tank, the Equal Opportunity Foundation,[253] which hosts the CEO, formed in late 1994. Whereas the foundation addresses civil rights issues in the broadest sense (opposing the Americans with Disabilities Act and the Civil Rights Act of 1990),[254] CEO focuses more narrowly on race. Staking out a place at the heart of a debate that was growing intense after the congressional elections of 1994 and the passage of the anti-immigrant Proposition 187 in California, CEO declared itself "the first think tank in Washington devoted exclusively to race, ethnicity, immigration, and public policy."[255]

Like Ward Connerly's American Civil Rights Institute, the Center for Equal Opportunity operates in the arena of public opinion and political pressure. Although the group does some litigation, CEO primarily tries to influence policy via the media and direct intervention rather than through traditional means of litigating or lobbying.

CEO has been criticized for focusing almost exclusively on media outreach. As one author has observed:

> In recent years, however, a new strain of . . . think tanks has taken root and turned the traditional model on its head. Rather than being collections of scholars generating ideas, these new groups are based solely on a single person's opinions, personality and ambitions. Others in the think tank community have dismissively dubbed these organizations "ego centers." Given that it produces more than 10 times as many opinion pieces as research papers, the function of CEO appears to be the promotion of Chavez's previous works and her weekly syndicated column, rather than rigorous intellectual development or continued examination of her ideas in the manner of traditional think tanks. Indeed, it would be easy to conclude that CEO exists largely to keep Chavez and her ideas in the public spotlight.[256]

Working in a style reminiscent of the think tanks Chavez is familiar with (she was a Manhattan Institute fellow for six years) and sometimes directly in conjunction with them (for example, the Cato Institute),[257] CEO works with likeminded academics to produce ideologically driven "research," then pushes the findings into the public debate through seminars, congressional testimony, and a network of media contacts long developed by the leaders of the group.[258]

CEO works on a variety of race-related issues, including bilingual and "Afrocentric" education,[259] racial districting, busing, and immigration.[260] With regard to affirmative action in particular, the center has studied several public university systems since 1996, including state schools in California, Washington State, Colorado, North Carolina, Michigan, and Virginia, as well as the service academies at West Point and Annapolis, and has issued requests for admissions data to other states. Taking advantage of existing public records laws, CEO demands detailed information on admission policies at public colleges.[261] Then, in virtually every case, the center claims that the institutions favor black applicants.

CEO has targeted medical schools in particular, claiming in a 2001 report that they routinely admit black and Latino students with less impressive grades and lower scores than whites and Asians on the Medical College Admission Test (MCAT).[262] Affirmative action in admissions to undergraduate schools has also been targeted. For example, CEO published a study undermining the expert report of Patricia Gurin in the crucial *Gratz v. Bollinger* University of Michigan affirmative action case, reinforcing a similar document issued under the auspices of the National Association of Scholars (see above). In the CEO-sponsored report, *A Critique of the Expert Report of Patricia Gurin in Gratz v. Bollinger,* the authors, Robert Lerner and Althea K. Nagai, explicitly thank Thomas Wood and Malcolm Sherman of the National Association of Scholars for sharing their report with them, and Roger Clegg for editing their own work.[263] Lerner and Nagai had previously analyzed undergraduate admissions to the University of California at

Berkeley, and their data were relied upon by political scientist (and Randolph Foundation trustee) James Q. Wilson to defend Prop 209, who pronounced that "The argument for diversity is a sham."[264]

CEO's studies are strategically targeted and carefully timed to serve the interests of local campaigns, and the group works directly with organizers. Just weeks before voters in Washington were to go to the polls on Initiative 200—banning affirmative action in the state—CEO released a study of the academic qualifications of undergraduate applicants to the University of Washington and Washington State University, concluding that both schools "discriminate" in favor of African American applicants. The study's release in Washington, D.C., was cosponsored by the Washington Institute Foundation, on whose board sits John Carlson, chairman of the I-200 campaign.[265]

For its Wisconsin study, CEO worked with the Wisconsin branch of the National Association of Scholars (two of whose California members authored Proposition 209—see above). CEO and the Wisconsin Association of Scholars sought admissions data on the University of Wisconsin system's thirteen four-year campuses,[266] but this attempt was rejected by the Wisconsin Court of Appeals on August 30, 2001.[267]

In Massachusetts, CEO requested similar information from public institutions over five years, working closely with Stephan Thernstrom, a Harvard history professor (coauthor of *America in Black and White: One Nation, Indivisible,*[268] with his wife, Abigail, who sits on CEO's advisory board). "Massachusetts might well be the last state to pass something like 209," he told the press, referring to California's anti-affirmative action proposition, "but it's certainly not impossible to have something like that here."[269] The Thernstroms (regular recipients of Olin Foundation support[270]) are also active in the Olin-funded National Association of Scholars.[271]

While the Center for Equal Opportunity rarely files lawsuits as the lead plaintiff itself, it does file *amicus* briefs (for example, with the antifeminist Independent Women's Forum in *Piscataway Township v. Board of Education*[272]), and it actively solicits clients for legal actions, for example, with Internet alerts such as the following:

ACTIVIST ALERT

The Center for Equal Opportuntiy [sic] *is currently seeking to interview people who have had a negative experience with bilingual education programs, especially parents. Call CEO toll free at 1 (800) 819-2343.*[273]

Parents in New Mexico, with the assistance of CEO, filed suit against their school district, seeking to end bilingual education in Albuquerque.[274] CEO also works with conservative legal organizations, in particular the Pacific Legal Foundation (PLF) (see below)—itself a recipient of major underwriting from conservative foundations. PLF often cites CEO studies in its briefs, and has filed petitions on CEO's behalf, proposing regulations to force compliance with California Proposition 227 (against bilingual education) and Proposition 209, and opposing waivers on implementation at the state and local levels.[275]

Policing Compliance: The Project for All Deliberate Speed

Well aware of the power of a highly public inquisition, CEO specializes in enforcement efforts, pursuing state law enforcement officers as aggressively as the group has targeted college administrators. In 1998, CEO sent all fifty state attorneys general a letter requesting "information on their role in any litigation challenging state programs that use racial or ethnic classifications."[276] The letter is part of the ongoing "Project for All Deliberate Speed," the aim of which, according to Chavez, is to urge state governments to end so-called racial preferences and other forms of discrimination in their laws and programs "with all deliberate speed." CEO's cosponsors on the Project are Clint Bolick, Ward Connerly, and Edwin Meese.[277]

Linda Chavez spoke at the Civil Rights workshop at the Federalist Society National Lawyers Conference in November 1998 about the Project for All Deliberate Speed (whose title draws cynically on the language of 1960s Civil Rights Act enforcement). She asked "those who remember the Civil Rights era" to recall that there has always been "massive resistance to Civil Rights law." As of that meeting, CEO had received replies from all but seven of the states. "The next job is to inform the public" about who is complying and who is not, and who is withholding information, Chavez continued.[278]

CEO already has sent letters to the federal judges who supervise school districts that remain under federal desegregation orders, asking them to "investigate whether there is still evidence that these schools are segregated in violation of the Constitution." If not, says Chavez, "we called on them to end federal judicial supervision." The court orders, as Chavez points out in her monthly memo on CEO's website, "make it difficult or impossible to adopt reforms such as school choice, charter schools, and school vouchers." In one state, says Chavez, the presiding judge distributed CEO's letter to the district's lawyers.[279] Since much of the work of the civil rights movement was implemented through court-supervised, rather than legislative, intervention, this legal approach is an effort to roll back the gains of the 1960s and 1970s in integrating education.

Chavez has also used this tactic to influence electoral redistricting. In a letter dated March 7, 2001, she urged "state officials all over the country not to use race and ethnicity when redrawing voting districts after the [2000] Census," declaring such use "racial gerrymandering." The contact persons for the letter were Roger Clegg of CEO and Edward Blum, the legal affairs director of ACRI. The letter relies upon legal arguments developed by Daniel Troy (see below), who has served as a steering committee member of the Washington, D.C., chapter of the Federalist Society, and served on the board of the Campaign for a Color Blind America along with Paul Weyrich. It was signed by Susan Au Allen of the U.S. Pan Asian American Chamber of Commerce; Phyllis Berry Myers of the Center for New Black Leadership (see below); Edward Blum; Clint Bolick; Lynn Hogue of the Southeastern Legal Foundation (see below); Terry Pell of the Center for Individual Rights; Kimberly Schuld of the Independent Women's Forum; and Abigail Thernstrom of the Manhattan Institute.[280]

Corporations may be next. "It's time to turn up the heat" on corporations that support affirmative action, Chavez told Federalist Society lawyers in 1998. "We could learn a thing or two from our opponents," she conceded, suggesting activists attend stockholder meetings of corporations like Boeing and Microsoft (which took out ads opposing Initiative 200 in their home state of Washington) to make them "pay a price for funding preferences."[281]

Apart from the Project for All Deliberate Speed, CEO has worked with the Institute for Justice on several projects. It was the Institute's Clint Bolick who led the attack on Lani Guinier, President Clinton's nominee to head the civil rights division of the Justice Department in 1993. And it was Bolick, CEO's Roger Clegg, and Heritage's Edwin Meese who collaborated against President Clinton's nominee for Associate Attorney General Bill Lann Lee, who ultimately received a recess appointment.[282]

As noted earlier, Chavez formed the Citizens' Initiative on Race and Ethnicity with Ward Connerly and Clint Bolick, a publicity-seeking committee brought together to provide a platform for critics of Clinton's Initiative on Race (along with Gerald Reynolds—see above). Vice-chair of the Initiative is Abigail Thernstrom, who has served on both the board of the Equal Opportunity Foundation (EOF) and the board of the Institute for Justice (Chavez and Thernstrom are also both supporters of the Independent Women's Forum).[283] With the coming to power of the second Bush administration, the "Citizens Initiative" seems to have run out of steam.

Center for Equal Opportunity and Equal Opportunity Foundation

The Equal Opportunity Foundation (EOF) Board of Directors includes Linda Chavez, Abigail Thernstrom, John Miller, and Arch Puddington (see bios below).[284] A relative newcomer to the EOF board is Rosalie Porter, author of *Forked Tongue: The Politics of Bilingual Education*.[285] On January 1, 1999, the Equal Opportunity Foundation acquired the Institute for Research in English Acquisition and Development (READ), an Amherst, Massachusetts–based program Porter had headed (in relative obscurity) since 1989.[286] READ opposes bilingual education programs nationally through publishing research, "servicing school districts with advice and information, and enhancing the public dialogue." Jorge Amselle is executive director of READ and vice president for education at CEO.[287]

For all CEO's talk of race "neutrality" and economics, it is important to remember that the group is rooted not only in neoconservative economic ideology, but also in the desire to wage the "culture wars." Chavez's position on the advisory board of the Catholic League for Religious and Civil Rights illustrates her connections with the broader political right. Among those who sit with her on the League board are Dinesh D'Souza (Heritage Foundation protégé and author of *The End of Racism*) and Thomas Monaghan. (The late William E. Simon also served on the board with Chavez.) Monaghan, founder and former CEO of Domino's Pizza, is a major funder of aggressive anti-choice campaigns in the U.S., and was on the advisory board of the 1996 presidential campaign of Pat Buchanan, another vigorous opponent of affirmative action.[288] Monaghan has pledged over $50 million to a new law school—the Ave Maria School of Law in Ann Arbor, Michigan—that is aggressively promoting conservative Catholic "natural law" theories.[289]

Simon, whose Olin Foundation heavily backed Chavez's efforts, had been president of the Olin Foundation since 1982, and was also on the board of trustees of the Heritage Foundation[290] and the advisory board of the Reason Foundation.[291] Secretary of the treasury and administrator of the Federal Energy Office in the Nixon administration, Simon was a key decision maker during the Reagan administration and played a crucial role in setting up right-wing legal organizations in the 1970s.[292] In 1994 he was finance chair of the Citizens Committee to Confirm Clarence Thomas.[293]

In 1995, Chavez was one of seventeen participants in a three-day colloquium sponsored by the Claremont Institute in Laguna Niguel, California. At its conclusion, Chavez signed a manifesto authored by then Claremont president Larry Arnn (a board member of CADAP—see above). The manifesto includes the following:

> The Founders of America built the first nation dedicated explicitly to the rights of all men under the laws of nature and nature's God. . . . Our problem today consists simply in this: Many of our leaders—intellectual, cultural and political—have abandoned the moral and natural law. If we do not repudiate this error, we will suffer a collapse that is both complete and irrecoverable. It ended with a flourish: The developing conflict over culture is a battle for the soul of America. We call upon all like-minded Americans to fight it, and to win it.

Cosigners with Chavez included Richard Brookhiser, senior editor of the *National Review*; Angela "Bay" Buchanan, sister of Patrick Buchanan and chair of Buchanan's presidential campaign; Edwin Meese; and Ralph Reed, Jr., then executive director of the Christian Coalition.[294]

CEO Funding

Through its parent group, the Equal Opportunity Foundation, CEO receives money from the leading foundations underwriting the conservative movement. In 2000 the Olin Foundation granted $330,000 to EOF to run CEO,[295] building on longtime support.[296] The Sarah Scaife Foundation granted the EOF $50,000 in 2000, $75,000 in 1999, $60,000 in 1998, $60,000 in 1997, $75,000 in 1996, and $75,000 in 1995.[297] The Lambe Foundation, with libertarian funder Charles G. Koch on its board, granted $100,000 to Chavez's organization in 1998.[298]

The Leadership of the Center for Equal Opportunity: Board of Directors

LINDA CHAVEZ

> I have been a beneficiary of affirmative action. You can't be a minority woman today without being a beneficiary.[299]

Conservative columnist, anti-communist, former Young Socialist turned high-ranking Reagan administration official, Linda Chavez helped to found the Center for Equal Opportunity in 1995 and currently serves as the group's first president.[300] She is a member of the Council on Foreign Relations,[301] the Board of Advisors of the Catholic League for Religious and Civil Rights,[302] and the National Advisory Board of the Capital Research Center. Of Mexican-American as well as Irish Catholic heritage, Chavez is monolingual in English and a vigorous opponent of bilingual education. Nominated to be labor secretary by George W. Bush, Chavez's nomination went down in flames after it was revealed that she might not have obeyed the law in hiring a domestic worker.[303] She has rededicated herself to CEO, continuing to speak out vigorously against affirmative action.[304]

In the late 1980s, she headed the highly controversial organization U.S. English, which came under a torrent of criticism for racism (see below), and in the 1990s, she advised Ron Unz on his successful campaign to bar bilingual teaching in California's public schools (Proposition 227).[305] Chavez is the author of *Out of the Barrio: Toward a New Politics of Hispanic Assimilation*.[306] She is a contributing editor at *Crisis*, the Catholic conservative magazine, and a former fellow at the Manhattan Institute. She has also served on the Board of Directors of Greyhound Lines, Inc., and ABM Industries, a building-maintenance firm.[307]

Chavez has been associated with affirmative action and multiculturalism issues since she was an undergraduate at UCLA in the early 1970s.[308] A graduate of the University of Colorado (1970) and UCLA (1972), Chavez worked for the House Judiciary Subcommittee on Civil and Constitutional Rights from 1972 to 1974,[309] then in the Carter administration as a consultant to the civil rights section at the Office of Management and Budget.[310] From 1977 to 1983 she came under the influence of various conservative movement ideologues at the American Federation of Teachers—primarily Albert Shanker, the union's aggressively anti-affirmative action, anti-bilingual, anti-busing president; but also Jeane Kirkpatrick, Robert Bork, and William Bennett, all contributors to *American Educator,* the union's journal of which she was the editor.[311]

In 1983, with the strong backing of veteran conservative activist William Bennett,[312] Ronald Reagan named Chavez staff director at the U.S. Commission on Civil Rights as part of a stormy reorganization in which he replaced three liberal members with conservatives.[313] Chavez led the charge (along with William Bradford Reynolds at the Justice Department) to reverse the government's civil rights program, taking positions against affirmative action and mandatory busing[314] and for limits on the implementation of Title IX.[315] Chavez's first steps as commissioner included canceling a study of the effects on minorities of cuts in student aid, and commissioning a report on the "general decline in academic standards" that she said coincided with the advent of affirmative action in higher education. She proposed a commission statement opposing court-ordered affirmative action plans in the Detroit police department. As for what she called the "radical" idea that men and women should receive equal pay for comparable work, if that idea were accepted, she wrote, it would "alter our existing . . . economy."[316] After her appointment to a White House position, she changed her party affiliation from Democrat to Republican.[317]

Chavez's actions at the commission so enraged its constituency that in 1985 the heads of the Hispanic and Black caucuses and Patricia Schroeder, chair of the Congressional Caucus on Women's Issues, proposed a complete cut-off of funds for the commission. The critics said the commission sought to change the meaning of civil rights "without the benefit of any hearings or investigative studies."[318]

Chavez's credo: "Many people confuse civil rights with social concerns—unemployment, poverty, housing, and other problems. Social problems and economic hardships have nothing to do with civil rights." The problems "facing minorities today, and blacks in particular," she told the *Washington Post* in 1986, were the result of social factors, and "cannot be solved by civil rights laws."[319] Chavez has cited "the problem of out-of-wedlock births" as an example of the type of problem that cannot be solved by government action.[320] Following her tenure at the commission, Chavez did a stint as White House director of public liaison (1985), working closely with movement conservatives such as chief of staff Donald T. Regan and communications director Pat Buchanan.[321]

A devout Reagan disciple, Chavez favored the Strategic Defense Initiative (Star Wars), opposed sanctions against South Africa, was against the Equal Rights Amendment, and is opposed to abortion rights.[322] On that platform, in 1986, with help from top Republican consultant Edward J. Rollins,[323] Chavez ran a hardball campaign for the U.S. Senate in Maryland against Democratic Representative Barbara Mikulski, whom she labeled a "San Francisco-style

Democrat" and urged to "come out of the closet."[324] She was roundly defeated at the polls but boosted in national recognition.

Chavez, whose family has not spoken Spanish since the 1870s,[325] was hired in August 1987 by Dr. John Tanton to give a new public profile to U.S. English, a group committed to making English the official language of the United States. Chavez was president of U.S. English from 1987 to 1988.[326] U.S. English was founded in 1983 by S. I. Hayakawa (a defender of the internment of Japanese-Americans in World War II)[327] and Tanton, an ophthalmologist from Petoskey, Michigan. It was heavily funded by Cordelia Scaife May (Richard Mellon Scaife's sister and a major funder of right-wing population control projects and anti-immigration causes).[328] Tanton also founded the Federation for American Immigration Reform, a recipient of support from the Pioneer Fund—which has sponsored research by scientists who have, critics charge, aimed to show that blacks are intellectually inferior to whites (see below).[329] He is the founding chairman of ProEnglish, an organization that has announced plans to sue President Bush, Attorney General John Ashcroft, and Health and Human Services Secretary Tommy G. Thompson to overturn Executive Order 13166, signed by President Clinton, which requires federal agencies and recipients of federal money to ensure that the inability to speak English does not have the effect of barring individuals from gaining access to federally funded programs.[330]

U.S. English aggressively lobbied states and presented an amendment promoting English as the sole official language in the U.S. Among other efforts, it sponsored a write-in campaign to support Chavez's advocate, Secretary of Education William Bennett, in his attacks on the Bilingual Education Act in 1985 to 1986.[331] After the *Arizona Republic* broke the story of a secret memorandum in which cofounder Tanton outlined the dangers of a Hispanic population explosion, Chavez resigned.[332] In 1998, Chavez supported Arizona's English-only law and defended the state's right to legislate the use of English for non-English speakers. "Language is a mutable characteristic. It can be changed," Chavez told the *Arizona Republic*. "People learn different languages."[333]

After the U.S. English debacle, Chavez returned to Washington as a fellow at the Manhattan Institute. With a Bradley Foundation-funded fellowship, Chavez was able to research and write *Out of the Barrio*, and she became a regular commentator on *The McLaughlin Group*, *CNN & Co.*, *To the Contrary*, and the *PBS NewsHour*. She was also named director of the Center for the New American Community, a group based in Manhattan, to address the assimilation issue "as a counterweight to the multicultural movement."[334]

Chavez served as a U.S. expert on the United Nations Commission on Human Rights from 1992 to 1996, and resumed a more active role in politics when conservatives in California sought her support for Proposition 209 and Ron Unz's campaign for Proposition 227, the latter a measure barring bilingual education in California's public schools.[335] At a low point in the Prop 209 campaign, six months before Ward Connerly was persuaded to take the helm, Chavez addressed "a small gathering of supporters" in Los Angeles, telling them the initiative "represents the best opportunity for signaling an end to the nation's slide into preferential policies."[336]

CEO is but the latest vehicle of a long career. Reflecting on her position in the conservative universe, Chavez once remarked: "I became a Republican because of Ronald Reagan, and I guess I'm more of a Reaganite than anything."[337] Chavez is married to Christopher Gersten, formerly political director of the American Israel Public Affairs Committee (AIPAC), the most powerful pro-Israel lobby. Gersten is also a founding director of the Institute for Religious Values, an organization that attempts to build support for antiabortion positions in the Jewish community.[338]

ABIGAIL THERNSTROM

Thernstrom, who in addition to sitting on the board of Equal Opportunity Foundation serves on the Board of Directors of the Institute for Justice, has become one of the most prominent critics of affirmative action and the feminist movement. Since January 2001 she has served on the U.S. Commission on Civil Rights, where she became involved in the successful but controversial Bush administration effort to seat a fellow opponent of affirmative action, Peter Kirsanow, former head of the right-wing Center for New Black leadership (see below).[339] A senior fellow at the Manhattan Institute, together with her husband Stephan (a Harvard historian), Thernstrom has penned one of the most straightforward academic attacks on affirmative action in print—*America in Black and White*.[340] The book was financed by the Olin, Bradley, Earhart, Smith Richardson, and Carthage Foundations. Roger Clegg of CEO and Ricky Silberman of the Independent Women's Forum assisted with the manuscript.[341]

Thernstrom has been writing on race issues for two decades, having weighed in as early as 1979 with an article in *Public Interest* magazine, arguing, in the midst of a debate on enforcement of the voting rights act of 1965, that federal attempts to ensure representation for racial groups lead to political polarization.[342] Thernstrom, an early and vocal critic of affirmative action,[343] also opposed minority-voting districts.[344] She is also a longtime opponent of bilingual education.[345] She serves on the national advisory board of the Independent Women's Forum along with affirmative action opponents Jennifer Braceras (now on the U.S. Civil Rights Commission), Linda Chavez, and Lisa Schiffren;[346] and is thanked for assisting with Clint Bolick's most recent book, *Transformation*. In April 1999 she spoke before the Milwaukee lawyers chapter of the Federalist Society and the Wisconsin Forum on race issues.[347] Thernstrom was projects director of the Twentieth Century Fund from 1981 to 1986, a member of the domestic strategy group of the Aspen Institute (1992–1997), a member of the education policy committee of the Hudson Institute (1994–1997), and is a member of the advisory board of the American Friends of the Institute for Justice in London.[348]

JOHN MILLER

John Miller rose from college editor of the University of Michigan's conservative *Michigan Review*[349] to a Bradley Fellow at the Heritage Foundation,[350] to his current position as national political reporter for William F. Buckley's *National Review*.[351] He has also been a Manhattan Institute Fellow[352] and vice president of CEO. He remains on the Board of Directors of the Equal Opportunity Foundation.[353]

Miller's first book, *The Unmaking of Americans: How Multiculturalism Has Undermined America's Assimilation Ethic*, was published by the Free Press in July 1998, and received positive reviews from former New York Housing and Urban Development administrator and fellow Manhattan Institute Fellow Roger Starr in the *Washington Times*.[354] A stout defender of Linda Chavez after her failed nomination for labor secretary in early 2001,[355] Miller's articles in *National Review* regularly deal with the battle against affirmative action.

Described as "one of the brightest young thinkers on the right" by *American Prospect*[356] magazine, Miller is often quoted in the media on issues relating to immigration. Speaking as a supporter of Congress's 1996 Welfare Reform Bill that stripped legal immigrants of food stamp, Medicaid, and SSI benefits, Miller said "there ought to be meaningful distinctions between citizens and non-citizens, and this (welfare reform) can be one of them."[357] An opponent of dual citizenship, Miller claims that if an individual has two passports, "it's akin to polygamy."[358]

ARCH PUDDINGTON

Puddington, a board member of EOF, is vice president of research at Freedom House, a New York-based conservative think tank,[359] and a self-described "professional cold warrior."[360] Old red-baiting habits seem to die hard with Puddington, and he has brought these into the debate on affirmative action. Writing in the *Washington Times* in 1998, he noted that those who say "that a cutback of affirmative action violates the rights of blacks" remind him that "during the Cold War, those demanding economic and social rights often harbored a hidden agenda: socialism."[361] Puddington criticizes the AFL-CIO's support for affirmative action, warning of its penetration by "operatives from left-wing splinter groups."[362] In the wake of the New York City police killing of an unarmed African immigrant, Amadou Diallo, Puddington also rejected suggestions that the New York City police department needs to consider implementing an affirmative action program to address racial tension between itself and minority communities, writing that "problems with misconduct and incompetence [have resulted elsewhere] as standards have been lowered to bring minority officers into the ranks."[363] Puddington suggests that we should "jettison altogether the concept of diversity."[364]

Formerly with Radio Free Europe and Radio Liberty, Puddington once served as executive director of the League for Industrial Democracy, a Cold War labor group. Like Linda Chavez, Puddington is a former Social Democrat,[365] and he has written attacks on affirmative action for her as far back as 1984, when he contributed an article on the legal primacy of the principle of seniority to that of racial balance for *New Perspectives* (which Chavez edited), the quarterly magazine published by the U.S. Commission on Civil Rights when Chavez was staff director.[366]

BRIAN W. JONES

Three days after the September 11 terrorist attacks, and in the midst of a storm of congressional sentiment to accommodate Bush, Brian W. Jones, an African-American attorney, was confirmed by the Senate as the Department of Education's general counsel, despite the vigorous opposition of civil rights advocates.[367] Before taking up his post at the DOE, Jones was in private practice with Curiale, Dellaverson, Hirschfeld, Kelly, and Kraemer in San Francisco.[368] Earlier, in 1998, he served as deputy legal affairs secretary to California Governor Pete Wilson.

Jones has served as a board member of Linda Chavez's Foundation for Equal Opportunity; was cofounder, director, and former president (1995–1997) of the Center for New Black Leadership (see below);[369] and was an executive committee member of the Federalist Society's Civil Rights Practice Group (see below).[370] He was also a member of the national advisory council of Project 21, a "national leadership network of conservative African Americans" run by the National Center for Public Policy Research.[371] From his post at the Center for New Black Leadership, and helped by the promotional efforts of Project 21, Jones became one of the leading voices of black conservatism, acting as a commentator on MSNBC from 1997 to 1998. "In the media and in public, black moderates are drowned out by liberal leaders," he told the *Wall Street Journal* in 1997. "Mr. [Ward] Connerly's challenge is to figure out how we can mobilize the same kind of passion on our side that defenders of affirmative action feel."[372] In 1997 he served as counsel to the U.S. Senate Judiciary Committee, advising committee chair Orrin Hatch (R-UT) on nominations and on constitutional and civil rights affairs.[373] Hatch went on to assume the role of cochair, along with Robert Bork, of the Federalist Society's Board of Visitors (formerly known as the Board of Trustees).

As an undergraduate at Georgetown University, Jones was president of the College Democrats, but not long after graduating law school at University of California–Los Angeles he was already deeply ensconced in the Right. In 1993, when Paul Weyrich launched National Empowerment Television, the twenty-seven-year-old Jones was general manager.[374]

CEO Staff

ROGER CLEGG

Roger Clegg currently serves as vice president and general counsel for CEO. In November 2001 he was elected chairman of the Civil Rights Practice Group of the Federalist Society.[375] He graduated from Yale Law School and received his B.A. from Rice University. Soon after finishing law school, Clegg swiftly moved through the ranks of the U.S. Justice Department, working under William Bradford Reynolds (see above).[376] He began his career in the department as the acting assistant attorney general in the Office of Legal Policy, and then became associate deputy attorney general before working as assistant to the solicitor general. From 1987 to 1991 he served as deputy assistant attorney general for civil rights, before moving to the Environment and Natural Resources Division, where he served as a deputy assistant attorney general as well. Clegg rose through the Reagan/Bush bureaucracy, reaching the second-highest position in the civil rights division in 1987 before switching to the natural resources division of the DOJ in 1991. Before joining CEO, Clegg was assistant treasurer, vice president, and general counsel for the National Legal Center for the Public Interest in Washington, D.C., which was instrumental in setting up the national infrastructure of the legal right wing (for more on the National Legal Center, see above).[377]

Along with Anita Blair, executive vice president and general counsel of the Scaife-funded Independent Women's Forum, he authored an *amicus* brief before the Supreme Court in support of Sharon Taxman in *Piscataway Township v. Taxman.* In his brief, Clegg argued that this case involved reverse discrimination.[378] Testifying before the House Judiciary Subcommittee on the Constitution, Clegg derided President Clinton's decision to have "a cabinet that looks like America" as an example of the "irrational and unfair practices" of so-called race- and gender-based preferences, "driving Americans apart."[379] Under Clegg's leadership, in 2001 CEO filed an *amicus* brief, along with the Pacific Legal Foundation, in the *Alexander v. Sandoval* case, arguing that there is no private right of action to bring disparate impact[380] claims under Title VI and that disparate impact regulations are invalid.[381]

Clegg also has targeted outreach programs aimed at attracting minority students to schools and universities. In a *Washington Times* opinion article adapted from the Heritage Foundation's *Policy Review* journal, Clegg warns that "proponents of colorblind affirmative action need to beware of ostensibly race-neutral programs that are really preferences. In any instance where a government agency weighs race, ethnicity, or gender in granting a benefit, it is using unconstitutional preferences. This is true even if the preference is used only for outreach or recruitment."[382]

JORGE AMSELLE

In 1992, Jorge Amselle, then president of the University of Maryland College Republicans, pronounced among the first of what was to become many sound bites from him in the national media. "I'm hoping Buchanan makes a good showing and makes Bush more conservative," Amselle told the *Baltimore Sun.*[383] Out of the background of his early support for one of the more "nativist" and xenophobic presidential candidates in American history, Amselle emerged in 1995 as a "policy analyst" for CEO[384] and as its communications director from 1996 to 1998.[385]

Currently billed as CEO's vice president for education,[386] Amselle has risen through CEO's ranks by making a crusade out of ending bilingual education programs. In March 2000 he published a long attack on bilingual education in Sun Myung Moon's *The World and I* magazine.[387] Amselle began publishing his views in the *Washington Times*, the *Weekly Standard*, and the Heritage Foundation's *Policy Review*.[388] In 1996 he testified before the Senate Committee on Labor and Human Resources,[389] and he continues to be cited in congressional debates as an expert on bilingual education.[390] While delivering CEO's official message to the press, he simultaneously began to contribute editorials and opinion pieces to newspapers and magazines—occasionally listed as CEO's "Project Director for Bilingual Education Programs,"[391] an oddly named post indeed.

Hugh Joseph Beard, Jr.

As a delegate and member of the Rules Committee at the Republican National Convention in 1980, Hugh J. ("Joe") Beard supported a proposal to release delegates "pledged" to support a specific candidate for president to vote for whomever they wished. "No Republican's conscience," Beard told the *Washington Post*, "should be burdened with having to vote for a left-wing lunatic like John Anderson."[392]

Beard passed away in July 2002. Beard, who left his post in 2000 as senior counsel at Center for Equal Opportunity[393] and took a position as a career attorney in the voting rights section of Ashcroft's Justice Department,[394] was no stranger to rhetorical excess or to the more extreme elements of the Right. A teenage veteran of the Goldwater campaign, Beard graduated in 1971 from the University of North Carolina Law School, working briefly as an assistant U.S. Attorney before opening his own law practice in Charlotte, N.C.[395]

He served as a delegate to the 1976 and 1980 Republican National Conventions, managed the Charlotte branch of Jesse Helms's Senate campaign in 1978, and was executive director of the North Carolina Fund for Individual Rights from 1973 to 1981. Beard litigated a number of cases challenging affirmative action and other "liberal" policies of educational institutions, including several suits brought against his alma mater, the University of North Carolina. In one such case, he tried to argue that the use of state money to support the student newspaper, the *Daily Tar Heel*, given its consistently liberal editorial policy, amounted to an unconstitutional establishment of religion.[396]

These accomplishments prepared Beard to accept a position in the Reagan administration in May 1981 as deputy general counsel of the Department of Education, where Clarence Thomas was getting his start in government service as assistant secretary for civil rights. Beard stirred up more controversy when the press obtained his internal memo suggesting tactics for getting the administration's proposed restrictions on education funds for the disabled enacted.[397] Beard cautioned that his plan "to divide the enemy" might run into trouble if "Congress [found] this to be a trick, which it definitely is." Secretary of Education Terrel H. Bell had to publicly disavow Beard's comments on national television, hastening to assure Senator Lowell Weicker (R-CT) that "that person has been reprimanded over it."[398]

In 1984, Beard was transferred to the Department of Justice, where he worked as special assistant to the assistant attorney general for civil rights, William Bradford Reynolds, a position he held until September 1992. Beard worked on anti-busing litigation at DOJ,[399] and found time to argue on his behalf unsuccessfully before the North Carolina Supreme Court, challenging his suspension from the North Carolina bar for failing, on principle, to pay a required $50 per year to a Client Security Fund.[400] He became president of the Equal Opportunity Foundation on December 1, 1992.[401]

Beard was also well-known as one of the original members of the Pro-Life Alliance of Gays and Lesbians (PLAGAL),[402] from which he received an award for his decade-long service as secretary and treasurer.[403] Beard proudly asserted, "my ability to get into philosophical arguments is unsurpassed in D.C. ['s gay community]," and argues against any alliance between the gay rights and pro-choice movements: "How many babies would you kill in order to be able to sleep with your boyfriend?"[404] In 1998, Beard introduced a resolution that led to the D.C. Log Cabin Republicans bestowing their "Spirit of Lincoln" award on Ward Connerly, champion of the California Civil Rights Initiative, a move which drew strong protests from some Log Cabin members.[405]

C. Right-Wing Ethnic and Gender-Based Groups in Anti-Affirmative Action Campaigns

Center for New Black Leadership (CNBL)

The rapid success of three of the leaders of the Center for New Black Leadership since it was founded in May 1995 indicates how well connected this organization is to the top levels of the conservative establishment. Gerald Reynolds, Brian Jones, and Peter Kirsanow—who all served as board members of CNBL—were selected in 2001 by the Bush administration for high-level posts dealing with civil rights and diversity issues. The Washington-based CNBL, whose executive director is veteran affirmative action opponent Phyllis Berry Myers, is attempting to position itself as the major voice of conservative black opinion on policy issues in the United States. CNBL is an outgrowth of the Center of the American Experiment, a conservative think tank founded by Minneapolis-based lawyer and lobbyist Mitchell Pearlstein.[406] Kirsanow and Reynolds ran into heavy opposition for their nominations to, respectively, the U.S. Civil Rights Commission and the Department of Education's Office of Civil Rights. Reynolds has been active in the Federalist Society's civil rights practice group. According to its mission statement, "The Center is a public policy research and advocacy institute that seeks to promote a new vision of leadership on public policy questions having a racial dimension . . . it emphasizes the primacy of market-oriented, community-based solutions to the nation's problems."[407]

The Center of the American Experiment, which received $20,000 from the Bradley Foundation to support its breakfast and luncheon forum series in 2000,[408] has made school vouchers one of its two main issues, and this concern is shared by CNBL.[409] CNBL phrases its voucher support ambiguously in its mission statement, which claims the Center is dedicated to "promot[ing] the use of publicly-financed scholarships for disadvantaged students," but proudly takes credit for an *amicus* brief in the Milwaukee school voucher case filed by Michael L. Williams, a CNBL board member.[410] Not only does CNBL share an agenda with its progenitor, Pearlstein, it shares funding sources as well. Both the Center of the American Experiment and CNBL have received grants from the John M. Olin Foundation and the J.M. Foundation.[411] The Donner Foundation gave CNBL $56,250 in 1998.[412]

Independent Women's Forum

The Independent Women's Forum (IWF) originated as a loosely tied group of women cobbled together to promote the nomination of Clarence Thomas to the Supreme Court,[413] one of the most successful instances of cooperation among the Christian, neoconservative, and libertarian right in recent American politics.[414] IWF is frequently described as a secular conservative organization and has established itself as the premier antifeminist women's group in Washington.[415] But it has done so with major funding from key financial backers of the religious right, such as the Bradley Foundation ($165,000 in 2000),[416] the North Carolina-based W.H. Brady Foundation ($125,000 in 2000),[417] the Randolph Foundation ($400,000 in 1999),[418] and the Sarah Scaife Foundation ($250,000 for general operating support in 1999).[419] Theodore Olson, now solicitor general and a longtime political ally of Richard Mellon Scaife, served on the national advisory board of the IWF, as did his late wife, Barbara Olson, who had become a ubiquitous hard-line conservative talk show presence before her death in the terrorist attacks of September 11. Ricky Silberman, the wife of prominent right-wing judge Laurence Silberman,[420] is chair of the IWF board of directors.[421] Mary Ellen Bork, wife of Judge Robert Bork, one of only two women who sit on the board of the Catholic Campaign for America, has served on the IWF Board of Directors, along with Lynne V. Cheney, Midge Decter, Kate O'Beirne of *National Review*, and Louise V. Oliver. All have now taken emerita status.[422] Louise Oliver is on the Board of Trustees of the Donner Foundation, which supported the IWF in 1998, along with Nicholas Eberstadt of the American Enterprise Institute.[423]

Active members of the Board of Directors include Heather Richardson Higgins,[424] Kimberly O. Dennis, Wendy Lee Gramm, and Sally C. Pipes of the Pacific Research Institute (see below). IWF's current president and CEO is Nancy

Mitchell Pfotenhauer, a former director of Koch Industries' Washington, D.C., office. As noted above, through their foundations, David and Charles Koch have heavily backed two of the main organizations attacking diversity policies: Linda Chavez's Center for Equal Opportunity and Clint Bolick's Institute for Justice. Pfotenhauer is a former senior economist at the Republican National Committee and served as economic counsel to former Senator William L. Armstrong (R-CO, 1979-1991, now vice chair of Paul Weyrich's Free Congress Foundation).[425]

Laura Ingraham, one of the founders of the group, first gained notoriety as editor in chief of the *Dartmouth Review.* According to published accounts, while Ingraham was editor, the *Review* sent a writer to infiltrate Dartmouth's new Gay Students Association. The *Review* published a portion of the transcript of the meeting, and, according to Ishmael Reed writing in Salon.com, sent secretly recorded tapes to the parents of the members of the group.[426] From college, Ingraham went to the White House, then to the EEOC, where she worked for Clarence Thomas.

The group's former executive director, lawyer Anita Blair, took the side of the Virginia Military Institute against a plaintiff contesting the school's right to exclude women. In 1995 she complained, as the Vatican had, about the use of the word "gender" in the U.N. Conference on Women's Platform For Action.[427] In a report questioning whether the U.S. government should promote a gender-based agenda that "reflects the Marxist roots of feminist ideology,"[428] IWF claimed that the use of the word would lead to a "sexual free for all."

IWF board member emerita Midge Decter also sits on the advisory board of the Capital Research Center (CRC, also funded by the Scaife, Bradley, and J.M. Foundations), which aims to defund liberal institutions.[429] Decter has sought to bridge the neoconservative and the religious right. The Capital Research Center launched a sharp attack on the National Organization for Women and the Feminist Majority Foundation after the two organizations took on Promise Keepers in 1997.[430] Also on the CRC advisory board are other mainstays of the far right, such as Kenneth Cribb (see above), an Edwin Meese protégé who is president of the Intercollegiate Studies Institute (ISI) (founded in 1953 by columnist William F. Buckley, Jr., to promote conservative values among college students and now funded by the Scaife, Bradley, J.M., Coors, Olin Foundations, and the ultraconservative Earhart Foundation).[431] IWF board member Louise Oliver is chair of the ISI Board of Directors.[432] ISI's vice-chairman, Richard M. Larry, was the longtime president of the Sarah Scaife Foundation,[433] and sat on its board along with Richard Scaife, Heritage's Ed Feulner, and Kenneth Cribb.[434]

Although IWF experienced a debilitating upheaval due to a power struggle between Barbara Ledeen[435] and Anita Blair in 2000 (Blair won and Pfotenhauer took over),[436] veterans of the organization are very influential with the new Bush administration. Lynne Cheney, the vice president's wife and a former National Endowment for the Humanities director, is working on education issues; Elaine Chao has become secretary of labor; and Paula Dobriansky has been appointed undersecretary of state for global affairs.[437]

Chapter 4

The Legal Battle:
Strategic Litigation and Networking

> This is not just about winning a lot of law cases. This is all the marbles, this is
> a fight for what kind of country this is. And if you want to be in that fight you
> have to have alliances that hold and real political constituencies that put some
> muscle behind the struggle.
>
> —Michael S. Greve[438]

A. Center for Individual Rights (CIR)

The Center for Individual Rights (CIR) is perhaps the most politically extreme of
the groups challenging affirmative action, civil rights, and racial equality in the
United States today. Though relatively small in size, it has raised to a fine art the
strategy of combining a virulently hostile attitude toward the civil rights gains of
the post-World War II period and a cynical vocabulary that turns the very language of civil rights on its head.

The origins of CIR can be found in the incubators of the Reagan Justice
Department and several of the key private right-wing legal advocacy groups, in
particular the Washington Legal Foundation (WLF) and the American Legal
Foundation (ALF), both founded by Daniel Popeo, in 1976 and 1980, respectively. Michael McDonald and Michael Carvin—recent law school graduates who
would become two of the four key figures in the formation of CIR—met each

59

other at ALF in 1982-1983, where Carvin was executive director and McDonald was legal director.[439]

As discussed above, immediately after the 1980 election, Meese (as head of the Department of Justice transition team), Parker (as head of the EEOC transition team), William French Smith (as Reagan's attorney general), and William Bradford Reynolds (as assistant attorney general in charge of the Reagan Justice Department's Civil Rights Division) began establishing a team of conservative enthusiasts at DOJ for their planned rollback of the civil rights movement, among other items on the right-wing agenda. In assembling his highest level advisors, Smith brought with him from the Los Angeles office of his law firm Gibson, Dunn & Crutcher, a young partner, Ted Olson, who had sharpened his movement credentials by, among other things, chairing California Lawyers for Reagan.[440] Olson was tapped by Smith to head the Justice Department's critically important Office of Legal Counsel (OLC) as assistant attorney general, where he served as Smith's counselor and was involved in some of the most notorious policy decisions of the era.[441]

In 1983, both McDonald and Carvin were recruited to the Justice Department. While McDonald's tenure as a staff attorney at Justice was brief, returning after a few months to his base at ALF,[442] Carvin stayed on, serving as special assistant to Reynolds's protégé, Charles Cooper, who was deputy assistant attorney general in the Civil Rights Division from 1983 to 1985. By late 1984, when Olson followed Smith back into private practice at Gibson, Dunn & Crutcher (Smith back to L.A., and Olson becoming managing partner of the firm's D.C. office), it was time to pass the OLC baton.

The baton was passed to Charles Cooper, who moved from deputy assistant attorney general in the Civil Rights Division, to become assistant attorney general in charge of OLC under the new attorney general, Edwin Meese.[443] Cooper brought along to OLC his assistant from the Civil Rights Division, Michael Carvin, who became his deputy assistant attorney general in the Office of Legal Counsel.

Meanwhile, the third and fourth key figures in the formation of CIR met at Cornell. German immigrant Michael Greve arrived in the U.S. in 1981 on a Fulbright scholarship to Cornell University's School of Government, where he studied under and was groomed by ultra-conservative constitutional scholar, CIR cofounder Jeremy Rabkin.[444] From 1986 to 1988, Greve served as a program officer at Smith Richardson Foundation (one of CIR's first funding sources),[445] and then became a resident scholar on a one-year fellowship at McDonald's Washington Legal Foundation.[446]

By 1988, with ultra-conservatives skeptical about the first Bush administration's commitment to carrying through the full agenda they developed during the Reagan years, plans were being nurtured to flank the new administration from the right.[447] That year, McDonald left WLF, and by April 1989, CIR was launched, with Michael McDonald, Michael Carvin, and Jeremy Rabkin as founding board members. Greve joined CIR immediately as executive director.

CIR took the lead in the courtroom to advance the right-wing movement's monumental efforts to rip the heart out of affirmative action. Its first foray into those controversial waters was the infamous *Hopwood* case in Texas, which ultimately resulted in a Fifth Circuit ruling ending affirmative action in Texas, Louisiana, and Mississippi. It was not by chance that Greve, on behalf of CIR's leadership, chose Ted Olson, who by then was president of the D.C. chapter of the Federalist Society, to argue the appellate case, after CIR failed at the lower court level. Olson agreed to take the case up through the Fifth Circuit to the Supreme Court for free. "This was some rinky-dink discrimination case" at that point, Greve recalled in discussing his approach to Olson. "It's not so natural that someone of Ted's stature would commit that much energy and time to it . . . it took a lot of political courage."[448]

CIR is continuing to pursue its radical litigation agenda, having filed suit against the University of Michigan's affirmative action programs, and initially won a lower court decision holding that there is no compelling state interest in achieving a diverse student body.[449] Although reversed in a bitterly divided opinion by the Sixth Circuit Court of Appeals, it is widely expected that the circuit split now created by *Hopwood* and *Michigan* will be heard by the same Supreme Court which gave Olson, Carvin, Flanigan, et al., their victory in *Bush v. Gore*. Should CIR succeed in convincing the Supreme Court to review these conflicting rulings, it will have set the stage for radically limiting or potentially overturning affirmative action throughout the United States.[450]

In seeking to promote "colorblindness" through "appropriate lawsuits,"[451] CIR represented Californians Against Discrimination And Preferences (see above), the sponsors of Proposition 209, and was counsel for Katuria Smith, who unsuccessfully sued the University of Washington Law School in a class action lawsuit under circumstances similar to Cheryl Hopwood.[452] CIR's strategy is divisive. In nearly all of its high profile cases involving alleged favoritism toward African Americans and Latinos, the lead plaintiffs have been white women—a two-edged sword: undermining the idea that women have likewise benefited from affirmative action, and co-opting the vocabulary of the civil rights movement in order to undermine historic public concern about the effect of discrimination against racial minorities.

Major backing from the foundations of the Right has enabled CIR to play a critical strategic role. It is interesting to note that CIR in its early years was funded by the Pioneer Fund, which provided funding "to conduct or aid in conducting study and research into the problems of heredity and eugenics in the human race generally and such study and such research in respect to animals and plants as may throw light upon heredity in man, and research and study into the problems of human race betterment with special reference to the people of the United States."[453] Critics of the Pioneer Fund, such as Bob Herbert of the *New York Times*, have charged that it "has spent more than half a century promoting the idea that whites are genetically superior to blacks."[454] The foundation's original charter set forth its mission as "race betterment" and aid for people "deemed to be descended primarily from white persons who settled in the original thirteen states prior to the adoption of the Constitution of the United States."[455] Other Pioneer Fund recipients have included leading Anglo-American race theorists such as Linda Gottfredson,[456] J. Philippe Rushton,[457] Arthur Jensen,[458] and Roger Pearson's Institute for the Study of Man.

CIR's website lists the following officers: Michael P. McDonald, President, Founder, and Director of Litigation; Terence J. Pell, Chief Executive Officer; Michael E. Rosman, General Counsel; Curt A. Levey, Director of Legal and Public Affairs; Hans Bader, Associate Counsel; and Silvio A. Krvaric, Associate Counsel.[459] The other members of CIR's Board of Directors (along with its founding members) are Terence Pell, Michael McDonald, Larry Arnn (see above), James Mann, and Gerald Walpin.[460]

Greve is aware of the protracted nature of the battle CIR is facing. "This is not the kind of battle you win overnight," he has acknowledged. "This is so deeply woven into the fabric of American society."[461] Nevertheless, he believes that CIR is winning: "I'm vastly more optimistic than I was even five years ago. The debate and the law have moved much, much faster than we had any reason to hope, and I'm fairly sanguine that the momentum will continue to go in our direction. It will be the death by a thousand cuts."[462] A sustained campaign, he believes, "depends on small but tangible victories that build political support and demoralize the opposition."[463]

Greve brushes off the potential impact that cases like *Hopwood* would have on the admission of blacks and Latinos on campus. "It will affect numbers of minorities that get in. Is that a social cost of the decision? Sure it is. But there is cost on the other side. There has been tremendous alienation and divisiveness [caused by affirmative action], and that is serious social cost."[464] While many opponents of affirmative action recognize, if only for practical political reasons, that some form of governmental action is necessary to correct racial and gender imbalances in society, CIR is absolutist on this point. "It looks intransigent to say absolutely no consideration of race ever," says Greve. "But you have to say that has to be the legal baseline, period. And then you have to live with the fact that nobody is going to play by the rules anyhow. The NAACP learned that in the sixties, and we'll learn that now."[465]

CIR taps heavily into the "angry white male" mythology of racial victimization. "The only legalized discrimination in this country is against whites and males," Greve believes.[466] In the same manner that the political implications of fanning such resentment was seized upon in 1994 by Newt Gingrich and other conservatives, Greve understands the potential political stakes of such a race-baiting strategy. "People have the perception that the Democratic Party now consists largely of feminists, racial minorities and labor unions—that that's what they're down to," he has been quoted as saying. "To the extent you can reinforce that perception, the civil rights issue is a very good issue for the Republicans."[467]

CIR has chosen to focus on three key areas: free speech (which has involved mainly hate[468] or sexist speech), sexual harassment (McDonald favors "challenging the fanatical application of sexual harassment regulations"), and civil rights (i.e., opposing affirmative action).[469]

CIR's Legal Victories

The Center for Individual Rights litigated twenty-two cases in 2001.[470] Among its major earlier victories are:[471]

Coalition for Economic Equity, et al. v. Wilson, et al. (9th Cir., 1997),[472] in which CIR successfully defended the California Civil Rights Initiative (Prop 209) against constitutional challenge. The U.S. Supreme Court declined to review this decision, allowing Proposition 209 to go into effect.

R.A.V. v. St. Paul (U.S. Supreme Court, 1992).[473] CIR obtained a landmark Supreme Court ruling striking down a city ordinance aimed at the suppression of politically disfavored "hate speech." This led to the invalidation of dozens of campus speech codes.

CIR has, as noted, taken the potential landmark case of Jennifer Gratz, a white honor-roll student who says she was denied admission to the University of Michigan because of her race, and has extensive case materials, media transcripts, and articles on these cases.[474] CIR also supported, in an *amicus* brief in which it joined with National Religious Broadcasters, a 1998 case in which the conservative Lutheran Church–Missouri Synod (LCMS) successfully challenged the Federal Communications Commission's thirty-year-old rules governing minority hiring at radio stations.[475]

The Well-Coiffed Victim as Plaintiff

CIR's modus operandi in selecting test cases and lead plaintiffs is quite carefully considered. Although its leaders—McDonald, Greve, and Terence Pell (once an aide to the director of President Reagan's Office of Drug Control Policy, William Bennett)—like to present CIR's lead plaintiffs as victims of political correctness or government intervention gone mad, in fact they are carefully selected. The *Washington Post*'s account is instructive in this regard:

When the group decided to sue [the University of Michigan], staffers pored over resumes and biographies of about 100 potential plaintiffs, information sent to them by sympathetic state legislators in Michigan. After paring the list, McDonald flew to Detroit, settled into a hotel room and held a series of interviews. The group's search for a camera-ready lead plaintiff ended when Gratz, a blonde homecoming queen from a blue-collar family, walked in the door. She had stellar grades, no apparent political leanings and good looks to boot. CIR staffers tipped off the *New York Times* about her suit, and soon a long line of print and television journalists formed. CIR staffers vetted interview requests and flew Gratz to Washington to pepper her with likely questions. When she showed up on the "Today" show, Terry Pell was sitting next to her, and he was on a speakerphone when reporters visited Gratz's home in a Detroit suburb. The trick, according to Greve, was making sure she had good answers that didn't come across as coached. "You can overdo it," said Greve, flashing a mischievous grin. "If she sounds like some lawyer made her say something, well, that's not advantageous for us, either."[476]

McDonald has persuaded a former law school classmate, Kirk Kolbo, a partner at Maslon, Edelman, Borman & Brand in Minneapolis, to take on, pro bono, the University of Michigan lawsuit challenging affirmative action. Besides the 1997 case it brought against the University of Washington School of Law in Seattle, and in addition to the Gratz case, CIR has played a crucial role in suing the University of Michigan Law School alleging admissions policies that set aside slots for African Americans, Hispanics, and others whose qualifications are lower than those of some whites who were denied admission.[477] This case is likely to reach the Supreme Court by 2003. CIR does not select its cases lightly. Greve reportedly searched hard for financial support for the *Hopwood* litigation.[478]

A Litigation "Boutique"

CIR opposed the Violence Against Women Act, which it asserted is unconstitutional because it addresses conduct by private citizens, rather than official government conduct, and because it doesn't affect interstate commerce. CIR represented one of the football players sued under the act for raping a woman.[479] After the case was dismissed, CIR again won on appeal.[480]

CIR has been active on other constitutional law fronts. The lines between the secular and religious right have been blurring for some time now, and CIR has been working to erode the constitutional separation between church and state. For example, CIR represented Christian students at the University of Virginia, (*Rosenberger v. The Rector and Visitors of the University of Virginia*) who demanded that the university pay $5,900 to print their monthly Christian student magazine *Wide Awake*.[481] CIR won the case before the U.S. Supreme Court.[482] Commenting on the victory, Greve said, "The newspapers predict that libertarians and the Christian right will divide conservatives. I don't think that's true. Both realize that big government is the main enemy."[483]

CIR has also opposed the use of clandestine testers (e.g., a white individual sent into a potential employment situation soon after an African American candidate, to see if they are treated equitably) to check for employment discrimination.[484] Greve has said that in the next few years "the hard-core discussions over affirmative action will be over employment discrimination."[485]

CIR vs. the Universities: Intimidation through Litigation?

> We'll sue you for punitive damages. We will attack your integrity. We will nail you to the wall.
>   —Michael Greve, to universities practicing affirmative action[486]

In January 1999, CIR launched a national campaign against affirmative action by urging students to sue their colleges for racial discrimination in admissions. The effort's National Press Club kickoff featured none other than former education secretary William J. Bennett and Nat Hentoff, a columnist with a reputation as a progressive pundit and an outspoken civil libertarian.

On January 26, 1999, CIR placed advertisements in fifteen campus newspapers, including papers at Columbia, the University of Chicago, Dartmouth, Duke, Virginia, Rutgers, James Madison, Pennsylvania, North Carolina, and Stanford. The full-page ads advised students to download or send for a free handbook on how to tell whether their college is breaking the law. "Guilty by Admission," the ads declare.[487] "Nearly Every Elite College in America Violates the Law. Does Yours?" The handbook tells students how to use freedom of information requests and acquire data from their university to compile complaints, then how to find a lawyer to bring a suit, courtesy of CIR. In this manner, CIR and its allies are setting the stage for universities and colleges to become mired in potentially expensive legal trouble for attempting to promote diversity. It will also serve their interests if conservative students break up the pro-diversity consensus that remains strong on campuses nationwide. To create further stress for educators, CIR intends to mobilize college funders with parallel ads in the *Chronicle of Higher Education* and *Philanthropy Magazine*. "We think the trustees have an interest in getting involved," Pell said at a press conference, "to avoid personal liability."[488]

Killing affirmative action is just one part of CIR's agenda. According to its 1997–1998 annual report, the organization's long-term objective is "the re-invigoration of meaningful constitutional constraints on government." Government-enforced desegregation is a case in point. CIR's principles have included the right to self-segregate: "CIR advocates a limited application of civil rights laws that would preserve private citizens' rights to deal or not deal with other private citizens."[489]

On the "free speech" front, CIR defended a Georgetown University Law Center student, Timothy Maguire, a "self-described Reaganite and a member of the law school's conservative Federalist Society,"[490] who publicly disclosed admissions information "that among accepted black applicants the average LSAT score was 36 of a possible 48, while the average score for accepted white applicants was 43."[491] In 1995, CIR argued that anti-discrimination law is narrowed by the First Amendment, and won a Supreme Court decision on behalf of its client—the organizers of Boston's St. Patrick's Day Parade—which had excluded an organization of Irish-American lesbians and gays (*Hurley v. Irish-American Gay and Lesbian and Bi-Sexual Group of Boston*).[492]

CIR's Funding

CIR was founded in 1989 by McDonald and Greve, a former program officer at the Smith Richardson Foundation, which gave them initial funding of $180,000.[493] Its first year budget totaled only $250,000.[494] By 1991 it had a $300,000 budget, 90 percent of which came from right-wing foundations, including the Olin Foundation, the Smith Richardson Foundation, the Scaife Foundation, the Bradley Foundation, the J.M. Foundation, the E.L. Wiegand Foundation, and the de Tocqueville Institute.[495]

By 1995 it had an annual budget of $800,000. The Smith Richardson Foundation gave $570,000 between 1989 and 1995, and the Scaife-directed Carthage and Bradley Foundations gave $450,000 each in the same period.[496] By 1997 it had grown to six full-time employees and a budget of $1.3 million, according to Greve, with nearly half coming from five large foundations: Smith Richardson, Olin, Carthage, Bradley, and Randolph. Olin, the center's largest single donor (headed by the late William E. Simon), contributed $200,000.[497] In 1999, CIR received $145,000 from the Randolph Foundation.[498]

In 2000, CIR received $150,000 from Olin,[499] $150,000 from Bradley, with another $50,000 earmarked,[500] and $150,000 from the Sarah Scaife Foundation.[501] CIR's budget was $1.4 million in 2000.[502] Corporate donors include Archer Daniels Midland Corp., ARCO Foundation, Chevron USA, Adolph Coors Foundation, Pfizer Inc., Philip Morris Cos. and Philip Morris USA, Texaco, USX Corp., and the Xerox Foundation.[503]

The Leadership of the Center for Individual Rights

MICHAEL S. GREVE

Greve was the cofounder and executive director of CIR, until he left in 2001 to join the American Enterprise Institute, where his mentor, Jeremy Rabkin, serves on the Council of Advisors. Born in West Germany, he came to the United States in 1981 on a Fulbright scholarship, and received a Ph.D. in government from Cornell studying under conservative scholar Jeremy Rabkin.[504] Greve was a resident scholar on a one-year fellowship at the Washington Legal Foundation, which he left with Michael McDonald to form CIR.[505] He also served as a program officer at the Smith Richardson Foundation,[506] and has worked with the Center for Land Use and Environmental Studies at the Claremont Institute.[507]

Greve is co-author of *Environmental Politics* with Fred Smith, president of the Competitive Enterprise Institute, and is the author of *The Demise of Environmentalism in American Law* (1996), the arguments for which were first put forth at a 1992 conference of the Federalist Society.[508]

MICHAEL MCDONALD

McDonald, an attorney, is the cofounder (in 1989) and president of the Center for Individual Rights. He received a bachelor's degree in political science from Catholic University in 1978[509] and a Juris Doctorate from George Washington University in 1982, and is a member of the D.C. and Supreme Court bars. After joining the Washington Legal Foundation straight out of law school, in 1983 McDonald served briefly as a staff attorney in the Reagan Justice Department, before becoming legal director of the American Legal Foundation (ALF), a right-wing law firm specializing in media issues. ALF was housed in WLF's row house, until ALF was absorbed by WLF in 1986, and McDonald rejoined it,[510] launching its Legal Studies Division in 1987.[511] ALF filed a suit in 1985 supporting a separate Central Intelligence Agency suit against the American Broadcasting Corporation for allegedly violating the "fairness doctrine" by reporting that the CIA had attempted to assassinate an American businessman.[512]

MICHAEL A. CARVIN

A founding member of the CIR board, Carvin was a partner at Cooper, Carvin & Rosenthal, from which he withdrew in April 2001 to join Jones, Day, Reavis and Pogue. He received his law degree from George Washington University in 1982. In 1983, Carvin directed the American Legal Foundation, which was founded in 1980 by the Washington Legal Foundation's head, Daniel Popeo. Carvin worked with McDonald at ALF.[513] Carvin then went to work as special assistant attorney general for Charles Cooper, then assistant attorney general in the Reagan Justice Department's Civil Rights Division under William Bradford Reynolds. Carvin then followed Cooper into DOJ's Office of Legal Counsel, serving as deputy assistant attorney general, again under Cooper (see above). Along with Cooper, Carvin has litigated a number of important affirmative action cases. Cooper & Carvin represented Californians Against Discrimination and Preferences (CADAP) in the Proposition 209 constitutionality case,[514] as well as representing supporters of prayer at public school graduations[515] and the National Rifle Association's political wing[516] before the Supreme Court. Carvin also successfully argued the Census 2000 sampling case before the Supreme Court,[517] and was a member of the all-star litigating team, including Tim Flanigan and Ted Olson, who represented George W. Bush in the case of *Bush v. Gore*, the success of which by a 5-4 majority installed Bush as president of the United States.

Terence J. Pell

Pell, CIR's senior counsel, joined CIR in 1997. Born in 1953, Pell received his Ph.D. from Notre Dame in 1996, his J.D. from Cornell Law School in 1981, and his B.A. from Haverford College in 1976.[518] Prior to working for CIR, Pell worked as an attorney with the firm of Arent, Fox, Kintner, Plotkin & Kahn. He was a deputy assistant secretary of education for civil rights under William J. Bennett[519] and later served as general counsel and chief of staff under Bennett at the Office of National Drug Control Policy.[520]

Michael E. Rosman

Rosman, CIR's general counsel, joined CIR in March 1994. He graduated summa cum laude from the University of Rochester in 1981, majoring in economics and political science; he received his J.D. in 1984 from Yale Law School, and worked as an associate at Rosenman & Colin from 1984 to 1993.[521] Rosman worked on the *Hopwood* case that sharply curtailed the use of affirmative action in the admissions process at the University of Texas Law School; and also on *Brzonkala v. Morrison*, in which Rosman mounted a successful constitutional challenge to the 1994 Violence Against Women Act, which previously allowed rape victims to sue their attackers in federal court.[522] In addition to serving as cocounsel to Cooper & Carvin on the Proposition 209 case, Rosman has represented religious colleges seeking state grants.[523]

Hans F. Bader

An associate counsel at CIR, Bader received his J.D. from Harvard Law School in 1994 and a B.A. in history and economics from the University of Virginia in 1991. Before joining CIR in 1996, he clerked for federal district judge Lawrence Lydick.

Silvio A. Krvaric

Krvaric joined CIR as an associate counsel in February 2001. He received his J.D. from Santa Clara University Law School in 2000 and his B.A. from Vesalius College at the Vrije Universiteit, Brussels, Belgium, in 1996. Krvaric has clerked for the AIDS Legal Services at the Santa Clara County Bar Association Law Foundation.[524]

B. Institute for Justice (IJ)

The Institute for Justice was established in September 1991 by two right-wing legal activists, William "Chip" Mellor[525] and Clint Bolick (see above). IJ pursues what it calls "cutting-edge litigation" on school vouchers and property rights issues. Bolick's diatribe, *The Affirmative Action Fraud*, is probably the most important book directly attacking the subject.[526] What distinguishes IJ is its ideology: Its seed money came from David Koch, who with his brother Charles could be said to be the co-parents of the contemporary libertarian renaissance.

Charles and David are co-owners of the Wichita-based Koch Industries, an oil company and the country's second-largest business still in private hands.[527] Their father, Fred C. Koch, was a founder of the John Birch Society,[528] but the younger Kochs put their money into libertarianism. In 1977, Charles G. co-founded the D.C.-based Cato Institute, where David sits on the board of directors.[529] David is also a trustee of the Reason Foundation[530] and a major underwriter of *Reason* magazine, the libertarian movement's most influential publication. In 1992 the Koch family contributed $700,000 to IJ—70 percent of the organization's 1993 budget.[531] Today, IJ's annual budget stands at over $5 million, up from $3.1 million in 1997-1998.[532]

From 1999 to 2000 the David H. Koch Charitable Foundation gave $500,000 to Bolick and Mellor's organization.[533] In 2000 the Charles G. Koch Charitable Foundation granted Cato—which published *The Affirmative Action Fraud*—$750,000.[534] Along with Bolick and Mellor, IJ's Board of Directors includes Robert Levy, Abigail Thernstrom, Arthur Dantchik, Mark Babunovic, James Lintott, Gerrit Wormhoudt, and Stephen W. Modzelewski. The board chair is David Kennedy, president of the Earhart Foundation.[535] Founded in 1929, the Earhart Foundation has played a low profile but vital role in funding the organizational infrastructure of the right wing, including the American Enterprise Institute and the Intercollegiate Studies Institute (for more on Earhart, see "David B. Kennedy" below).[536] Kennedy also has served on the Board of Directors of the Philanthropy Roundtable, an umbrella funding organization of the Right.[537]

Although the Institute for Justice attempts to project a public profile as an ardent defender of the individual and small entrepreneur against the pernicious effects of government regulation, its agenda is far broader, encompassing the entire public interest establishment and indeed government itself. IJ describes itself as fighting "foes like the AFL-CIO, the National Education Association, much of the civil rights establishment, and federal, state, and local governments nationwide."[538] This broad-based opposition to government itself locates the Institute for Justice among the most extreme of the right wing's legal organizations.

Bolick is responsible for state initiatives as a member of the Federalist Society Civil Rights Practice Group.[539] Bolick has announced plans to create IJ state chapters in Washington, Oregon, Minnesota, Arkansas, and North Carolina. The first state chapter already has been set up in Arizona, in cooperation with the Goldwater Institute. Among the characteristics IJ looks for when deciding whether to set up a state chapter are active chapters of the Federalist Society, an ample supply of right-wing attorneys to assist IJ lawyers, a favorable state constitution with strong provisions protecting property and individual rights, and a reasonably large central city in which to set up shop.[540]

The Institute for Justice does not at present litigate affirmative action cases, but Bolick continues to speak out forcefully on affirmative action. IJ's litigation strategy is carefully designed to gnaw away at the same web of broadly defined government policies and constitutional foundations upon which affirmative action rests. Bolick, vice president and director of litigation at IJ, charged in *The Affirmative Action Fraud* that the Civil Rights Act of 1964 "sanctioned an unprecedented intrusion into individual autonomy."[541] IJ was one of the strongest advocates for repeal of affirmative action at the federal level in 1997.[542] In 1995, Bolick worked with Newt Gingrich to cut off funding for 160 affirmative action provisions in federal law.[543]

Bolick is a member, along with Ward Connerly and Linda Chavez, of the so-called Citizens Initiative on Race (see above), and he was one of three Washington legal advisors to the sponsors of California's Proposition 209.[544] But Bolick and IJ's long-term goal is libertarian: to free individual relations from all but the most minimal government mediation. To accomplish that end requires an erosion of the government's authority to legislate for the social good. For the Right, the one person, one vote democratic impulse of representative government is anathema to the countervailing wealth-weighted (and historically white male) impulse of unaccountable private corporate power.

Both Mellor and Bolick had worked at the Mountain States Legal Foundation (Mellor from 1979 to 1983, Bolick from 1982 to 1985), the law firm founded by Joseph Coors that unsuccessfully sought to keep the reverse discrimination *Adarand v. Mineta* case alive before the Supreme Court in 2001.[545] From there, Bolick went on to acquire media savvy and hone his cynical approach to affirmative action, working from 1985-1986 as the special assistant to Clarence Thomas, chairman of the Equal Employment Opportunity Commission (1985–1986). Bolick then worked as an attorney in the appellate section of the Civil Rights Division at the Department of Justice from 1986-1987, and then as assistant to William Bradford Reynolds, the assistant attorney general from 1987-1988. After serving as director (1988-1991) of the Landmark Legal Foundation Center for Civil Rights, he went on to form IJ with Chip Mellor in 1991.[546] In late December 2001, the parent organization Landmark Legal got involved in the battle over control of the U.S. Commission on Civil Rights (see below), calling in a letter to Attorney General Ashcroft for a federal investigation of whether Victoria Wilson, a member of the commission, violated federal law in refusing to leave office to make room for a new Bush appointee.[547] "I would rather sue bureaucrats than be one," Clint Bolick has said.[548]

Mellor worked at Mountain States from 1979-1983, first as a staff attorney (1979-1982), then as president (February 1982-September 1983), taking over for his predecessor, James Watt. At Mountains States he worked, as had Watt, to open government-owned natural resources to more private exploitation and opposed taxpayer spending on disarmament activities.[549] After his stint at MSLF, Mellor went to the Department of Energy from 1984-1986, and served as president of the Pacific Research Institute from 1986-1991. In September 1991, Mellor and Bolick came together to form IJ to engage in "cutting-edge litigation," legal training, media outreach, and advocacy work, though they had broached the idea of such an organization five years earlier to David Kennedy, head of the Earhart Foundation.[550] Picking up where the older generation of legal groups left off, they gave the institute a specifically ideological mission as "the nation's premier libertarian public interest law firm."[551]

Think tanks such as the Cato Institute were set up specifically to push libertarian policy options. Just as *Reason* is the libertarians' communication mechanism, IJ is the movement's legal arm. And all exploit popular (and media-exacerbated) confusion about their liberal-sounding message. As IJ puts it, "once people turned first to the ACLU whenever government violated their rights. No longer. . . . [The] alternative is the Institute for Justice."[552]

IJ brags that the *Wall Street Journal* has dubbed its lawyers the "new civil rights activists," and it's a title the staffers clearly relish.[553] "We are in the courts across the country preserving freedom of opportunity," their leaflets assert. Their goal is to secure "economic liberty, school choice, private property rights." Clint Bolick refers to himself as a "bleeding-heart conservative."[554]

Through the strategic selection of clients and cases, IJ has been able to win against existing, but relatively marginal, municipal ordinances that appear excessive or absurd. In so doing, however, the group advances its mission, namely, to justify the wholesale elimination of government administrative responsibility. By focusing attention on the absurdity of some regulations, IJ (aided by the media), forestalls serious discussion of the broader implications of striking down laws that are genuinely in the public interest.

IJ's Voucher Cases

IJ's key areas of litigation have been civil rights, small business, and the promotion of schemes for pushing tax dollars into private religious and secular schools through voucher systems. In Milwaukee, in an early case shaping law in this area,[555] IJ teamed up with the Landmark Legal Foundation in "an effort to transform the terms of the debate in the area of civil rights." On September 25, 2001, the Supreme Court accepted for review another case in which the Institute for Justice represented five parents who intervened in a lawsuit to help defend the use of a voucher system[556] in Cleveland's public school system (*Zelman v. Simmons-Harris*). Nine months later the Supreme Court ruled in favor of the state of Ohio and IJ's plaintiffs, and Clint Bolick and his "merry band of litigators" were cracking open a case of Dom Perignon donated by a board member to celebrate their victory in the most significant ruling on education policy and church-state separation in decades.[557] The decision could have a significant impact on the constitutional issues surrounding George W. Bush's "faith-based initiative."[558] Bolick joined IJ's Chip Mellor, Richard D. Komer, and Robert Freedman, and former Reagan solicitor-general Charles Fried (see above) in writing a key brief in the case. Oral argument was presented by, among others, Solicitor General Ted Olson[559] representing the United States as *amicus curiae* in support of the state and IJ's clients.

The libertarian obsession with legal boundaries between government and private activity notwithstanding, IJ senior litigation attorney Richard Komer represented Parents for School Choice and several inner-city families in their quest to expand Wisconsin's voucher program to include religious schools. Komer left the Equal Employment Opportunity Commission in 1990, where he had served as special assistant to Chairman Clarence Thomas, when he was appointed deputy assistant secretary for civil rights policy under George H.W. Bush education secretary Lauro F. Cavazos.[560] IJ has also promoted "faith-based healing" by forcing the Texas Commission on Alcohol and Drug Abuse to remove licensing requirements from Teen Challenge in San Antonio, an important project of the religious right to recruit youth.[561]

One of the key litigators in the first round of the important 1998 Milwaukee school voucher case was Kenneth W. Starr. Bolick and Starr were recruited to then-Governor Tommy Thompson's "legal dream team" to defend his school voucher plan—with Starr representing the state of Wisconsin, and Bolick representing the pro-voucher parents, before the Wisconsin Supreme Court.[562] Although many expected this to become the Supreme Court's landmark test case on the church-state issues involved in the school voucher issue, the Supreme Court declined to review the case, instead deciding the issue in its 2002 *Zelman* decision.

Other litigation of interest to Thompson, now secretary of health and human services, includes IJ's defense of private welfare reform efforts, including Wisconsin's controversial and severe "W-2" welfare-to-work program.[563] When NOW and the ACLU and Legal Services Corporation sought to establish a constitutional right to welfare support, IJ represented the American Legislative Exchange Council (ALEC) and the Empowerment Network Foundation (ENF) "to prevent the creation of a positive right to welfare and to preserve the greatest possible flexibility for state welfare reform efforts."[564]

A Long-Term View

A close reading of the institute's legal arguments reveals its long-term vision. In *Ricketts v. New York City*,[565] for example, IJ represented a private (African American-run) commuter van company against the New York Metropolitan Transportation Authority, private bus companies with city franchises, and the public transportation workers union. The case appeared to be one where the biased issuing of franchise licenses operated against an underprivileged group, but IJ used it to attack a series of landmark constitutional decisions collectively called the Slaughter-House cases.[566] Slaughter-House has long been a target of the anti-affirmative action conservatives because it expanded the role of the state in regulating discriminatory and unjust practices by private entities.

In the *Ricketts* case, IJ's lawyers argued that the New York jitney drivers were held back by excessive regulation stemming from the Supreme Court's alleged misreading—in Slaughter-House—of the "the original understanding of the constitutional limits on government power." Thus, in challenging "legal restrictions on behalf of entry-level entrepreneurs struggling to pursue their American dreams," IJ attempted to overturn the long-recognized protections of the Fourteenth Amendment. "Our ultimate goal," according to IJ, "is to restore economic liberty as a fundamental civil right by overturning the Slaughter-House cases in the Supreme Court."[567] IJ lost the case to overturn municipal regulations preventing Hector Ricketts from operating his van on bus routes.[568]

With similar cynicism, IJ represented four African American construction contractors and three public housing tenant organizations in order to challenge the 1931 Davis-Bacon Act. "The Davis-Bacon Act was passed in 1931 in order to prevent migrant black construction workers from competing with white union labor," argues IJ. That's one angle. The passage of Davis-Bacon also established that the Department of Labor was authorized to mandate "prevailing wages" be paid to workers by contractors receiving federal funds. In a libertarian world, there are no federal minimum wage regulations—and no Labor Department. Hence IJ's interest in the case.[569]

IJ sponsors seminars in "natural rights and public interest litigation" several times a year, offering programs "tailored to law students, lawyers, and policy activists." Faculty participants in these seminars include leading conservative attorneys.[570] The Institute covers all tuition, housing, and meals, and offers some travel scholarships.[571] It also arranges clerkship and sabbatical programs for participants in this so-called Human Action Network.[572] At last count, IJ claimed to have 249 young lawyers, activists, and advocates on board. It's a strategic investment. "Our calculation: if we trained 15 lawyers a year, and only half of them litigated only one case, over ten years we would have 75 additional cases litigated." [573]

IJ also publishes a monthly newsletter, *Law and Liberty*, and conducts the Court of Public Opinion, its online public relations arm.

IJ Funding

IJ's office in Washington has the sleek, designer look of the lavishly endowed, and today it is backed by the same conservative foundations underwriting the rest of the contemporary Right. The Institute for Justice raises $5.4 million in annual revenue including generous grants from foundations: Bradley ($240,000 in 2000),[574] Olin ($225,000 in 2000),[575] Jacqueline Hume,[576] Sarah Scaife Foundation ($100,000 in 2000),[577] and others.

The Leadership of the Institute for Justice

CLINT BOLICK
> If we as conservatives have learned anything . . . it is that you can't win without an offense.[578]

Bolick is cofounder, vice president, and director of litigation of the Institute for Justice. Along with Chip Mellor, he is a member of the Board of Advisors of the *Texas Review of Law and Politics*.[579] Bolick is a member of the conservative Citizen's Initiative on Race and Ethnicity[580] and author of *Changing Course: Civil Rights at the Crossroads*,[581] *Unfinished Business: A Civil Rights Strategy for America's Third Century* (see below for a fuller discussion of this seminal work),[582] *Grassroots Tyranny: The Limits of Federalism*,[583] *The Affirmative Action Fraud*, [584] and *Transformation: The Promise and Politics of Empowerment*.[585]

Raised in New Jersey, Bolick attended Drew University, and then the University of California at Davis Law School (1979–1982),[586] where he arrived just one year after the 1978 *Bakke* decision, in which the Supreme Court held that while places could not be set aside for minority students, race and ethnicity could be factors in admissions. His first job out of law school was at the Mountain States Legal Foundation in Denver (see above). There, Bolick specialized in cases that challenged affirmative action and that promoted vouchers for private schools, which has become perhaps the major litigating concern of the Institute for Justice.

At Mountain States, Bolick met William "Chip" Mellor, at the time president of the organization (a position Mellor took on when James C. Watt resigned as Mountain States' founding president to join the Reagan administration as secretary of the interior). At this time Bolick also came to the attention of Dr. Roger Pearson (see above). In the early 1980s, Pearson added Bolick and another Mountain States official to his *Journal of Social, Political and Economic Studies*, where Bolick's name appeared on the masthead in the fall of 1984.[587] Also in 1984, Bolick (while still at Mountain States) authored a report for the Cato Institute on cable deregulation.[588] The work at Mountain States "was so exhilarating," he said, "I couldn't wait to come to work every day."[589]

From Mountain States, Bolick moved to Washington, working from 1985 to 1986 at the Equal Employment Opportunity Commission (EEOC), then under the direction of Clarence Thomas. In early 1986, Bolick played an active role in the successful effort to win Thomas a second term as EEOC chair, acting as his "unofficial aide" and campaign guru. Because in his first term as EEOC chair Thomas had blasted affirmative action and comparable worth, and massively cut down on the number of class actions the commission would consider, civil rights leaders were loudly critical. After his stint at the EEOC, William Bradford Reynolds, the assistant attorney general for civil rights in the Reagan administration, hired Bolick as an assistant at the Justice Department's civil rights division, where he served from 1986 to 1987.

Preferring, unlike Reynolds, to sit out the first Bush administration, Bolick instead chose to critique it from the wings.[590] In May 1988, Bolick founded a Washington, D.C., affiliate of the Landmark Legal Foundation, called the Landmark Center for Civil Rights.[591] Conservatives "must go forward and set forth a positive alternative civil rights agenda," said Bolick[592] from his new perch at the Landmark Center for Civil Rights.[593] While there, Bolick articulated conservative criticism of, among other things, Bush's nominees to head the Civil Rights Division. He raised concerns, for example, that Michael Martinez, a past president of the Hispanic National Bar Association, "would not energetically support a program based on individual rights and racial neutrality."[594] Attacking Bush from the right, Bolick hoped to neutralize and possibly drown out critics from left of center.

Bolick subsequently played a key role in securing for Thomas nominations and confirmations first to the D.C. Circuit and then to the Supreme Court. When in 1989, Clarence Thomas was nominated for his D.C. Circuit judgeship, Bolick's Landmark Center for Civil Rights submitted an early assessment of Thomas's record as chairman of the EEOC to the American Bar Association, concluding that he was well qualified. "Conservative groups have never responded to the ABA in a formal manner to the liberal critique" of a nominee, said Bolick.[595]

At the end of the 1980s, it was to Bolick that the Heritage Foundation turned to lay out a civil rights agenda for the future. Included in its tenets were an end to affirmative action, a crackdown on crime, and the killing of federal income supports. Bolick wrote, "Creative incentives designed to free Americans from the welfare-fueled cycle of dependency and despair are an important component of giving minorities genuine equality of opportunity." His language became the clarion call of welfare-enders for the decade that culminated in the passage of so-called welfare "reform" under Clinton in 1996 and beyond.[596]

Bolick's cynical and libertarian "race-neutral" civil rights agenda had two parts. If, on the one hand, conservatives were to continue to condemn racial preferences and other desegregation policies, he reasoned, then, on the other hand, they simultaneously would have to develop what he called "empowerment strategies to secure for people—particularly economically disadvantaged people—greater control over their lives."[597] For that reason, Bolick pursued a handful of media-friendly, strategically chosen lawsuits, and won, among others, a landmark suit on behalf of black shoe shiners, overturning a D.C. law banning outdoor shoeshine stands.[598]

As two writers on this period describe it, Thomas's subsequent fight in 1991 to win a seat on the Supreme Court was the natural consequence of the Reagan administration's defeated attempt in 1987 to confirm Robert H. Bork to the Supreme Court. Thomas's campaign was "conceived by people determined never to let another nominee be 'Borked.'"[599] And Bolick, a close protégé of Thomas and now an administration outsider, was the perfect person to orchestrate this campaign.

With the support of Thomas's backers, Edwin Meese and Reynolds, Bolick crafted Thomas's up-by-his-bootstraps personal story in such a way as to discomfort his black critics from the start of the Supreme Court confirmation battle. Bolick even arranged for a busload of Thomas supporters to travel from the south, as if on their own initiative, to lobby, something that most of the media missed. In fact, Bolick's Landmark Center for Civil Rights paid most of the bus expenses, and Christian right activist and Reagan White House aide Gary Bauer helped foot the bill for the group's motel.[600] The group was entirely stage-managed and recruited, but able, as Bolick put it, to "monopolize the media at the time people's impressions were being formed about Thomas." The pro-Thomas effort was victorious and its lessons were well learned.[601] Thomas, meanwhile, became Bolick's close friend and the godfather of Bolick's youngest son. Says Bolick of Thomas, "He's one of my mentors."[602]

Bolick was the driving force behind the devastating assault on Lani Guinier, President Clinton's nominee to head the civil rights division of the Justice Department in 1993. According to the *Washington Post*'s Michael Isikoff, "Working out of a small suite of offices across the street from the Justice Department, Bolick and colleague Chip Mellor became what they call 'information central' for the Guinier battle, [distributing] more than 100 copies of her articles to key Senate staff aides, journalists, editorial writers and other 'opinion leaders.' They also produced a drumbeat of press releases, reports and op-ed articles that portrayed the . . . law professor as a pro-quota, left-wing extremist bent on undermining democratic principles."[603]

Bolick led the attack against Guinier's nomination in an op-ed in the *Wall Street Journal*, dubbing her one of "Clinton's Quota Queens."[604] He repeated the routine in 1994, when he unleashed a predictable torrent of rhetoric against Deval Patrick, who had been nominated to head the civil rights division—dubbing him "Quota Clone." (The Senate confirmed Patrick anyway.)[605] In 1997, he led the fight that blocked Bill Lann Lee's nomination to head the Justice Department's civil rights division (Clinton ultimately gave Lann Lee a recess appointment). He was a principal strategist in the nearly two-year fight that held up passage of the Civil Rights Act of 1991—opponents called it a quota bill. Not ones to give up, Chavez's CEO and Bolick's IJ together released a report on Lee's term as assistant attorney general for civil rights just as Lee's candidacy was due to be resubmitted to the Senate by Clinton.[606]

Bolick has continued in his role as a high-visibility, quotation-rich source of support for right-wing legal initiatives. In March 2001, when President Bush ended the American Bar Association's (ABA's) fifty-four-year advisory role in vetting candidates for the Supreme Court and other federal judgeships (and supplanted it with the Federalist Society), in part because of the ABA's stance on welfare reform, Bolick cheered. "The action is proper and long overdue, the ABA is a liberal advocacy group," Bolick was quoted as saying. "Even the criteria it uses, which include 'compassion' and 'sensitivity,' can be viewed through a liberal prism to disqualify highly qualified conservative nominees."[607] As Chavez describes him, "In terms of Washington-based groups, he is the person who is most active in these legislative fights. He really has been giving leadership on these issues."[608] Others view him differently. The *Nation* magazine accused Bolick of waging a "smear campaign" against Lani Guinier.[609]

WILLIAM H. "CHIP" MELLOR

President and general counsel of the Institute for Justice, Mellor has been an anti-regulatory lawyer since he graduated the University of Denver School of Law in 1977. He received his B.S. from Ohio State University in 1973.[610] He practiced at the Denver law firm of Balaban and Lutz.[611]

In 1979, Mellor went to practice law with Mountain States Legal Foundation in Denver, an anti-regulatory legal organization (see above), underwritten by the Coors family and other right-wing foundations.[612] From 1979-1982, Mellor was a staff attorney at Mountain States where he handled all of the group's major litigation, and from 1982-1983, Mellor served as vice president and acting president for the organization. As president, Mellor took over from his boss who was the group's first president, the evangelical and anti-environment James Watt, later Ronald Reagan's controversial interior secretary.[613] Under Watt, Mountain States went to court to fight discount utility rates for the elderly and disabled in Colorado, federal strip-mining regulations, a plan to designate part of a Wyoming oil field a protected wilderness area, and a National Park Service ban on motorized rafts in the Grand Canyon.[614]

In 1984, Mellor was appointed deputy general counsel for regulation by Energy Secretary Donald Hodel (a member of the Federalist Society Board of Visitors, formerly its Board of Trustees, and a former president of the Christian Coalition).[615] In a move that consolidated what had been two positions, he was subsequently given additional responsibilities—handling environment and conservation as well as renewable energy and legislation.[616] These were heady days at the Department of Energy (DOE), when massive protests took place at nuclear plants from Hanford to Oak Ridge. Among other projects, as the deputy general counsel responsible, Mellor handled a DOE plan to shorten the selection process for the nation's first high-level nuclear waste site at Yucca Mountain in Nevada.[617] During his tenure, Mellor received the department's Exceptional Service Award for his work on energy deregulation and environmental compliance.[618]

In 1986 Mellor became president of the Pacific Research Institute for Public Policy,[619] a conservative think tank in San Francisco,[620] which he left to form the Institute for Justice with Bolick in 1991. Under his leadership, the Pacific Research Institute commissioned and published books on civil rights, property rights, and technology-related First Amendment issues. One of the first publications was an edited collection, *Taxation and the Deficit Economy*,[621] in which Eric Mack of Tulane University argued that "all existing and prospective tax schemes of the U.S. government and its political subdivisions . . . involve . . . impermissible seizures— seizures that, from the perspective developed here, have the same moral status as banditry." Instead of taxes, the book argued, every public service should be paid by those who benefit, with the nation's defense paid by those who need it and are willing to pay.[622] An end to all taxation is "obviously a radical concept," conceded Mellor. "But it is one that is made radical not by the fact that it is wrong but because people have come to accept as normal something which deserves fundamental questioning."[623]

DAVID B. KENNEDY

Institute for Justice board chairman David Boyd Kennedy also serves as president and trustee of the Earhart Foundation.[624] Born in 1933 in Ann Arbor, Michigan, Kennedy attended McGill University and the University of Michigan before serving in the U.S. Army from 1954 to 1957. He received his A.B. from Indiana University in 1958, followed by an L.L.B. from the University of Michigan in 1963. He was admitted to the Bar in Michigan as well as Wyoming, where he worked in private practice from 1964 to 1984. From 1967 to 1972, Kennedy served in the Wyoming House of Representatives, and he was state attorney general from 1974 to 1975. His mother is the former Elizabeth Earhart, and he became president of the Earhart Foundation in 1985.[625]

With assets of nearly $70 million, the Earhart Foundation was incorporated in 1929 and is the legacy of Harry Boyd Earhart, founder of White Star Refining Co., now part of the Mobil empire. White Star pioneered the service station business.[626] In 1995, Earhart spent more than $2 million funding organizations such as the American Enterprise Institute and the Intercollegiate Studies Institute in support of free-market social policy research and education.[627] More recently Earhart has supported research and education focusing on the judiciary, for instance the Montana-based Foundation for Research on Economics and the Environment, which organizes educational retreats for judges.[628] In 1995 it co-sponsored a joint Goldwater Institute/Federalist Society symposium on "Federalism and Judicial Mandates."[629] Kennedy also sits on the board of trustees of the Citizens Research Council of Michigan;[630] is a member of the Mont Pelerin Society, formed after World War II to oppose nearly all forms of government economic intervention; and has served on the Board of Directors of the Philanthropy Roundtable, a conservative umbrella organization for coordinating policy on foundation giving.

GERRIT H. WORMHOUDT

Born in Iowa in 1926, IJ board member Gerrit Wormhoudt received a B.S. from Northwestern University in 1950 and an L.L.B. two years later from the same university.[631] Later in 1952 he sat for the Bar in Kansas, where he has practiced law ever since as a member of Fleeson, Gooing, Coulson, and Kitch.[632] Among the areas handled by this Wichita-based firm are white-collar criminal and civil defense.[633] As a partner, Wormhoudt has argued anti-discrimination cases on both sides. In 1989 he successfully represented black former chair-car attendants in a Title VII suit against the United Transportation Union and the defunct Santa Fe Railroad.[634] He has also defended two school districts in Fourteenth Amendment and Title IX cases, respectively.[635]

ROBERT A. LEVY

In August 2001, IJ board member Levy came out against a proposal by the ABA for public financing of judicial campaigns, pointing to affirmative action as an example of why the ABA is "responsible for politicizing the profession it purports to represent."⁶³⁶ Since 1996, Levy has been a senior fellow in constitutional studies at the Cato Institute, a libertarian public policy think tank. In this capacity Levy has been highly visible in defending high-profile corporations resisting government regulation, such as Microsoft in its recent anti-trust litigation, and tobacco companies.⁶³⁷ He has called for the abolition of the anti-trust laws.⁶³⁸ Levy was awarded a Ph.D. in business from American University in 1966; he founded CDA Investment Technologies upon graduation and served as its chief executive officer for the next twenty-five years. Upon retirement, Levy returned to law school and received his J.D. from George Mason University in 1994. From 1994 to 1996 he clerked for Judge Royce C. Lamberth, U.S. District Court, in Washington, D.C., and then for Judge Douglas H. Ginsburg, U.S. Court of Appeals for the D.C. circuit. Levy recently donated $1 million to George Mason University, its largest alumni gift ever, to create an endowment for the Robert A. Levy Fellowships in Law and Liberty. The fellowships are designed to facilitate the development of the law and economics movement by encouraging economists to obtain law degrees at George Mason University.⁶³⁹

C. The Federalist Society and Civil Rights: A Constitutional Challenge to Fairness

Federalist Society Civil Rights Practice Group

As the conservative movement develops its challenge to fundamental institutions in the American body politic, it has not ignored the legal front. Extreme conservative legal organizations sponsoring a combination of right-wing litigation and advocacy are opening the way for a radical transformation of the American legal system.

One of the most significant developments has been the emergence of the Federalist Society for Law and Public Policy Studies, formed in 1982 and based in Washington, D.C. The Federalist Society has emerged as the most significant organization of the legal right wing in the United States.⁶⁴⁰ This organization has developed comprehensive challenges to a broad range of constitutional principles, and it is targeting the courts, law schools, and the American Bar Association (ABA). The society brings together on its Board of Visitors (formerly its Board of Trustees) the most influential group of right-wing jurists and political activists of the day, including cochairs Robert Bork and Orrin Hatch, and C. Boyden Gray, Edwin Meese, Donald Paul Hodel, William Bradford Reynolds, and Gerald Walpin (also on CIR's Board of Directors). T. Kenneth

Figure 4.1. Federalist Society for Law and Public Policy

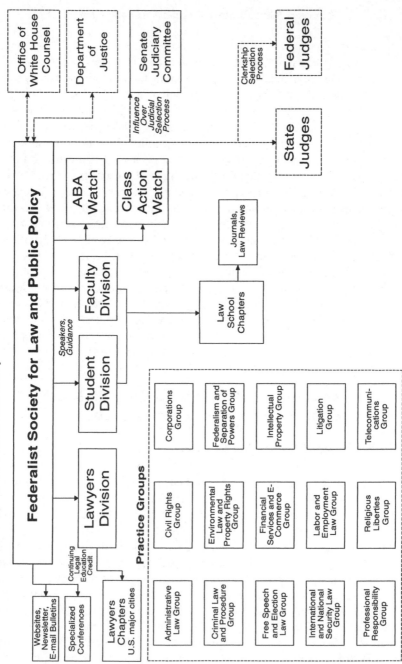

Source: © Institute for Democracy Studies 2002.

Cribb, Jr., who has served as a trustee of the Scaife Foundation, serves as the society's counselor and as a member of its Board of Directors, along with Steven Calabresi, who is the national cochair of the Board of Directors. The Bush administration's new White House legal team is largely composed of Federalist Society veterans.[641]

Although it craves mainstream respectability and has carefully cultivated an image of fostering high-quality discussion, the Federalist Society is promoting breathtakingly radical changes in America's constitutional structure through the immense organization it has built over twenty years, that now includes members who hold high-level positions throughout the United States government. With chapters in more than 150 law schools, lawyers' chapters throughout the country, and affiliates in many major law firms nationwide, the Federalist Society has emerged as a serious rival to mainstream umbrella legal organizations such as the American Bar Association, of which it is a vociferous critic. Recent participants in the activities of the Federalist Society lawyers' chapter include Rep. Bob Barr (R-GA), Linda Chavez, Ward Connerly, Charles Fried, Justice Clarence Thomas, Dr. Charles Murray, Edwin Meese, Sen. Thad Cochran (R-MS), and former California governor Pete Wilson.[642]

With a grant from the E.L. Wiegand Foundation of Reno, Nevada,[643] the Federalist Society established fifteen Practice Groups in 1996, which sponsor educational and networking events, publish newsletters, and monitor legal developments in various areas of the law. In 1999 the Wiegand Foundation granted the Federalist Society $150,000 to enhance its Practice Group program.[644] In 2000 the Federalist Society spent $268,458 on Practice Group activities.[645]

The Civil Rights Practice Group, according to its first newsletter, emerged "at what is likely a defining moment" in the development of the Right's attack upon the civil rights law of the last thirty years.[646] The Practice Group takes no official positions on specific issues and handles no litigation directly. Its executive committee, however, is a virtual "Who's Who" of conservative lawyers, including many Justice Department veterans of the Reagan administration, who are deeply active in lawsuits, research, and political activity on a number of interrelated fronts. The Civil Rights Practice Group is divided into five subcommittees: Education, Electoral Process, Employment and Contracting, Second Amendment, and State Initiatives.[647]

The Executive Committee of the Civil Rights Practice Group

CHARLES J. COOPER was chairman of the Practice Group from its founding, and has recently been replaced by his former law partner, Michael Carvin.[648] He is also on the steering committee of the Federalist Society's Washington, D.C., lawyers' chapter, and is a member of the National Security Council's Policy Review and Planning and Coordinating Groups. Cooper served as counsel to the 2000 Bush campaign, and his partner at Cooper, Carvin & Rosenthal, Michael

Carvin argued on behalf of Bush in the November 13, 2000, Florida State Supreme Court hearing on the election dispute.[649] His other membership affiliations include the Standing Committee on Rules of Practice and Procedure of the Judicial Conference of the United States—the body by which the federal court system governs itself on the national level.[650]

Cooper was born in Dayton, Ohio, in 1952. He was editor in chief of the *Alabama Law Review*, 1976–77.[651] From 1977 to 1978 he clerked for Judge Paul H. Roney, U.S. Court of Appeals for the Fifth Circuit, St. Petersburg, Florida.[652] He then served as law clerk to now-Chief Justice William H. Rehnquist from 1978 to 1979.[653] In 1981, Cooper served as special assistant to the assistant attorney general for civil rights, W. Bradford Reynolds, and later became his chief deputy the following year. From 1985 to 1988, Cooper was promoted to assistant attorney general for the Office of Legal Counsel, the constitutional law advisory group within the Justice Department, where he helped define Reagan administration policy on numerous civil rights questions. He also chaired Reagan's working group on federalism.[654] Cooper had a close personal relationship with Reynolds; they were daily running partners[655] and, according to his own account, Cooper helped shape Reynolds's attitude against affirmative action.[656] Since leaving the Justice Department in 1988, Cooper has been in private practice in Washington, D.C., and founded his own firm, Cooper, Carvin & Rosenthal, in 1996 (now Cooper & Kirk). He has testified before numerous congressional committees.

MICHAEL A. CARVIN is chairman of the Practice Group.[657] Currently at Jones, Day, Reavis and Pogue, Carvin is a founder of the Center for Individual Rights. During the legal battle over the Florida results in the 2000 presidential election, Carvin played a major role in representing the Bush team on behalf of Cooper, Carvin and Rosenthal.[658] According to veteran legal journalist Jeffrey Toobin, Bush confidant Ben Ginsburg sent Carvin down to Florida because he was "a dedicated Washington conservative" who could be trusted to "keep an eye" on Florida attorney Barry Richard, who had been retained by the Bush team.[659] Carvin worked from 1985-1987 under William Bradford Reynolds in the Civil Rights Division of the Justice Department along with Cooper. He went on to serve as deputy assistant attorney general in the Office of Legal Counsel from 1987-1988 (a post in which Cooper preceded him), where he worked on the Bork nomination to the Supreme Court.

Together, Cooper and Carvin have litigated crucial affirmative action cases and worked for other right-wing causes. In 1991, for example, Carvin argued against gender-inclusive affirmative action policies in the granting of broadcast licenses by the Federal Communications Commission (in *Lamprecht v. FCC*— before a U.S. Court of Appeals, D.C. Circuit panel consisting of Clarence Thomas, James Buckley, and Abner Mikva).[660] From 1991 to 1993 he was a partner at Shaw Pittman, along with Cooper. Carvin argued *Harding v. Gray*, a 1993 reverse discrimination case in which a white carpenter alleged that he was discriminated against in a promotion in favor of a black woman;[661] and another Center for Individual Rights reverse discrimination case, *Henry Painting Co. v. Ohio State University*, which resulted in Ohio State University agreeing to pay a white contractor $368,000 in damages and attorneys' fees and cancel its affirmative action program for painting contracts.[662] Carvin also filed an *amicus* brief on behalf of the Knights of Columbus in a key U.S. Supreme Court church-state separation case, *Board of Education of Kiryas Joel v. Grumet,*[663] and he successfully argued the Census 2000 sampling case before the Supreme Court.[664] In 1996, they formally became partners and formed the law firm of Cooper & Carvin, which became Cooper, Carvin & Rosenthal in 1998. In 2001, Carvin (and Rosenthal) left the firm, which is now Cooper & Kirk.

ROGER CLEGG, chairman-elect, was born in 1955 and is presently counsel to the Center for Equal Opportunity. While working in the Reagan Justice Department from July 1982 to January 1993, including four years as a deputy for Bradford Reynolds in the Civil Rights Division (1987-1991), he led the battle within the administration to get the Supreme Court to overturn *Roe v. Wade.*[665]

NOEL FRANCISCO, while no longer on the Executive Committee of the Civil Rights Practice Group, formerly served as chair of its Subcommittee on Employment Law and Government Contracts. He is currently the assistant counsel in the Office of White House Counsel. Francisco attended the University of Chicago and went on to receive his J.D. from its School of Law in 1996. He clerked for Hon. J. Michael Luttig of the Fourth Circuit (often mentioned as a potential Bush nominee for the Supreme Court), and then Justice Antonin Scalia, 1997-1998. Before joining the administration, he was with the law firm of Cooper, Carvin & Rosenthal, started by Federalist Society Civil Rights Practice Group leaders Charles Cooper and Michael Carvin—also two of the leaders of the right-wing "public interest" law movement. In his short career, Francisco already has credentialized himself with the Right through his work with Cooper on a school desegregation case in which they sought an end to federal oversight of previously segregated schools.[666]

ANDREW W. LESTER, codirector for membership, heads the law firm of Lester, Loving and Davies in Oklahoma City, where he specializes in municipal law, representing numerous cities and municipalities in Oklahoma. Born in Minneapolis in 1956, Lester received his law and foreign service degrees from Georgetown University in 1981, but not before serving on President Reagan's EEOC transition team from 1980 to 1981. He currently serves as the president of the Oklahoma City chapter of the Federalist Society and as a member of the Defense Research Institute, a pro-police legal group established by Edwin Meese.

CURT A. LEVEY, director for pro bono outreach, is the director of legal affairs for the Center for Individual Rights.

JODI BALSAM, codirector for membership, is counsel for operations and litigation for the National Football League.

CLINT BOLICK, in charge of state initiatives (one of the subcommittees of the Practice Group), is head of the Institute for Justice (see above).

GAIL HERIOT, director for education, is a vigorous opponent of affirmative action (see below). She is a 1981 graduate of the University of Chicago Law School, and has held the position of law professor at the University of San Diego since 1989. She was also an active public proponent of Proposition 209.[667]

JENNIFER BRACERAS, in charge of publications for the Practice Group, was recently appointed to the U.S. Civil Rights Commission (see below).

M. MILLER BAKER, chairman of the Electoral Process Subcommittee, was born in Houma, Louisiana, in 1962. After graduating from the Tulane University Law School in 1984, Baker held several positions in the Reagan Justice Department, including in the Office of Legal Policy and the Civil Rights Division. At his current Washington firm of Carr, Goodson and Lee, Baker worked on the landmark election law case declaring Louisiana's open primary unconstitutional.[668] He also defended the alleged rights of the Virginia Leadership Council and a member of the Concerned Women for America to distribute voter information pamphlets despite the legal restrictions associated with the tax-exempt status of these organizations.[669]

NELSON LUND, chairman of the Second Amendment Subcommittee, is a 1985 graduate of the University of Chicago Law School and currently professor of law at George Mason University. His legal scholarship on the right to bear arms as a basis for political liberty has been influential in conservative legal circles.[670]

Activities of the Practice Group

The Practice Group maintains no official agenda; when group leaders and members act on various projects, they do so in their own names rather than that of the Federalist Society. Nevertheless, the tenor of its *Civil Rights News* bulletin reveals a clear direction in favor of overturning numerous government measures designed to prevent or remedy civil rights discrimination. For example, issues have chronicled in heroic tones the efforts to pass California's Proposition 209 and to defend it in the courts;[671] and its website regularly keeps members informed of controversial issues bearing on civil rights.[672] The November 2001 panel of the Practice Group at the Federalist Society's National Lawyers meeting was a key event for the legal arm of the conservative movement to assess the progress of the Bush administration on race and gender issues. Through the Practice Group's speakers' program, prominent members of the Practice Group also speak nationwide at law schools and other venues.

Prominent figures of the Right have used *Civil Rights News* as a vehicle to reach the key movement leaders. Clint Bolick reported in *Civil Rights News* on the struggle to defeat the nomination of Bill Lann Lee as assistant attorney general for civil rights.[673] Bolick, now responsible for state-level initiatives for the Practice Group,[674] describes how he, with the assistance of a University of Texas law student, organized a group of "two dozen anti-preference groups" that approached Senate Judiciary Committee Chairman Orrin G. Hatch (R-UT), announcing their opposition. Hatch is the national cochair of the Board of Visitors of the Federalist Society, and his staff member for nominations at the time, Brian W. Jones, was a member of the executive committee of the Civil Rights Practice Group and editor of *Civil Rights News*. The "well-prepared" Republican committee members, armed with detailed information on Lee's record prepared by Bolick's coalition, "subjected Lee to tough but courteous questioning," which Lee was, according to Bolick, unable to withstand. A "blistering expose" in a column by George Will turned the tide (the implication being that Will's piece was largely based on the coalition's research).

The Civil Rights Practice Group, like the Federalist Society more generally, gives the Right a preexisting network of like-minded individuals and organizations that can be mobilized into action quickly when an opportunity, like the Lee confirmation hearings, presents itself. Through its newsletter, formal presentations,[675] and informal contacts, the Practice Group keeps its membership informed about current issues, and connects the disparate elements of the legal right to leverage their power effectively.

D. Pacific Legal Foundation (PLF)

In some respects, the story of the Pacific Legal Foundation (PLF) is the story of the right-wing legal movement itself. According to a *Yale Law Journal* article by Oliver A. Houck, Pacific Legal was born indirectly out of discussions in 1971 between future Supreme Court associate justice Lewis F. Powell, Jr.,[676] and members of the U.S. Chamber of Commerce.[677] After listening to the Chamber's concern over the difficulties corporations were having in the social and legal environment of the time, Powell produced a memorandum entitled "Attack on American Free Enterprise System." According to Houck, Powell's memo explained that:

> [I]ndependent and uncoordinated activity by individual corporations would not suffice. Moreover, "there is the quite understandable reluctance on the part of any one corporation to get too far out in front and to make itself too visible a target." This is where the Chamber came in. It should launch scholars and speakers, an "evaluation of textbooks" to address problems in schools, "constant surveillance" of the media and, "in the final analysis," the "pay-off" area: action in politics and the courts. The judiciary "may be the most important instrument of social, economic and political change."[678]

In addition, the memo states, according to Houck, "As with respect to scholars and speakers, the Chamber would need a highly competent staff of lawyers. In special situations it should be authorized to engage lawyers of national standing and reputation to appear as *amicus* counsel in the Supreme Court. The greatest care should be exercised in selecting cases in which to participate, or the suits to institute."[679] Powell's memorandum was read by Chambér members throughout the country, including the West Coast—where construction, energy, mineral, and oil industrialists were locked in battles with environmentalists and regulatory agencies.[680] The president of the California Chamber of Commerce, Fred Hartley, was also the president of Union Oil Company. Hartley spoke with James Archer, president of the California Bar, who in turn spoke with William French Smith,[681] who would later become President Ronald Reagan's first attorney general. In addition to then-Governor Reagan, William French Smith had another client who would become significant, J. Simon Fluor of the Fluor Corporation, a major contractor for the Alaska pipeline, the construction of which had been delayed by litigation brought by the environmental movement. After reading Powell's memorandum, another top-level Chamber member, Roy Green (who would later become PLF's first executive vice president), suggested that the Chamber should have its own non-profit law firm.[682] Discussions ensued, and a recommendation was made to create such an organization.

Pacific Legal was founded on March 5, 1973, as the first in a series of right-wing "public interest organizations—the same year and with some of the same funders as the Heritage Foundation."[683] In addition to Fluor, who became PLF's first chairman of the board,[684] PLF received initial funding from Richard Mellon Scaife,[685] advised by his then-chief aide, Richard M. Larry.[686] The Chamber originally housed PLF,[687] and all fifteen founding members of PLF's board of directors served on the advisory committee of the Chamber.[688]

At the time, Edwin Meese[689] served as Governor Reagan's chief of staff. Meese, along with William French Smith, helped found PLF,[690] and Meese continued to help it as an advisory board member[691]—indicating the level of backing from what they claim to be "mainstream thinking"[692] benefited. When in 1998 Meese was asked about the monthly meetings of conservatives that he organized at the Heritage Foundation, he stated, "It really started in California while Ronald Reagan was governor. . . . He was trying to reform welfare so as to get those who were not eligible off the rolls. . . . There were two groups attempting to thwart those reforms: the liberal think tanks, and some so-called public-interest law firms. . . . But there were no resources on the other side to represent true public interest—the taxpayer. . . . So in 1973 the Pacific Legal Foundation got started. That was the first of what I call the real public-interest law firms—the ones that represent the taxpayers."[693] According to the *Philadelphia Inquirer,* "Scaife provided Meese with $1.9 million to start the Pacific Legal Foundation."[694] Further immersed in Reagan's inner circle, PLF retained early on longtime Reagan aide (and future Reagan deputy chief of staff) Michael Deaver's public relations firm, Deaver & Hannaford, Inc.[695]

Although headquartered in Sacramento, Pacific Legal has other offices in Anchorage, Bellevue (Washington), Portland, Honolulu,[696] and Miami. Specifically founded to protect "economic and individual liberty," PLF's mission emphasizes "private property rights; freedom from excessive government regulation; free enterprise; balanced environmental policy; and nonwasteful, productive, and fiscally sound government."[697] According to Oliver Houck, PLF initially engaged in strategic litigation on energy issues while maintaining "remarkably close" relationships with Pacific Gas & Electric and other California energy companies.[698] PLF also defended the use of herbicides in the national forests and the use of DDT.[699] A resolutely pro-business, 501(c)(3) non-profit, PLF's primary orientation is to litigate (or threaten to litigate) against pro-environmental measures. However, Pacific Legal's fierce anti-government agenda also has led it to participate in the English Only (see above) movement in both California and Arizona,[700] and in the critical battle over diversity policies.

In the civil rights arena, Pacific Legal's activities were becoming increasingly significant by the late 1980s. In 1989, PLF filed an *amicus* brief in *Martin v. Wilks,* in which the Supreme Court held that so-called victims of "reverse discrimination" had the right to challenge affirmative action plans in their workplace resulting from consent decrees.[701] Additionally, in *Associated Gen. Contractors v. Secretary of Commerce,*[702] PLF challenged the federal Public Works Employment Act on behalf of the Associated General Contractors (one of PLF's founders[703]) and construction companies.

By 1999 the *Washington Post* had referred to Pacific Legal as the "oldest and perhaps most influential of the conservative public interest law firms."[704] As exemplified by its business-oriented Board of Trustees and reflected consistently in its litigation, PLF does not represent the average American. PLF's litigation indicates a clear agenda: to dismantle regulations put in place to protect the public interest. According to Pacific Legal's property rights attorney, James Burling, PLF is pursuing a property rights agenda using the Takings Clause of the Fifth Amendment[705] to "get rid of the regulatory state established under F.D.R.'s New Deal."[706] This seems hard to square with Pacific Legal's protestations in the civil rights arena about the impropriety of a so-called activist judiciary supposedly using the courtroom to change settled law. Douglas Kendall, executive director of the Community Rights Counsel in Washington, D.C., states, "PLF's demand that judges broadly interpret the Takings Clause is difficult to reconcile with PLF's simultaneous demand that judges narrowly interpret the Equal Protection Clause to exclude all forms of affirmative action."[707]

Activities of the Pacific Legal Foundation

The Legal Practice Groups
Pacific Legal is organized into three "legal practice groups." PLF's war on diversity is a major focus of its Individual Rights practice group. In addition to at-

tacking diversity policies, the group has used both litigation and administrative proceedings to oppose bilingual education; change tax policies; fight for so-called reforms in education, welfare, and immigration; and support "a strong national defense"[708]—a big issue in California, where so much of the defense industry is located.

Before its war on diversity policies began, PLF was best known for its relentless pursuit of economic deregulation regardless of consequences to the public interest. This type of litigation is the focus of the remaining two practice groups, Environmental Law and Property Rights. These two practice groups concentrate on bringing strategic litigation to challenge the traditional understanding of the Fifth Amendment's Takings Clause in order to erode government oversight of the use of private property. Although claiming a balanced approach, PLF states: "The wholesale introduction of environmental extremists into the executive branches of state and federal government has caused an indiscriminate hodgepodge of new and exacting environmental rules and regulations that completely disregard private property rights and the need for the public to bear the cost of public benefits."[709]

In addition to the three groups, PLF has a number of smaller projects in such areas as government abuse, limited government, judicial responsibility, tort reform, education reform, rent control, the Pacific Northwest, and victims' rights.[710]

Publications

PLF's main quarterly newsletter, *Guidepost*, updates a national audience about PLF activities and related news items. Its *Action Report* is a periodic publication highlighting key actions in the courts or by PLF, and is designed specifically for Pacific Legal's "Guardian Donors"—those who donate $1,000 or more. PLF also issues newsletters specific to the regional projects: *Northwest Center Dispatch, Atlantic Center Dispatch,* and *Project Hawaii Dispatch.* PLF also publishes *At Issue,* a monthly bulletin that discusses and comments on a single issue that PLF is currently litigating. *Liberty Watch* is a quarterly publication that summarizes and updates everything in which PLF is currently involved. In addition, PLF issues one or two monographs each year on issues central to its mission.

1-866-END-BIAS

On May 8, 2001, PLF launched "Operation End Bias" in order to further its efforts to eliminate the use of all diversity policies in the public sector throughout the state of California. Just a few weeks later, Operation End Bias was dubbed by the *Orange County Register* "a systematic watchdog effort against racial preferences."[711] PLF claims it launched the project "to identify jurisdictions around California that are violating Proposition 209, publicize those violations, and put offenders on notice."[712] Since the time Operation End Bias was launched, PLF has issued Freedom of Information (FOIA) requests throughout California, demanding to be told about any diversity policies in place. PLF says that by law these jurisdictions must respond within ten days.[713]

Proudly referring to itself as "the sole enforcer of California's Proposition 209,"[714] PLF also has implemented a series of measures directed at enlisting disgruntled members of the public in its opposition to diversity policies. Those measures include setting up a "whistle-blower hotline," 1-866-END-BIAS, "to report policies that play favorites by sex or skin color;"[715] a set of "strategically placed"[716] advertisements; public service announcements; and a separate website[717] to focus the public's attention on discovering diversity policies still in place. In *Capitol Weekly,* which is subscribed to by state employees throughout California, Pacific Legal has placed an advertisement that reads "STOP QUOTAS AND OTHER DISCRIMINATION" and encourages readers to "Report Violations."[718] As of November 5, 2001, PLF had received almost one hundred claims of alleged violations of California law under Prop 209.[719] After reviewing these so-called tips, PLF embarks on a letter-writing campaign. If PLF determines that in its estimation a public agency is still using diversity considerations in violation of Prop 209, it sends the agency a letter demanding that the policy be discontinued. If the agency does not end all diversity initiatives, PLF will review the potential case to determine whether or not to file suit against the agency.[720] According to Sharon Browne, PLF's lead attorney on this project, "Disobeying Proposition 209 could bring legal liability."[721]

Unraveling the Legacy of Bakke—The Litigation Onslaught of PLF

> The Connerly ruling, coupled with the California Supreme Court's decision in Hi-Voltage Wire Works, Inc. v. City of San Jose, gives PLF powerful ammunition to systematically dismantle costly programs throughout the state in which government discrimination is perpetuated under deceptive euphemisms like "affirmative action," "outreach," "goals and timetables," etc.
>
> — Pacific Legal Foundation[722]

Beginning with its involvement in the seminal 1978 case, *Regents of the University of California v. Bakke,*[723] Pacific Legal Foundation has been in the forefront of anti-affirmative action litigation throughout the entire country. In *Bakke,* PLF founding board member and attorney Ronald Zumbrun; another PLF attorney, John Findley; and William F. Harvey (an Indiana University Law School professor who served on PLF's advisory board)[724] filed an *amicus* brief on behalf of Pacific Legal urging the Supreme Court to hold the university's affirmative action polices unconstitutional. PLF has joined the foray against diversity by supporting cases once they reach the Supreme Court, as well as by taking a special interest in the anti-diversity propositions in both Texas and Florida.[725] However, it is in relation to California's controversial Proposition 209, cynically and misleadingly designed as a "civil rights initiative" in order to ensure its passage, that PLF has done the most damage to racial and gender justice. PLF's attack on diversity policies can be explained both by its antipathy to government regulation and its claims that diversity initiatives unduly burden the taxpayer.

PLF's proud claim to be "the leading force in California courts for enforcement of Proposition 209"[726] is supported by the sampling of its anti-diversity activity:

- *Attacking California's attorney general:* On the fifth anniversary of Prop 209, November 5, 2001, PLF issued a press release in which it joined the American Civil Rights Institute's Ward Connerly in giving California Attorney General Bill Lockyer an "F" for his enforcement of Prop 209 (incorporated into the California Constitution as Art. 1, Sect. 31). PLF Senior Vice President and General Counsel Anthony T. Caso demanded that California "[q]uit profiling job applicants by race and denigrating the value of individual merit and achievement."[727] PLF describes its role as that of a "private attorney general."[728] The press release listed fourteen state and local entities that PLF believed to be in violation of Prop 209 and presumably at risk of legal action by PLF; and it indicated that PLF used California's Public Records Act to obtain documents detailing the state attorney general's use of diversity policies in hiring within his department. One of PLF's letters requesting information used to decide whether or not it should pursue litigation was sent at the beginning of November 2001 to the state's Department of Justice,[729] suggesting that the state may be facing PLF in the courtroom in 2002.

- *Charging Los Angeles County with illegal conduct:* On May 8, 2001, Pacific Legal Foundation sent Los Angeles County a letter putting it "on notice" that PLF believed it was in violation of Prop 209 through county policies that establish goals and timetables for minority and female participation in its contracting with private contractors.[730]

- *Targeting the East Bay:* Also on May 8, Pacific Legal wrote a similar letter to the East Bay Municipal Utility District accusing it of imposing illegal race and sex preferences, and putting it "on notice" of violating Prop 209 in its "Contracting Objectives" policy detailing diversity targets for district contracts.[731]

- *Ending diversity outreach:* In 2000, Pacific Legal's attorney Sharon Browne filed the landmark case *Hi-Voltage Wire Works, Inc. v. City of San Jose,*[732] suing San Jose on behalf of a contractor, Hi-Voltage. In that case, PLF challenged state and local government diversity outreach programs such as San Jose's. PLF won when the California Supreme Court held that such diversity outreach programs and diversity "goals and timetables" violated the law. As PLF stated, the "decision marks the first time the California Supreme Court has interpreted the scope of Proposition 209 and carries major implications for thousands of state and local agencies throughout the state."[733]

• *Suing San Francisco, Part I:* In a lawsuit filed September 12, 2000, Pacific Legal represented a private firm, Coral Corporation, in charging the city and county of San Francisco with violating the California Constitution by employing diversity policies in awarding public contracts. At issue in *Coral Construction v. City and County of San Francisco* was a policy that required general contractors to at least make a "good faith" effort to meet diversity goals. However, even that minimal level of diversity awareness was more than PLF was willing to tolerate. "This kind of blatant discrimination is costing California taxpayers millions of dollars; it's got to stop," said a PLF attorney.[734]

• *Suing San Francisco, Part II:* Pacific Legal asked that the city of San Francisco's airport "Diversity Staffing Plan" be declared void and unenforceable in *Cheresnik v. City and County of San Francisco,*[735] an action brought in federal district court on September 7, 1999. PLF further requested an injunction against both the city's Airport Commission and its director in order to prevent them from continued implementation of existing diversity policies.[736]

• *Challenging Sacramento's "Equal Business Opportunity Program":* On June 20, 2000, Pacific Legal brought a lawsuit, *United Utilities, Inc. v. Sacramento Municipal Utility District,* on behalf of two businesses against the Sacramento Municipal Utility District for violating Prop 209 by utilizing an "Equal Business Opportunity Program" in its public contracting program.[737] On January 8, 2002, Sacramento Superior Court Judge Richard Park ruled in favor of PLF.[738]

• *Joining forces with ACRI's Ward Connerly:* In *Connerly v. State Personnel Board,*[739] Pacific Legal won a major victory representing the American Civil Rights Institute head, and Prop 209 sponsor, Ward Connerly. On September 4, 2001, the federal district court struck down California state government's and community colleges' diversity policies in hiring practices, as well as diversity initiatives by the state lottery and treasurer's office in contracting procedures. "We are heartened by this strong ruling for equal rights," said the winning attorney, PLF's Anthony Caso.[740]

• *Backing the Center for Individual Rights' case against the University of Washington Law School:* On May 17, 2001, PLF issued a press release about its involvement in *Smith v. University of Washington Law School.*[741] PLF had filed an *amicus* brief urging the U.S. Supreme Court to grant *certiorari* in the case in order to overturn the U.S. Ninth Circuit Court of Appeals, which held that Justice Powell's *Bakke*[742] opinion was controlling on the issue of diversity constituting a compelling governmental interest.[743] On May 29, 2001, the Supreme Court denied *certiorari*.[744]

• *Targeting the elementary schools:* On November 9, 2001, PLF filed a lawsuit against Gilroy Unified School District for alleged race, ethnicity, and sex discrimination in its operating procedures in the twelve elementary schools in the district. In *Cowles v. Gilroy Unified School District,* PLF's claim primarily referred to the district's use of diversity considerations in the placement of children and staff throughout the district's schools in an attempt to achieve racial and gender balance throughout the system. PLF alleged that Gilroy's policies are in violation of Prop 209.[745] The judge hearing the case, the Honorable William J. Elfving, ordered the school district to terminate all use of its diversity balancing policies by January 4, 2002, or to show cause why the district was unable to do so.[746]

Program for Judicial Awareness

Recognizing that the legal environment in which a case is argued can help shape a judge's response, PLF has set up the Program for Judicial Awareness, directed by PLF attorney R. S. Radford. Its stated aim is to counter "American law school faculties . . . dominated by the ideological Left" and the so-called "leftist" bias of published legal theory.[747] PLF designed this program "to help redress this imbalance"[748] by selecting topics that PLF determines to be the most beneficial to its agenda, and then funding a writing competition, offering cash prizes of up to $5,000 per essay,[749] which produces theory and documentation for PLF's own purposes. The cash prize serves as an obvious incentive for law students, who welcome the unusual opportunity to write a law review article and be paid for it. Topics in the 2001 competition closely hew to PLF's property rights and laissez- faire agenda: (1) the relevance of investment-backed expectations in takings law in light of the 2001 Supreme Court case *Palazzolo v. State of Rhode Island* (see below); (2) the constitutionality of state-funded school voucher programs; and (3) the current limitations of the Commerce Clause with respect to enactment and enforcement of environmental regulations.[750]

PLF's "Well-Coiffed Victim"

PLF is savvy in choosing the ideal plaintiff. In discussing the case of a PLF plaintiff who was an eighty-three-year-old widow from Nevada, PLF chief executive officer Robert Best said, "those are the cases that frequently make precedent," because "it's 'not the big developer against the poor bureaucrat trying to protect the environment.'"[751] PLF "take[s] only those cases that, when resolved, would set key legal precedents that eventually would add new layers of protection for individual rights."[752] Rather than protecting the rights of disenfranchised or disempowered individuals who lack adequate resources to protect themselves, Pacific Legal's overarching mission is the protection of private ownership of property from government regulation. PLF utilizes a one-sided pro-property approach, thus guaranteeing that at least some measure of the business sector's economic priorities prevail—regardless of the cost or consequences to other individuals or the environment.

"Public Interest" Law Veers to the Right

Douglas Kendall and Charles Lord, authors of an important study of how right-wing organizations have sought to clothe their efforts to gut environmental regulation in the garb of the civil rights struggle, write:

> [T]ypically, PLF will monitor cases from around the country, weigh in with an amicus brief as a case reaches a federal appellate court or a state supreme court, and then, if the case has a sympathetic plaintiff and presents an important issue upon which PLF desires Supreme Court review, PLF will assist the landowner in petitioning the Supreme Court to review the case. PLF has filed a brief in favor of the property owner in every important Supreme Court regulatory takings case that has been heard by the Court since the mid-1970s.[753]

PLF is forthright about its goals: "We only take precedent-setting cases.... Our effort is to change the law," stated Richard R. Bradley, who directs strategy and development at PLF."[754] Most notably, PLF won a highly significant victory for the property rights movement in *Palazzolo v. Rhode Island*, in which the Supreme Court held that the Fifth Amendment's "just compensation" clause entitled private property owners to compensation for land regulations that affect the value of the property even when the regulations in question were in place before the property was acquired.[755] PLF claims to have on average between 100 and 125 active cases, either in research or litigation.[756]

PLF Funding

Over the past two decades the major right-wing foundations have demonstrated their clear support for Pacific Legal to emerge—as it has—as the most formidable conservative litigation group on the West Coast. According to Media Transparency, from 1987 to 1992 the Bradley Foundation gave Pacific Legal $300,000 for specific work to support follow-up on PLF's landmark anti-environment, property rights victory: *Nollan vs. California Coastal Commission.*[757]

According to the *Washington Post*, Scaife money constituted at least half of PLF's budget in its early years.[758] Pacific Legal also has always had considerable ability to tap into both individual and private industry resources. Early corporate contributions came from the Knudsen Corporation, Southern Pacific Co., Santa Fe Railway Co., Sperry Corporation, and Borg-Warner Corporation, in addition to the Lilly Endowment and the William Randolph Hearst Foundation.[759]

Pacific Legal's initial budget was $240,000 in 1973; in 1979 it was $1.25 million;[760] by 1996 PLF had a $4 million annual budget, with corporate contributors including Castle and Cooke Properties in Hawaii, Boeing, Ford Motor Co., Exxon, and Philip Morris.[761] When PLF wanted to open its Florida office in 1997, it embarked on a four-city, two-day tour that raised $350,000[762] with the help of developers, individuals with an interest in property rights law, and the Sugar Cane Growers Cooperative of Florida.[763] A spokeswoman for the Sugar Cane Growers stated, "We don't have a specific project in mind. . . . [But] we can't help but want to give to organizations that have the same kind of philosophy."[764] As the *Palm Beach Post* stated in response to PLF's successful fund-raising efforts in Florida, "[t]he Pacific Legal Foundation may find clients who look like pawns on the chessboard of regulation, but the kings and queens who dominate the board will be paying for the cases."[765] "This demonstrates that PLF is really following the money," said Dan Barry of the D.C.-based Clearinghouse for Environmental Advocacy and Research; "there's big money for them to start these legal cases."[766] By calendar year 2000, PLF's total revenue was $5,507,082 and its net assets totaled $11,031,803.[767] In 2000 alone, PLF spent $3,840,309 directed solely at program services.[768]

Furthermore, Media Transparency has reported that the Sarah Scaife Foundation donated $2,205,000 and the Olin Foundation gave $545,000 to PLF between 1985 and 2000.[769] Between 1992 and 1996, the Murdock Foundation gave Pacific Legal $600,000.[770] Pacific Legal is still funded in large part by key right-wing foundations: Scaife, Olin, and Castle Rock (Coors family). In 1999 the Sarah Scaife Foundation gave $300,000 for general support;[771] the John M. Olin Foundation authorized $120,000 "for litigation and public education on freedom and equality before the law"[772] (and another $60,000 allocated for calendar year 2000);[773] and the Castle Rock Foundation gave $80,000[774] (an additional $50,000 was given for the tax year 12/1/99–11/30/00).[775] Pacific Legal also received $30,000 in 1999 from the Weyerhaeuser Company Foundation—a forest products company—for "unrestricted support,"[776] and another $30,000 for calendar year 2000.[777] In addition, PLF was awarded $300,000 in 2000 by the M. J. Murdock Charitable Trust for "program expansion—for legal research on environmental issues."[778]

Leadership of the Pacific Legal Foundation

RONALD A. ZUMBRUN is the former president and cofounder[779] (along with Roy Green) of Pacific Legal Foundation. When he stepped down from his position at Pacific Legal in 1995 to be succeeded by his law partner (and former PLF lawyer Robert Best), Zumbrun agreed to continue serving Pacific Legal as president emeritus.[780] Zumbrun had begun to move away from PLF in 1991 when he announced the formation of a private law firm that specialized in "public issue" litigation, Zumbrun, Best & Findley.

Before beginning Pacific Legal, Zumbrun served as the deputy director of legal affairs for the California Department of Social Welfare.[781] According to the *New York Times,* PLF stated that Zumbrun "was responsible for the legal aspects of the designing, implementation and defending of California's . . . welfare reform program."[782] He has been called "one of the chief legal architects of Reagan's anti-poor actions, particularly in denying health and welfare benefits to the poor."[783] Zumbrun was a key figure in using California in the early 1970s as an important testing ground for so-called welfare reform in the implementation of the landmark Welfare Reform Act of 1971.[784] Al Meyerhoff, who served as regional counsel for California Rural Legal Assistance, stated that Zumbrun "has spent his career in defending attacks on the poor and then in defending business interests."[785]

In 1981, Zumbrun was President Ronald Reagan's first choice for chair of the board of the Legal Services Corporation. At the time, Robert L. Gnaizda of Public Advocates, Inc., charged that Zumbrun believed that the Legal Services Corporation, which grants federal funds for legal aid for the poor, should be abolished.[786] Reagan had asked Congress to abolish it, but was unsuccessful. A controversy then unfolded in which Zumbrun was accused by a lawyer representing two environmental groups of making a "highly irregular request for direct collusion" to the Justice Department regarding DOJ's assistance to the Interior Department in a case involving Secretary of the Interior James G. Watt (who was founder and former president of Mountain States Legal Foundation).[787] The charge of impropriety, denied by Zumbrun, was based on a letter Zumbrun sent to the Justice Department, in which he wrote, according to the *New York Times*, that "we were informed that the filing of this lawsuit was received with favor" by the Reagan administration, and requested the DOJ's help in framing questions that Interior Secretary Watt "would feel comfortable in answering" for use as evidence in a case centering on the issue of granting access to a Montana wilderness for the purposes of exploring gas and oil reserves.[788]

Eventually, Reagan instead nominated William J. Olson,[789] who was confirmed. Of counsel to Olson's small three-attorney firm, William J. Olson, P.C., is Herbert W. Titus—the founding dean of Pat Robertson's Regent University's College of Law and Government.[790] Zumbrun has continued his long affiliation with conservative legal interests. Since 1998 he has been serving as the vice chairman for pro bono outreach of the Federalist Society's Environmental Law and Property Rights Practice Group.[791]

Past PLF Advisors of Interest
In addition to Zumbrun and members of PLF's Board of Trustees, other notable conservatives have served Pacific Legal in varying capacities in the past. The following descriptions reflect the key associations and positions each individual has held:

CURRENT PLF OFFICERS[792]

Thomas G. Bost,
chair of the board.

Richard R. Albrecht,
vice chair: Former general counsel of the U.S. Treasury Department, Presidents Nixon and Ford (1974–76). Currently counsel, Perkins Coie LLP.

James L. Cloud,
secretary-treasurer.

Robert K. Best,
president and chief executive officer.

Anthony T. Caso,
general counsel and assistant secretary-treasurer.

CURRENT PLF BOARD OF TRUSTEES[793]

Richard R. Albrecht, *vice chair: Former general counsel for U.S. Treasury Department, Presidents Nixon and Ford (1974–76). Currently counsel, Perkins Coie LLP.*

Robin P. Arkley, *president/owner, Security National Holding LLC.*

Thomas G. Bost, *professor of law, Pepperdine University School of Law; partner, Latham & Watkins.*

James J. Busby, *president and owner, Security Owners Corporation.*

James L. Cloud, *executive vice president, National Bank of Alaska.*

Greg M. Evans, *president and general manager, Evans Management Services.*

Ben J. Gantt, Jr., *Graham & Dunn.*

Timothy R. Hall, *owner, T. R. Hall Land & Cattle Co.*

John C. Harris, *chairman/chief executive officer, Harris Farms, Inc.*

Gail A. Jaquish, *president, Jurix, Inc.; former assistant professor at Notre Dame.*

Thomas C. Leppert, *chairman and chief executive officer, The Turner Corporation;*

White House Fellow under Reagan assigned to the Department of Treasury; board member, Hawaii Business Roundtable.

Robert E. McCarthy,[794] *of counsel, McCarthy & Rubright, LLP.*

Kile Morgan, Jr., *Ponderosa Homes, Inc.*

April J. Morris, *former vice president, finance, chief financial officer, and secretary, Standard Pacific.*

Jerry W. P. Schauffler, *president, W.S.I. Builders, Inc. (retired).*

Jeffrey T. Thomas, *Gibson, Dunn & Crutcher LLP.*

Charles W. Trainor, *Trainor Robertson; member of Urban Land Institute.*

Ronald E. Van Buskirk, *Pillsbury Winthrop LLP.*

Brooks Walker, Jr., *general partner, Walker Investors.*

Richard D. Williams, *Charlston, Revich & Williams LLP.*

Donald Joe Willis, *Schwabe, Williamson & Wyatt.*

- WARD CONNERLY: Has served on the board of trustees, Pacific Legal Foundation; chairman of the American Civil Rights Institute; contributor to Federalist Society Civil Rights Practice Group newsletter.
- MARC SANDSTROM: Has served as vice chairman of PLF; current vice president, Sharpe Health Care; former executive vice president and general counsel, San Diego Federal Savings & Loan; former Reagan appointee on the Board of Directors of Legal Services Corporation.
- WILLIAM F. HARVEY: Has served on Board of Advisors for PLF College of Public Interest Law; former Reagan appointee as chair of the Board of Directors of the Legal Services Corporation. A longtime law professor at Indiana University who has drawn controversy for his hard-line conservative positions, Harvey wrote an *amicus* brief for Pacific Legal Foundation in the landmark *Bakke* case supporting the white plaintiff in the case. Harvey also supported a for-credit Indiana Law School Semester-in-Washington program that was administered by the Lincoln Center for Legal Studies.[795] He also served on the advisory board of the Institute for Government and Politics of Paul Weyrich's Free Congress Foundation.
- RAYMOND M. MOMBOISSE: Has served as PLF deputy director; one of three initial staff attorneys who helped start PLF;[796] former California deputy attorney general under Reagan; former general counsel to the Immigration and Naturalization Service under President Reagan.
- The late W. GLENN CAMPBELL: Served on advisory panel for PLF Fellowship Program; director emeritus of the Hoover Institution; former research director of the American Enterprise Institute; had consulted for the National Security Council; served as a member of Committee for a Free World; and served on the Board of Directors for the Committee on the Present Danger.[797]

Key Staff

ROBERT K. BEST is president and CEO of Pacific Legal. His areas of specialty include land use law, environmental law, regulatory agencies, the judiciary, and questions of federalism.[798] A Vietnam War veteran and former naval officer,[799] Best also serves as an adjunct law professor at the University of the Pacific McGeorge School of Law, from which he received his J.D. after completing his undergraduate degree in economics at Stanford University. In addition, Best is an associate faculty member[800] with the Lincoln Institute of Land Policy,[801] based in Cambridge, Massachusetts.

Best joined Pacific Legal in 1976 and served as both chief of the Environmental and Land Use sections and deputy director of PLF for the next twelve years. In February 1988, Best resigned from Pacific Legal for a brief period to serve under conservative Governor George Deukmejian as the director of the California Department of Transportation—an area he originally had worked in for ten years before joining PLF. Upon leaving his post in the California government in 1991, Best continued his practice in zoning, planning, and land use law and served as a founding principal with Ronald Zumbrun and John Findley in the Sacramento firm of Zumbrun, Best & Findley. In January 1995, Best returned to Pacific Legal as president and chief executive officer. The chair of the Board of Trustees at the time of Best's return, Jerry Schauffler, exhibited the utmost confidence that Best would further the Pacific Legal agenda.[802]

Best has published several articles relating to takings law, including: "The Supreme Court Becomes Serious about Takings Law" (parts 1 and 2),[803] "Evolution and Thumbnail Sketch of Takings Law,"[804] and "All Dressed Up but Where Do We Go?"[805] In legal circles, Best is perhaps best known for personally arguing on behalf of Pacific Legal for the plaintiffs in the 1987 *Nollan v. California Coastal Commission*[806] case that led to a historic Supreme Court victory for the property rights movement. *Nollan* weakened the Public Trust Doctrine by holding that requiring an easement for public beach access in order to obtain a permit to build on beachfront property violates the Takings Clause of the Fifth Amendment and the Due Process Clause of the Fourteenth Amendment. PLF attorneys have said that *Nollan* is "considered the most significant property rights and government regulatory case of the past half-century."[807]

ANTHONY T. CASO is PLF's senior vice president and general counsel. In addition, Caso serves as corporate counsel and oversees PLF's law program generally. Since joining PLF in 1979, his principal areas of focus have included civil rights and discrimination policies, employment policy, the judiciary, tort reform, free speech, government regulation relating to finance, and issues of federalism.

Caso is currently vice chairman for pro bono outreach of the Federalist Society's Free Speech and Election Law Practice Group, which is chaired by Prop 209 lawyer Manuel Klausner. In 2001 he coauthored an article with Robert John Corry, Jr.,[808] the former president of the Stanford chapter of the Federalist Society and a past PLF attorney. The article's title speaks for itself: "Whites Need Not Apply: The Conservative Pacific Legal Foundation Challenges College Classes Designed Exclusively for Minorities."[809] In an interview with the *Los Angeles Times*, Corry said that Supreme Court Justice Antonin Scalia advised him to go to work for Pacific Legal.[810] Corry is also a member of the Federalist Society's Criminal Law and Procedure Practice Group and its Civil Rights Practice Group.[811]

Caso received his law degree from the McGeorge School of Law and his undergraduate degree from the University of La Verne. Caso has participated in a number of notable cases. Along with Zumbrun and Findley, he filed an *amicus* brief on behalf of PLF against the diversity policies at issue in *Adarand v. Pena*. He has filed briefs in a number of other groundbreaking cases, such as *Shaw v. Hunt*[812] (along with Deborah J. La Fetra, also from PLF); *Romer v. Evans*[813] (with La Fetra);[814] *Rosenberger v. Rector & Visitors of the University of Virginia*[815] (with La Fetra); *United States v. Lopez*[816] (with former PLF attorney and president, Ronald Zumbrun); *Int'l Union, United Auto., etc. v. Johnson Controls*[817] (with Zumbrun);

and *Metro Broadcasting, Inc. v. FCC*[818] (with Zumbrun and Sharon Browne).[819] Caso also handles the recruitment for PLF's College of Public Interest Law, which offers fellowships of $52,000 to law school graduates to do litigation with PLF.[820]

Caso has been heavily involved in PLF's anti-diversity litigation since the beginning. In response to the Supreme Court's first hearing of *Adarand v. Pena,* which declared a provision of the Small Business Act unconstitutional because of its diversity policies, Caso stated, "The High Court's message is clear: Equality cannot be achieved through a system of discrimination; justice cannot prevail by perpetuating injustice."[821] In the historic *U.S. v. Lopez*—a case in which the Supreme Court overturned a Federal gun control law because, it ruled, Congress exceeded its power under the commerce clause of the Constitution (the commerce clause plays an important role in Federal anti-discrimination legislation)—Pacific Legal filed an *amicus* brief on behalf of Lopez. Caso commented, "*Lopez* has the potential to be very significant in terms of how this Supreme Court is going to define the relationship between states and the federal government and Congress' power to intrude. . . . We think there are some limits to congressional power and hope the court will recognize that."[822]

On October 5, 2001, on behalf of Pacific Legal, Caso signed an ominous letter to California community college presidents suggesting that employees who continue to engage in diversity practices could be held personally liable for discrimination in violation of California law:

> Although it is true that someone is likely to appeal this ruling to the Supreme Court, this fact does not insulate your college or the individuals that take part in the hiring process from potential significant liability. . . . Thus, those actually involved in the hiring process (interview panels, affirmative action officers, screeners, and final decision makers) are all subject to personal liability for compensatory and punitive damages. . . . We urge you not to risk the scarce resources available for education at your college by continuing to enforce regulations that a California Court of Appeal has characterized as not even close to being constitutional. It is our hope that you will immediately cease any discriminatory hiring practices called for by the regulations without need for further legal action. [823]

The American Civil Rights Institute (ACRI—see above) headed by Ward Connerly placed Caso's letter on its website. In addition, in 2001, Caso wrote a featured article for the Federalist Society's Free Speech and Election Law Practice Group entitled "Supreme Court Preview: Compelled Financing of Expressive Activities."[824] Showing his strong libertarian bent, Caso (along with senior PLF property rights attorney James Burling)[825] has joined the Lone Mountain Coalition—a high-powered group of individuals committed to the libertarian precepts of the Lone Mountain Compact.[826] The principles of the Compact include a determined commitment to free market ideas, decentralized development, and a radical conception of private property rights.[827]

SHARON L. BROWNE is principal attorney for PLF's Individual Rights Practice Group. Browne has spent the past seventeen years waging an attack on diversity and affirmative action through her work at PLF. Like Best and Caso, Browne is a graduate of the McGeorge School of Law. She joined PLF in 1985 and has been there ever since, with the exception of 1991 to 1995, when she worked as a senior attorney at the "PLF private firm" of Zumbrun, Best & Findley in Sacramento.[828] During the 1980s, Browne worked with Ronald Zumbrun, Timothy A. Bittle, and Robert Best to fight regulatory initiatives[829] that grew out of PLF's win in *Nollan v. California Coastal Commission.*[830] Browne spent this period at PLF seeking to enforce private property rights against the rights of the public to access natural resources, such as the ocean, that traditionally have been viewed by the courts as within the public domain.[831]

Since her return to PLF in 1995, Browne has served as the lead attorney for litigating the right-wing version of "individual rights." As part of Pacific Legal's agenda, Browne battles against diversity remedies, affirmative action, and bilingual education. Browne has also been a key player in the litigation supporting the expansion of the Prop 209 attack on affirmative action in California. Browne is listed in the Heritage Foundation database as a "policy expert" on "racial preferences," bilingual education, and charter schools.[832]

In 1986, Browne worked to support the judicial activist idea that judges take control of school security under a state constitutional amendment created by the Victims' Bill of Rights.[833] Browne said of the judge-imposed plan, "It was necessary in the integration plans, and I think it's going to be necessary in the school safety plans. Somebody has to step in to protect the children, if the school district is dragging its feet."[834]

Working with Mark T. Gallagher, John Findley, Deborah La Fetra, and Stephen R. McCutcheon, Jr., Browne and PLF won the precedent-setting case *Hi-Voltage Wire Works, Inc. v. City of San Jose.*[835] In the lawsuit, they alleged a violation of Proposition 209 in the diversity policies used in contracting decisions.[836] Browne told the *Los Angeles Times* that even an outreach program such as the one in San Francisco amounts to an affirmative action program in violation of Proposition 209.[837]

Browne then launched an assault on the Los Angeles program, claiming that it violates Proposition 209 by calling for a 25 percent minority participation goal and by establishing numerical guidelines and timelines for participation in government contracts by women and minorities. Said Browne, "We call on [Los Angeles County] to get on the right side of the law by repealing their policies which treat some people more favorably than others because of color, ethnicity, or sex. Disobeying Proposition 209 could bring legal liability."[838] Browne accused the California attorney general of failing to enforce Proposition 209, claimed that PLF was "uphold[ing] the will of the people,"[839] and essentially threatened that PLF would seek to push the ruling in *Hi-Voltage* even further, in order to sweep up the Los Angeles program in its dragnet.[840]

With respect to the new admission policies under consideration in the University of California system, Browne questions the move toward evaluating a student's personal achievements as a backhanded method of boosting minority enrollment. "I really hope the regents consider carefully if they want to go down this road and embarrass the university again for discriminating on the basis of race,"[841] Browne told the *Los Angeles Times*. In a later interview she added, "There is a pretty good likelihood of a lawsuit. They have created a subjective standard, as opposed to an objective standard."[842] On this issue she has a clear difference with Ward Connerly, who sits on the Board of Regents of the University of California and has backed the effort to eliminate affirmative action in California. Connerly thought the shift in admissions criteria was a wise idea. "I believe that there isn't a hidden agenda here," Connerly said in an interview.[843]

In November 2001, Browne and PLF continued their relentless pursuit to abolish diversity policies and sued the Gilroy Unified School District, claiming that it relies on racial and ethnic factors when placing students in elementary schools.[844]

JOHN H. FINDLEY is principal attorney for the PLF Individual Rights Practice Group. After receiving his law degree from the University of California, Los Angeles, he began his career in government, serving as a deputy attorney general for California, special counsel for the U.S. Department of Health, Education, and Welfare, and staff counsel for the California Department of Social Welfare. Findley then joined Pacific Legal in 1973 and remained there until 1991, when he became a founding principal in the law firm of Zumbrun, Best & Findley, continuing to work with PLF on a part-time basis. In 1999 he rejoined Pacific Legal to specialize in individual rights.

DEBORAH J. LA FETRA is principal attorney at PFL. She joined Pacific Legal in 1990, after receiving a J.D. from the University of Southern California Law Center and a B.A. with honors in 1987 from Claremont McKenna College in political science and history. Her areas of specialty are civil rights and discrimination policies—in particular, equal protection and Proposition 209, the Voting Rights Act, the First Amendment, tort reform, and issues of federalism.

On behalf of PLF, La Fetra has participated in many of the recent civil rights cases that have overturned long-standing precedent. In reference to the controversial case *Miller v. Johnson,* which overturned Georgia's congressional redistricting plan, La Fetra commented, "Artificially dividing people along racial lines makes the ludicrous assumption that societal issues like crime, welfare, and education reform can only be resolved on the basis of skin color. . . Skin pigmentation is irrelevant to the effective representation of 'interests' of qualified voters in any given district. Thus, racial gerrymandering is not necessary for achieving moral equality in the voting rights context."[845]

E. Southeastern Legal Foundation (SLF)

The Southeastern Legal Foundation (SLF) was founded in Atlanta, Georgia, in 1976 as a "public interest law firm" advocating "limited government, individual economic freedom, and the free enterprise system in the courts of law and public opinion."[846] From the outset, SLF has portrayed itself as an organization designed to counteract the work of "activists" who had "so impeded the development of our economy and our energy resources that our nation's health and future are threatened."[847] A powerful instrument of legal activism, SLF identifies itself as both a "conservative alternative to the American Civil Liberties Union"[848] and, in the words of SLF's former president Matthew Glavin, "the liberal establishment's worst nightmare come true."[849] SLF litigates the majority of its cases in federal courts.

SLF functions as a southeastern corollary to the Pacific Legal Foundation, "[t]he foundation that started all the controversy."[850] The National Legal Center for the Public Interest (NLCPI), founded in 1975, helped to establish emerging conservative legal groups based on the PLF model, including SLF, Mountain States Legal Foundation, the Gulf and Great Plains Legal Foundation, among others.[851] NLCPI financially supported SLF, reporting that it raised funds in 1975 for SLF's launch.[852] NLCPI has also facilitated conservative networking, organizing annual meetings for the directors of each regional foundation.[853]

With the support of NLCPI, a group of conservative Atlanta political and business figures "who arrived at the conclusion that a public interest law firm was needed"[854] founded SLF. By 1977 foundations associated with United States Steel and United States Sugar, along with six other private foundations, had contributed to SLF—as well as "sixty-five of the largest oil, chemical, banking, lumber, construction, retail merchandise, and utility enterprises in the South."[855] By 1981 executives from Florida Power & Light, T. A. Jones Construction, United American Can, Gages Enterprises, and Linder Industrial Machine Company sat on SLF's board.[856] Its first board of trustees included a bevy of conservative sun belt political notables such as Edward E. Noble, James P. Poole, Robert L. Garges, Thomas V. Patton, and Charles B. West.[857] Its first president was former Republican U.S. Representative Ben Blackburn (R–Ga.), known for his far-right politics.[858]

Southeastern Legal Foundation's Activities

SLF takes on the battle of its financial and political backers—"beachfront property owners, stock-market tycoons, private-school parents and other haves against share-the-wealth government policies."[859] One of SLF's principal objectives, in its own words, is to "creat[e] binding legal precedent" and to implement what it considers "positive public policy change for all Americans."[860] This "public policy change" largely centers on economic and tax issues, including advocacy for the limitation of the Endangered Species Act;[861] the elimination of unemployment benefits, affirmative action programs, and benefits for same-sex and unmarried partners; and the rollback of court-ordered desegregation programs.[862]

Southeastern Legal's anti-government, anti-race consciousness stance has led it to emerge as the leader in dismantling census provisions in recent years. SLF prevailed in *Clinton v. Glavin*, a politically charged lawsuit filed in opposition to the use of statistical sampling in the 2000 U.S. Census.[863] The method of statistical sampling is designed to reduce census undercount, a problem that disproportionately affects people of color and results in an under-allocation of services and resources to communities often already underserved. In a decision described by the *New York Times* as "a victory for Republicans,"[864] the Supreme Court upheld SLF's argument[865] that rather than statistical sampling, the Constitution calls for a literal "actual enumeration" of the population.[866]

In addition, SLF members fought to pass a Republican-sponsored U.S. Senate resolution proclaiming "that no American will be prosecuted, fined or in any way harassed by the federal government or its agents for failure to respond to any census questions which refer to an individual's race, national origin, living conditions, personal habits or mental and/or physical condition."[867] SLF also resolutely opposed any mention of race on the census form, in a manner reminiscent of Ward Connerly's efforts to pass a "racial privacy initiative" in California that would make impossible the collection of statistics essential to monitoring diversity in social and institutional settings. In an April 2000 article, former SLF president Mathew Glavin was quoted as arguing that the Census Bureau should work as an "independent agency that only counts people," rather than as part of the U.S. Department of Commerce.[868] Glavin maintained that the census questions are "intrusive," claiming "[t]he government is trying to extort private information out of private citizens with a threat of prosecution. If a law enforcement agency can't do that, a $9-an-hour census worker can't."[869] SLF has announced that refusal to answer census questions pertaining to race and other such characteristics constitutes a form of "civil disobedience," which SLF would defend.[870]

Since its inception, SLF has written *amicus* briefs and represented clients in several key affirmative action cases, including *Metro Broadcasting v. FCC*,[871] *City of Richmond v. Croson*,[872] and *Northeastern Fl. Chapter Assoc. Gen. Contractors v. City of Jacksonville*.[873] According to Patricia Mayes of the *Macon Telegraph*, "annihilating affirmative action" has claimed "much of [SLF's] money and energy."[874] Southeastern Legal files suits—or threatens to—against city and county schools and government entities attempting to implement affirmative action policies. SLF has joined as counsel or submitted *amicus* briefs in several successful suits against diversity policies in school districts and minority business enterprise programs in government agencies.[875]

In 1979, SLF submitted *amicus* briefs on behalf of a class of non-minority Kaiser Aluminum employees in the important *Weber* case discussed earlier,[876] which challenged an affirmative action plan at Kaiser, this despite that fact that only 1.83 percent of the craft workforce was African American in a region where African Americans constituted 39 percent of the local workforce.[877] Ten years later, SLF filed *amicus* briefs in support of white contractors in one of the most important anti-affirmative action cases to date, *City of Richmond v. Croson*,[878] in which the U.S. Supreme Court struck down all race-based set asides in city-sponsored contracts, even where minority contractors held only .67 percent of contracts while 50 percent of the city's population was African American. The *Croson* decision has paved the way for virtually every subsequent attack on affirmative action programs.

In 1993, SLF represented the Northeastern Florida Chapter of Associated General Contractors in a suit against the city of Jacksonville, Florida, before the U.S. Supreme Court.[879] The Supreme Court found that a group of white public sector contract applicants whose bids were rejected had standing to bring suit.[880] The Court held that "a construction guild need not show that one of its members would have received a contract absent a local affirmative action ordinance."[881] Until *Northeastern Florida*, establishing standing against a race-based program required proof that "but for" the ordinance the applicants would have been granted the contract.[882] In *Bakke*[883] and in some non-education rulings prior to *Northeastern Florida*, the Court had granted standing based on a similar requirement.[884]

The Court has consistently granted standing to individuals who suffered injury due to government programs based on race, but the Court's protection of individuals rather than groups under the Equal Protection clause is in accordance with the new "colorblindness jurisprudence."[885] This decision is indicative of a trend toward acceptance of the colorblindness principle by the Supreme Court, stemming from an emphasis "not on whether a racial classification unfairly burdened the minority, but rather on whether it disadvantaged the majority."[886] It also tends to support University of Georgia Law School professor Michael Wells's argument that "conservative justices have a more accommodating attitude towards the standing of plaintiffs with substantive interest they favor."[887] This more expansive granting of standing has enabled many rejected non-minority applicants to file lawsuits without having suffered what traditionally has been considered "injury in fact." SLF has invoked this precedent in putting forth subsequent claims on behalf of aggrieved whites who have been denied contracts or admissions to colleges and universities.

Challenging Atlanta's Minority Enterprise Program

In August 1999, SLF filed suit against the City of Atlanta in federal court on behalf of four white contractors who alleged that they were denied contracts on the basis of their race in *Lee General Contractors, Inc. v. City of Atlanta, Georgia*.[888] SLF challenged Atlanta's affirmative action contracting program, which was designed to increase minority and female representation,[889] by seeking to grant 30 to 34 percent of its contracts to minority and female-owned businesses.[890] SLF threatened to sue the city if it did not dismantle its program within thirty days,[891] and placed an online petition on its website to Mayor Campbell demanding the elimination of the city's program.[892] SLF's role in promoting the litigation against minority contracting led the Georgia Black Chamber of Commerce to threaten a boycott of businesses that supported SLF.[893] The case was eventually settled in the summer of 2001 when the city replaced the existing program with one that did away with race and gender-based guidelines but included outreach to minority-owned businesses.

SLF has continued to challenge minority-contracting programs in other cities. In late 2001, SLF sent a letter to the mayor of Charlotte, North Carolina, demanding that the city's Minority and Women Business Development Program be rescinded and damages paid to a low-bid contractor that did not receive a city contract due to the program. SLF threatened to sue if the city did not take immediate action,[894] and then carried this threat through with support for a lawsuit filed in January 2002 claiming that the city's minority-contracting rules were unconstitutional. In a settlement that was reached in March 2002, the City of Charlotte agreed to pay $300,000 to the company involved in the suit (United Construction of Charlotte) and an additional $78,744 to cover attorney's fees.[895] SLF claimed victory in the case, in which attorney Lee Parks (see below) was cocounsel.[896]

In 1999, Southeastern Legal was involved in eliminating a twenty-year-old court-ordered busing program in DeKalb County, Georgia. SLF first threatened the school board with a lawsuit unless it eliminated a *voluntary* program that bused African American students to predominantly white and Latino schools.[897] The program, known as the Majority-to-Minority program (M-to-M program), worked to reduce the impact of residential segregation on county schools by permitting students who were in a racial majority in their own schools to be bused to county schools outside their neighborhoods in which they would be a racial minority.[898] Glavin asserted that the program violated the civil rights of whites, ironically citing the historic *Brown v. Board of Education* decision. After the school board agreed to eliminate the program, Glavin responded, "We're encouraged that the school board has taken this initial step to dismantle the M-to-M program based on our threat of litigation."[899] The elimination of the program did not provide for reducing significant disparities between the white and Latino neighborhoods (north DeKalb) and African American neighborhoods (south DeKalb), but instead returned 4,300 students to disproportionately crowded schools in south DeKalb.[900] The elimination of the DeKalb County program has significantly "paved the way for what could be a major redistricting of attendance boundaries."[901]

SLF also opposes any use of affirmative action in higher education, and in 2001 it filed an *amicus* brief in *Johnson v. Board of Regents of the University of Georgia,*[902] which challenges the freshman admissions process at the University of Georgia.[903] Current SLF president Phil Kent commented that the challenge to the admissions process was brought because "[b]asically some white girls were bounced from admission because of the quotas."[904]

SLF has also taken an interest in a range of issues outside the realm of civil rights, including challenging recent campaign finance reform proposals,[905] government policies and benefits conferred upon illegal immigrants,[906] and Atlanta's allocation of impact fees paid by city developers. It was also a leading advocate for the disbarment of former President Bill Clinton.[907]

The Money Trail

The importance of Southeastern Legal's role in the Right's legal assault on diversity policies is illustrated by the continuous, significant support it has received from major right-wing foundations. The Sarah Scaife Foundation has supported SLF for well over a decade, but in 1996 its donations reached a new level. According to Media Transparency, Scaife gave SLF $150,000 for each of the calendar years 1996, 1997, and 1998;[908] in 1999 it gave SLF $200,000;[909] and in 2000 it gave $100,000.[910] Moreover, in 1999, SLF received $75,000 from the John M. Olin Foundation for "a legal challenge to the government's plan to use statistical sampling in the 2000 census;"[911] in 1998, it received $40,000 from the Castle Rock Foundation;[912] and in 1997 it received $50,000 from the Samuel R. Noble Foundation.[913]

Southeastern Legal's reported revenue for 1999 totaled $2,063,525,[914] allowing it to spend $1,385,212 on "program services" and $338,880 on fund-raising expenses.[915] From 1995 to 1998, SLF's "gifts, grants, and contributions received" totaled $7,336,999.[916] SLF also received significant funding from private individuals. During 1999, SLF reported individual grants ranging from $5,000 to $200,000 that totaled $671,950.[917] According to David Kendall, who defended President Clinton in SLF's lawsuit seeking his disbarment, "Richard Scaife gives the foundation money, and [former independent counsel] Kenneth Starr helps raise money for it."[918] On January 3, 2002, Southeastern Legal announced that Starr and Edwin Meese were poised to wage a legal battle on its behalf in opposition to campaign finance legislation.[919] Subsequently, SLF became "co-counsel with Kenneth Starr and chief funder for the legal team in *McConnell et al. v. FEC*,[920] FCC Omnibus Constitutional lawsuit" filed in April 2002.[921]

Leadership of the Southeastern Legal Foundation

As of June 2000, Southeastern Legal's Board of Trustees included the following:[922]

KATHY BARCO is treasurer and former chair of SLF[923] and president of Barco-Duval Engineering, Inc., a contracting company based in Jacksonville, Florida, that reported over $15 million in business in 1999. Her parents, Charles and

Lynda Barco, founded the company in 1959.[924] Barco attended the University of Florida and completed several study units at the Harvard Business School Owner/President Management Program. Barco is a member of the Jacksonville Economic Development Commission, and is the immediate past president of the Northeastern Florida Region of the Associated General Contractors of Greater Florida,[925] which was the moving party in *Associated General Contractors v. City of Jacksonville*, the suit that paved the way for future litigation on behalf of white contractors challenging affirmative action programs for minority businesses.[926] Florida Governor Jeb Bush also appointed her citizen member of the Atlantic States Marine Fisheries Commission.[927]

Barco is part of a growing constituency of contractors who have actively opposed minority business enterprise (MBE) programs. She has recently expressed concern over Jacksonville's MBE program, commenting that it is problematic because "it just adds a whole new layer of bureaucracy." She proposes in its place a program directed toward "small businesses" in general.[928] Accordingly, Barco has worked through SLF to change the legal climate she feels threatens businesses such as her own.

GRIFFIN BELL, JR., former chair of SLF,[929] is the son of Griffin Bell, who served as the conservative attorney general during the Carter administration. The younger Bell has served as an active force within the Board of Trustees. He was considered "instrumental in bringing [Robert] Proctor, SLF chair from 1994-1996 (see below), and [Matthew] Glavin to the foundation."[930] Bell and former SLF board member Franklin Burke recruited both Proctor and Glavin in hopes of improving fund-raising and promoting activism.[931]

Bell currently serves as senior counsel with Fisher & Phillips of Atlanta, and gained a reputation as a pro-management labor attorney. He has been noted as a possible candidate for district attorney. He campaigned for Barry Goldwater in 1964 and refers to himself as "a Gingrich Republican."[932] Bell graduated from the University of Georgia with an A.B. in 1965 and received his J.D. from Emory University in 1970. Bell clerked for Judge Alexander A. Lawrence, U.S. District Court, Southern District of Georgia.

PHILIP A. KENT has been president of Southeastern Legal since April 30, 2001. Upon joining SLF he commented that Southeastern Legal Foundation picks its battles carefully, speaks plainly, and wins.[933] Prior to joining SLF, Kent served for twenty-five years as the "take-no-prisoners" conservative columnist,[934] editorial writer, and editorial page editor of the *Augusta Chronicle*,[935] which he joined immediately after graduating from the Henry W. Grady School of Journalism at the University of Georgia in 1973.

From 1981-1982, Kent served in Washington, D.C., as press secretary and public affairs advisor to U.S. Senator Strom Thurmond (R-SC). He rejoined the *Chronicle* as editorial page editor, but stepped down in 1999 after, as the *Augusta*

Chronicle itself stated, "he admitted to, and apologized for, using language from a national columnist without properly attributing the material to that columnist."[936] Kent is cofounder and chairman of the Board of Advisors of Editorial Information Network, a D.C.-based organization that provides information to the media about Capitol Hill.[937] Kent is also a member of the Board of Advisors for Coalition for a Voting America, the National Conference of Editorial Writers, and the Military Order of World Wars.

CARL LOOP, JR., has served as president of the Florida Farm Bureau since 1983.[938] He served as vice president of the American Farm Bureau Federation from 1995 to 2000, and still serves on the executive committee as the representative of the Southern Region. Loop is president of Loop's Nursery and Greenhouses—a specialized flower business that he founded in 1949—in Jacksonville, Florida. He is also an outspoken critic of the federal estate tax.[939]

MACK MATTINGLY is chair of the SLF Board of Trustees.[940] He served in the Air Force from 1951 to 1955 and received his B.S. from Indiana University in 1957.[941] Mattingly worked at IBM in Georgia as a marketing manager from 1959 to 1979, and was owner and president of M's Inc. (a computer company) of Georgia from 1975 to 1980.[942] In 1964, Mattingly entered politics as chairman of the 8th District Goldwater for President campaign, and in 1966 he unsuccessfully ran for U.S. Congress in the 8th District.[943] He then served as state chairman of the Georgia Republican Party between 1975 and 1977.[944] Mattingly went on to become the first Republican U.S. Senator from Georgia since 1871. Serving only one term, he lost in 1986 to Democrat Wyche Fowler. During his tenure he was known as "one of the more conservative members of the Senate, [who] voted with his party leadership more than 90 percent of the time."[945] After losing his bid for reelection, Mattingly was appointed by Reagan as assistant secretary general for defense support at NATO headquarters in Brussels, heading the department that addressed arms cooperation from 1987 to 1990.[946] In 1992, George H.W. Bush appointed Mattingly ambassador to the Seychelles for a term that lasted until 1993, when Clinton took office.

Mattingly has remained active in politics to this day. In 2000, Mattingly, seeking his old seat, ran as the Republican candidate for U.S. senator from Georgia, losing to Senator Zell Miller. On July 16, 2001, Mattingly was appointed the first chairman of the Prosperity Institute's Task Force on Information Exchange and Financial Privacy. The Prosperity Institute is chaired by fellow SLF board member Richard Rahn (for more on Rahn and the Institute, see below), and Ed Meese and Jack Kemp serve as senior advisers to the Task Force.[947] Mattingly and Rahn's connections extend into the private sector as well. Mattingly is a member of the Novecon Companies' Board of Senior Advisors, whose founder and chief executive officer is Rahn.[948]

EDWIN MEESE, III, former U.S. attorney general and former member of the

National Security Council, "was among President Ronald Reagan's most important advisors."[949] Meese is a well-connected member of several organizations: He is the Ronald Reagan Distinguished Fellow in Public Policy at the Heritage Foundation, a Distinguished Fellow at the Hoover Institution at Stanford, an adjunct Fellow of the Discovery Institute, and Distinguished Senior Fellow at the University of London's Institute of United States Studies. As chief of staff for Governor Ronald Reagan in California, Meese was instrumental in the creation of the Pacific Legal Foundation and the raft of right-wing "public interest" organizations that followed in its wake. He received his undergraduate degree from Yale University and his law degree from the University of California, Berkeley.

GUY MILLNER is a wealthy Georgia businessman with political aspirations. After graduating from Florida State University with a B.A. in political science in 1958, Millner moved to Atlanta and in 1961 founded Norrell Corporation, a temporary services agency that reported $1 billion revenue in 1996.[950] He unsuccessfully opposed Zell Miller for governor of Georgia in 1994 and 1998, and lost a bid for U.S. Senate against former Democratic Georgia Secretary of State Max Cleland in 1996. In his 1994 gubernatorial campaign, the Associated Press reported, the Georgia State Ethics Commission fined Millner a record $12,700 for "failing to correctly report hundreds of contributions and expenditures."[951]

Former Republican presidential candidate Steve Forbes endorsed Millner,[952] who supports the elimination of the Department of Education "because it is simply an arm of the National Education Association, a teachers union." He is an advocate of home schooling and has strong views about a traditional education: "I don't want a curriculum in Georgia that says a family is two men or two women."[953] He also supports the abolition of parole for all crimes and the privatization of prisons.[954]

Millner personally financed $1.6 million of $5.2 million spent on his 1994 gubernatorial campaign; over $6 million of $9.7 million spent on his 1996 Senate campaign; and $4.6 million of $6.7 million spent (through July 31, 1998) in his 1998 gubernatorial campaign.[955] According to the Associated Press, in the 1996 campaign season, Cleland publicized Millner's membership in a West Palm Beach country club that had a reputation for excluding African Americans and Jews.[956] After receiving considerable negative publicity, Millner pledged that he would leave the club, but did not do so until after the election was over.[957] Since his defeat, Millner has supported conservative Georgia political figures, including Rev. Ron Crews, a Georgia state representative supported by Ralph Reed, the former executive director of the Christian Coalition.[958]

EDWARD E. NOBLE has been identified by Edwin Feulner as one of the Heritage Foundation's three founding fathers (along with Joseph Coors and Richard M. Scaife).[959] Noble comes from the wealthy Noble family of Oklahoma, heirs to the Lloyd Noble oil fortune.[960] His brother was the late Oklahoma oilman Samuel R. Noble, former chairman of the board of Noble Affiliates and Noble Drilling

Group and figurehead of the Samuel R. Noble Foundation.[961] The Noble Foundation is an organization that funds plant genetics research and donates substantial amounts of money to conservative causes such as SLF ($50,000 in 1999),[962] the Heritage Foundation, and the Capital Research Center.[963]

Noble's initial and continuing support of the Heritage Foundation has been instrumental to its growth. Through the Samuel R. Noble Foundation, of which Edward Noble is a trustee,[964] Heritage received $5 million in 1998 "to finish a new building and fund research programs,"[965] and $7 million in 1999 "to retire the debt on its Capitol Hill office."[966] At a Heritage Foundation dinner in 1999, "Mr. [Joseph] Coors was being honored for his unfailing support for the foundation since he, Edward Noble and Richard Scaife kicked in the start-up funds for the storefront foundation that was then, as Mr. Feulner likes to say, the feisty new kid on the conservative block."[967]

Noble has long been involved in conservative causes. In 1967 he was appointed to the Board of Overseers of the Hoover Institute on War and Peace at Stanford University.[968] Noble is also a member of the Board of Governors of the Georgia Public Policy Foundation, which Glavin founded in 1990.[969] In the late 1970s, Noble opposed congressional legislation that sought to establish Synthetic Fuels Corporation, a government-sponsored agency designed to subsidize the development of a synthetic fuel industry in the wake of anticipated rising oil prices in 1980, when the cost of a barrel of oil was expected to exceed $75.[970] After Congress succeeded in establishing U.S. Synthetic Fuels Corporation in 1980, Noble headed a task force under Reagan that sought to dismantle it.[971] In 1981, Reagan appointed Noble as chairman of the board of Synthetic Fuels,[972] where he remained until 1986, when Congress dissolved the corporation after oil prices fell to less than $20 a barrel.[973] Noble also served as chairman of Reagan's transition team and was a member of Reagan's White House Council on Natural Resources and the Environment between 1982 and 1983.[974]

Noble graduated from the University of Oklahoma with a bachelor's degree in geology in 1951, and in 1981 he received an honorary Ph.D. from Hanyang University in Seoul. He is also known as an Atlanta real estate figure and founder of Noble Properties, which developed Atlanta's famous Lenox Square Mall and conducts business in Georgia, Oklahoma, North Carolina, West Virginia, and Ohio.[975] In addition, Noble serves as chairman of the Foundation of the Holy Apostles, a conservative offshoot of the Episcopal Church.[976]

THOMAS V. PATTON is chief executive officer of Atlanta-based Triton, Inc., a gas station and convenience store chain that he founded in 1962, which is now a real estate and development company. Patton is also trustee emeritus of the Georgia Tech Foundation, and has served on the board of the U.S. Chamber of Commerce and the Atlanta Chamber of Commerce.[977] Patton graduated from Georgia Tech in 1943.

RICHARD W. RAHN is an ultra-conservative economist who began his career as an adjunct professor of economics at George Mason University from 1974 to 1980. He was vice president and chief economist of the U.S. Chamber of Commerce during the Reagan and Bush, Sr., administrations, from 1980 to 1991,[978] and an economic advisor to Bush, Sr., during his 1988 campaign.[979]

Rahn is chairman of the Prosperity Institute,[980] which supports and disseminates research from organizations advocating free-market and limited government solutions to policy issues.[981] The Institute's first project is the Task Force on Information Exchange and Financial Privacy (chaired by Mack Mattingly and advised by Jack Kemp and Edwin Meese), advocating for global financial privacy and unlimited tax competition.[982] Dan Mastromarco and David R. Burton serve, respectively, as president and chief executive officer of the Institute.[983] Members of the Task Force include Brad Jansen of the Free Congress Foundation, Dan Mitchell of the Heritage Foundation, and Solveig Singleton of the Competitive Enterprise Institute.[984]

In the private sector, Rahn is founder of the Novecon companies[985] and serves as president of Novecon Ltd., vice-chairman of Novecon Technologies Corp., and chairman of the Board of Directors of Novecon Financial Ltd.[986] Rahn was married to Reagan speechwriter Peggy Noonan, from whom he was divorced in 1990.

In addition to personal business endeavors, Rahn has been directly involved in "transition to democracy" operations in Eastern Europe and the former Soviet Union. In 1990 he was U.S. cochairman of the Bulgarian Economic Growth and Transition Project, and he was a member of the U.S. Committee to Assist Russian Reform from 1992 to 1993.[987] He serves on the Board of Directors of the D.C.-based "pro-business" American Council for Capital Formation (ACCF),[988] where he was executive director from 1976 to 1980.[989] ACCF professes an anti-tax, anti-regulatory mission to "help redefine and restructure U.S. tax, trade, and environmental policies."[990] ACCF has published studies addressing the alleged high cost of environmental policies, which are ultimately geared toward replacing existing environmental policies with ones that "promote capital formation."[991]

As chief economist for the U.S. Chamber of Commerce,[992] Rahn was involved in seeking out future black conservative leaders who would promote the politics of the Reagan administration. Addressing this subject in a White House memo, Reagan political aide James Cicconi wrote, "For the immediate future, we must avoid the 'established' black leadership.... [T]hey cannot be expected to take a constructive approach.... They are personally and rhetorically linked to a philosophy which cannot be reconciled with our own."[993] Rahn advised his friend (and White House public liaison) Faith Whittlesey that the White House could recruit African Americans by "dealing with the right blacks," noting, "If you have credible people, they can be alternative leaders."[994] Rahn then proceeded to draw up a list of "credible people," who Whittlesey invited to a White House meeting, with the idea of excluding black Republicans "who have little clout in the black community."[995] The most successful recruit of the Reagan administration's efforts was Alan Keyes, who defended U.S. policy in South Africa, arguing that sanctions would be dangerous because it would "only stir racial turmoil in this country."[996]

Rahn is an adjunct scholar at the Indianapolis-based Hudson Institute, one of the leading think tanks formulating conservative social policy. The Hudson Institute published Clint Bolick's 1988 report, "Opportunity 2000," which called for private sector solutions to racial imbalances in the workforce.[997]

Rahn also serves as an adjunct scholar at the Cato Institute and as a senior fellow at the Seattle-based Discovery Institute, which through its Center for the Renewal of Science & Culture is currently funding researchers who disseminate "intelligent design theory"—a "scientific" version of creationism—at colleges and universities.[998] In addition, Rahn is a member of the advisory board of the Private Sector Council[999] and was executive vice president of the National Chamber Foundation (affiliated with the U.S. Chamber of Commerce) from 1985 to 1991.[1000]

Rahn received his B.A. in economics from the University of South Florida in 1963, his M.B.A. from Florida State University in 1964, and a Ph.D. in business economics from Columbia University in 1972.[1001]

Legal Advisory Board[1002]
- E. Lynn Hogue, Chairman (see bio, infra)
- Jackson H. Ables, III: Daniel, Coker, Horton & Bell, Jackson, MS
- Foster D. Arnett: Arnett, Draper & Hagood, Knoxville, TN
- Maxfield Bahner: Chambliss & Bahne, Chattanooga, TN
- Fournier J. Gale, III: Maynard, Cooper & Gale, Birmingham, AL
- Edwin S. Hopson: Wyatt, Tarrant & Combs, Louisville, KY
- Burke Kibler: Holland & Knight, Lakeland, FL
- Fletcher C. Mann: Leatherwood, Walker, Todd & Mann, Greenville, SC
- Walter H. Ryland: Williams, Mullen, Christian & Dobins, Richmond, VA

Southeastern Legal's Founding Father
BENJAMIN B. BLACKBURN was the first president of Southeastern Legal, serving from the time of SLF's inception in 1976 until 1985, when he accepted a federal government appointment. Known for his extreme conservative politics, Blackburn served as chairman of the Board of Trustees of the Heritage Foundation from 1974 until 1982[1003] with other conservative stalwarts such as the late William E. Simon, Sr.,[1004] J. Robert Fluor, Frank Shakespeare, and Shelby Davis.[1005] Fluor is J. Simon Fluor's nephew, and has assumed his uncle's position in the Fluor Corporation (see above).

In 1980, Blackburn served on the Reagan presidential transition team. In 1983 the Reagan administration offered Blackburn a position on the board of the Legal Services program after the Senate had refused to confirm several Reagan nominees who opposed the program. Blackburn turned down the offer, commenting that if he were nominated to the Legal Services board, "we'd be declaring war."[1006] According to the *Washington Post*, "The [*Atlanta Journal-Constitution*] reported that Blackburn once 'joked' with House colleagues about hanging public housing tenants, and later defended literacy tests to make sure voters are qualified to cast ballots."[1007] He later served as regional representative for the United States Department of Transportation from 1985 to 1989.[1008] Retired Rear Admiral William O. Miller replaced Blackburn as president of SLF in 1985.[1009]

Former SLF Board Members

WILLIAM H. FLOWERS, JR., was a founding member of Southeastern Legal [1010] and served as chairman of SLF from 1983 to 1987.[1011] Until his retirement in 1996, Flowers was chairman of the board of Flowers Industries, a corporation formerly known as Flowers Baking Company, which was founded by his father, William Howard Flowers, Sr. Flowers was active in both business and right-wing politics. He was a Georgia state senator from 1964 to 1968, during which time he drafted a "Georgia Plan" that proposed a balanced budget constitutional amendment.[1012] In 1984, Flowers became a member of the board of the National Legal Center for the Public Interest.[1013] Former SLF president Matt Glavin's Georgia Public Policy Foundation awarded Flowers its annual Freedom Award in 1994. Flowers graduated from Washington and Lee University with a B.A. in business administration in 1933. He died in May 2000.

MATTHEW J. GLAVIN was president and chief executive officer of Southeastern Legal.[1014] He left SLF in October 2000 after pleading guilty to a misdemeanor public indecency charge following an encounter with an undercover federal ranger in a Gwinnett County park.[1015] Originally from upstate New York, Glavin graduated from Columbia College of Sonora, California, with a degree in broadcasting. Following college, Glavin moved to Vermont, where he began a "marketing and communications firm," and later to Maine, where he hosted both television and radio talk shows.[1016] Before joining SLF, Glavin served as founding president of the Hannibal Hamlin Institute for Economic and Policy Studies of Hallowell, Maine,[1017] which is featured in the *National Journal*'s "New Rightist Think Tank Roster."[1018] Not unlike SLF, Hannibal Hamlin has been described as a "business think tank, backed by conservative corporations and foundations, [and] focused on property rights and privatization of state government services."[1019]

In 1988, Glavin managed the unsuccessful campaign of Linda Bean for the U.S. House.[1020] Bean is the granddaughter of L.L. Bean and a director on the L.L. Bean board. She was described by the Purple Panthers, a group of gay rights activists in Philadelphia, as a "conservative Republican" and a supporter of "right-wing causes and homophobes"—views that instigated a boycott of L.L. Bean by gay activists in Philadelphia in 1993.[1021] According to the *Portland Press Herald*, Bean contributed to a 1997 campaign by the Maine Christian Coalition to remove a prohibition on discrimination for sexual orientation from the state's human rights law.[1022] Glavin has donated thousands to conservative causes, such as Phyllis Schlafly's Eagle Forum and the Constitution Party (formerly known as the U.S.

Taxpayers Party), whose platform favors the abolition of the federal income tax, criminalization of abortion, and elimination of any federal role in education.[1023]

In 1990, Glavin moved to Georgia, where he established the Georgia Public Policy Foundation (GPPF),[1024] a conservative Atlanta-based advocacy group whose Board of Governors includes fellow SLF board member Ed Noble.[1025] The GPPF, like SLF, believes that "the solutions to most problems lie in a strong private sector, not in a big government bureaucracy."[1026] It presents an annual Freedom Award, which is given to a Georgian "who exemplifies the principles of free enterprise, personal responsibility, limited government and service to others."[1027] Recipients of the award include[1028] former U.S. Attorney General Griffin Bell; former SLF chairman of the board and chairman emeritus of Flowers Industries William Flowers, Jr.; Supreme Court Justice Clarence Thomas; Georgia Governor Zell Miller;[1029] Mrs. Deen Day Smith[1030] and Sen. Phil Gramm.

Impressed with Glavin's work at the Georgia Public Policy Foundation, SLF board members Griffin Bell, Jr., and Franklin L. Burke invited Glavin to join SLF. In 1994, Glavin became president and vice chairman of the board. After Glavin assumed his leadership role in SLF, annual fund-raising more than doubled.[1031] Glavin also increased SLF's media visibility by appearing regularly on national television and radio talk shows.

AMOS R. MCMULLIAN became chairman of Southeastern Legal in 1991,[1032] carrying on the Flowers tradition at SLF. McMullian is "the second head of Flowers Industries to have sat on the board of Southeastern Legal Foundation," following SLF founding member W. H. Flowers, Jr., who served for fourteen years.[1033] McMullian was appointed chief executive officer of Flowers Industries in 1981 and became chairman of the board in 1985. He resigned from SLF's Board of Directors following the Georgia Black Chamber of Commerce's (GBCC's) 1999 campaign against businesses supporting SLF, declaring that the boycott compelled him to put his company's economic interests ahead of his SLF board membership. McMullian received a B.S. from Florida State University in 1962 and began working for Flowers in 1963.[1034]

WILLIAM O. MILLER, retired rear admiral and former judge advocate general of the navy, became president of SLF in 1985.[1035] He was succeeded by Bob Barr in 1990, at which time Miller became vice chairman of SLF's board of trustees.[1036]

WILLIAM W. SPRAGUE, JR., was chief executive officer and chairman of the board of SLF until 1991, when Amos R. McMullian replaced him. He continued to serve on SLF's Board of Trustees and executive committee.[1037] Sprague was chief executive officer and chairman of the Board of Directors of Savannah Foods and Industries until he retired in 1995, when his son, William W. Sprague III, assumed the positions of president and CEO. In 1997, Savannah Foods and Industries was acquired by the Texas-based Imperial Holly Corporation. Like McMullian, Sprague resigned from the board in 1999 following the Georgia

Black Chamber of Commerce's campaign against SLF.[1038]

Sprague resigned from SLF's board only a few hours after Atlanta mayor Bill Campbell and the Georgia Black Chamber of Commerce threatened to boycott Savannah Foods and Dixie Crystals Sugar, both subsidiaries of Imperial Sugar. His son, Sprague III, objected to the threatened boycott on the grounds, he told the *Atlanta Constitution*, that Savannah Foods had "been sold to Imperial Sugar since his father retired and does not contribute money to the foundation."[1039] Savannah Foods was later withdrawn from consideration for the boycott after the Chamber received a letter from Imperial Sugar's general counsel, stating that William Sprague, Jr., was never associated with Imperial Sugar.[1040] Sprague's son resigned from Imperial Sugar in September 1999 to, as a company press release stated, "pursue other interests."

LARRY D. THOMPSON is currently U.S. deputy attorney general.[1041] A former member of SLF's legal advisory board (and also active in the Atlanta Federalist Society), Thompson protested SLF's position on affirmative action and resigned during the GBCC campaign, stating that his SLF involvement undermined his "representation of clients." He was the only African American member of SLF's legal advisory board.[1042] A close friend of Supreme Court Justice Clarence Thomas,[1043] he worked as the U.S. attorney for the Northern District of Georgia from 1982 to 1986, and became a partner at King & Spalding in Atlanta in 1986. He graduated from the University of Michigan Law School in 1974.

ROBERT L. BARR left his job as a Reagan-appointed U.S. attorney from the Northern District of Georgia in 1990 to become president of SLF in early 1990.[1044] Barr received a bachelor's degree from UCLA in 1970, a master's degree from George Washington University in 1972, and a J.D. from Georgetown in 1977. Barr worked for the CIA as an analyst from "the height of the Vietnam War" until 1978.[1045] Since 1994 he has been Georgia's 7th District representative in Congress. He is a member of the Pro-Life Caucus, the National Rifle Association (serving as a director), and the Federalist Society,[1046] and he has received the Christian Coalition's Friend of the Family award. He also has been named "Gun Rights Legislator of the Year" by the Citizens' Committee for the Right to Keep and Bear Arms and "Congressional Leader of the Year" by the American Shooting Sports Council.[1047] Barr was keynote speaker at the 1998 semi-annual convention of the Council of Conservative Citizens, which has been described by the Rev. Joseph Lowery (who founded the Southern Christian Leadership conference with Rev. Dr. Martin Luther King) as "the Ku Klux Klan with a coat and tie."[1048]

ROBERT PROCTOR was chairman of SLF between 1994 and 1996,[1049] but left because he feared that it had become "too partisan and was straying too much from its mission."[1050] Proctor later became concerned that SLF was addressing national issues while neglecting "the Southeast, or the Voting Rights Act, affirmative action and state and local tax issues." Proctor graduated from Vanderbilt with a B.A. in 1978 and received his J.D. from the University of Georgia School of Law in 1981. In a 1999 interview, Proctor publicly criticized Glavin's leadership of SLF, noting that Glavin has been more interested in national cases than he should be, creating a situation where "[t]here's been too much jumping into political cases rather than legal issues."[1051]

Personal grievances notwithstanding, Proctor's work at SLF generated significant media attention. He played an instrumental role as the head litigator in eliminating affirmative action programs in the Atlanta school system and in DeKalb County. In 1996 he sued the Atlanta Public School system three times, and won a case that enjoined the city of Atlanta from giving $18 million a year to the public school system through local sales taxes. Proctor has advocated the elimination of the Atlanta public school system and the creation of a private system in its place.[1052]

Key Figures

LYNN HOGUE is chairman of SLF's Legal Advisory Board,[1053] and served as interim president after Matt Glavin's departure—until Phil Kent assumed the presidency in spring 2001.[1054] He received his A.B. from William Jewell College in 1966, a Ph.D. from University of Tennessee in 1972, and his J.D. from Duke in 1974. Hogue has been a lieutenant colonel in the U.S. Army Reserve Judge Advocate General's Corps since 1979.[1055] In 1998 he filed a complaint against President Clinton with the Arkansas Supreme Court Committee on Professional Conduct on allegations of professional misconduct,[1056] eventually leading to Clinton's disbarment.[1057] Hogue is a professor of constitutional law at Georgia State University's College of Law and also serves on the Board of Advisors of the Federalist Society's Atlanta Chapter.[1058]

VALLE SIMMS DUTCHER serves as general counsel for SLF.[1059] Dutcher began her legal career working for Robert Proctor after she graduated from Pace University Law School in 1993. She graduated from Hollins College in 1969. Dutcher represented the plaintiffs in *Glavin v. Clinton* (1999), SLF's challenge to the Clinton census sampling plan. She litigates all of SLF's cases in the southeast and in the District of Columbia.[1060]

A. LEE PARKS, JR., is a senior partner at Parks, Chesin & Miller, an Atlanta-based law firm, and has frequently worked with SLF on key cases, such as the Charlotte reverse discrimination suit that settled in March 2002, on which he was cocounsel (see above). He received his B.A. from the University of Arizona in 1974 and graduated from Emory University School of Law in 1977. Focusing on affirmative action and civil rights attacks, Parks represented plaintiffs in *Miller v. Johnson*[1061] and *Abrams v. Johnson,*[1062] cases SLF describes as "the first successful constitutional challenges to majority black congressional and legislative districting plans as racial gerrymanders."[1063] He has also represented students in

2001 in critically important cases of reverse discrimination against the University of Georgia's admission policy,[1064] which he successfully argued was unconstitutional because it employed a formula "that boosted the chances of some minority applicants."[1065]

RICHMOND MASON BARGE serves as outside counsel to Southeastern Legal.[1066] He is also counsel for Parks, Chesin & Miller. Barge graduated from Emory University School of Law with Parks in 1977, and received his B.A. from Yale in 1974. His practice area is race and gender discrimination in business and educational institutions. He litigated a successful constitutional challenge to Fulton County, Georgia's, minority contracting program. Upon appeal, the Eleventh Circuit affirmed the prior ruling.[1067] Barge was also the first named attorney for the plaintiffs in *Webster v. Fulton County*,[1068] SLF's high-profile lawsuit against the city of Atlanta's Minority Business Enterprise program.

THOMAS G. GREAVES, JR., was a member of SLF's Legal Advisory Board from 1977 until his death in 2000. He was of counsel with Hand Arendall, L.L.C. of Mobile, Alabama. He graduated from the University of Alabama Law School in 1947 and received a B.S. in economics from the University of Pennsylvania in 1939. A fellow of the American Bar Foundation, Greaves was president of the Alabama State Bar (1975–1976), and an Alabama state delegate (1959–1974).

D. BURKE KIBLER III was a member of SLF's Legal Advisory Board from 1981 to 1999.[1069] He is chairman emeritus of the Holland & Knight law firm and general counsel for Florida House, of which he is a trustee, and a fellow of the American Bar Foundation.[1070] Kibler, a former chairman of the Board of Regents of the Florida state university system, is involved in the Florida Department of Education Facilities Task Force, of which he is chairman; the Governor's Commission for Government by the People Subcommittee on Education, of which he is a member; and the Governor's Council for a Sustainable Florida, for which he serves as an advisor.[1071] Between 1980 and 1990, Kibler served as member and chairman of the Post Secondary Education Planning Commission. He then served as a member of the governor's Transition Task Force on Education from 1990 to 1991. In 1989 the Independent Colleges and Universities of Florida presented Kibler both their Liberty Bell Award and their Champions of Higher Independent Education in Florida Award.[1072]

Kibler has served as general counsel of the Florida Citrus Commission and the Florida Phosphate Council.[1073] He was also a director of the James Madison Institute for Public Policy of Tallahassee. He received his B.A. from the University of Florida in 1947 and graduated from University of Florida Law School in 1949. Kibler also served as president and director of the University of Florida Foundation.

Chapter 5

The Assault on Diversity and the Coming to Power of the George W. Bush Administration

The national controversy over "diversity" has been dramatically affected by the climate produced by the September 11 terrorist attacks on the United States. Unlike some other issues, the manner in which America deals with ethnicity and tolerance was not put on the back burner by the shock of the attacks. Rather, it immediately leapt to the fore as the country reacted to the perceived threat. The question now for those concerned about civil rights is whether, as in the case of civil liberties, the hasty and emotional reflex for national self-protection produced by the events will overwhelm good judgment and be translated into bad law.

Some bedrock problems shaping the long-standing national debate on diversity have resurfaced with a vengeance: tolerance of ethnic and religious minorities in various communities; the scapegoating of minorities as a threat to "our" culture or physical security (long a motif in the segregationist south and suburban north); where the line is to be drawn between religious expression and stigmatizing behavior;[1074] the danger of bigotry working its way into decisions on racial profiling in law enforcement;[1075] the constitutional rights of immigrants; and tolerance for a diversity of views on university campuses.[1076]

Spinning 9/11 against Diversity

Opponents of diversity have not been slow to seize upon this new climate to give a populist spin to the assault on affirmative action.[1077] Shortly after the attacks, conservative commentator Ann Coulter penned a screed—"Affirmative Action for Osama"—complaining that "under the affirmative action program now pending before the Supreme Court in *Adarand Constructors v. Mineta*, each of the 12,000 boys born in Pakistan last year who were named 'Osama' would be granted preferential treatment over American-born whites."[1078] Coulter is a veteran opponent of civil rights protections and former lawyer at the Center for Individual Rights (CIR).

The national security argument has also been used opportunistically to attempt to force Senate confirmation of Bush nominees to the federal bench, several of whom have notoriously bad records on diversity issues. But legal positions *have* certainly been shaken up across the political spectrum by the events of September 11, not least on the question of racial profiling.[1079] Before 9/11 there were indications that the Right was actually thinking about ramping up a campaign *against* racial profiling (then largely concerned with police practices), the better to advance the cause of constitutionally prohibiting any judicial consideration of race—and, of course, doing away with affirmative action in the process. For example, Attorney General Ashcroft declared ending racial profiling as a top priority soon after his confirmation, prompting the media to wonder whether we were seeing "a new and progressive John Ashcroft, a champion of civil rights?"[1080] Since then, however, a firestorm of controversy has broken around Ashcroft over the detention of hundreds of alleged terrorist suspects in what critics charge is a blatant exercise in racial profiling. Center for New Black Leadership senior fellow Horace Cooper has leapt to Ashcroft's defense, suggesting that Ashcroft is firmer in opposing racial profiling than the "70 percent of blacks [who] now say they approve of racial profiling of Arabs and Muslims."[1081]

Roger Clegg, who in addition to his duties as general counsel at CEO is now chairman elect of the Federalist Society's Civil Rights Practice Group, went from writing in June 2001 that "racial profiling is wrong whether it is police stopping a black teenager or colleges telling an Asian teenager that they have 'too many' of them already,"[1082] to declaring in September 2001 that "first, it is not at all clear that what will be used really is racial profiling. And, second, so what?"[1083]

Getting Back to Business

Besides the obvious advantages that come from having comrades in arms elevated to exalted positions, right-wing opponents of diversity policies actively are taking stock of what the advent of the George W. Bush administration has meant, and of how far their agenda can be pragmatically pushed. Though all agree that control of the executive branch is a golden opportunity, a complicated debate, sometimes public but often behind the scenes, has ensued over the strategy, tactics, and timing of finishing off legally sanctioned efforts to promote diversity in business and higher education. Of critical importance in this debate is the understanding among some top figures in the Bush White House, including Karl Rove, of the electoral importance of African American, suburban liberal white, and especially Latino votes in some critically important swing states, which argues for a more cautious approach on the pace and scope with which the right wing pursues its anti-diversity agenda.[1084]

For some conservatives the record of the Bush administration has been a mixture of positive steps and lost opportunities, raising serious questions about its ideological bona fides and strategic vision. This perspective, which is shared by some in the administration, is rooted in a generation of struggle against the gains of the civil rights movement and diversity policies, focusing mainly on affirmative action. As noted earlier, Clint Bolick, head of the Institute for Justice, wrote one of the earliest papers nearly twenty years ago fixing the outlines of the "focused, aggressive legal agenda"[1085] that has since taken the form of a half dozen right-wing organizations fighting diversity polices. Perhaps somewhat surprisingly, Bolick's long-term take on strategy and tactics has translated into a generally sympathetic view of the Bush administration's efforts. When many on the Right expressed dismay that the Bush administration decided not to support the challenge of a white contractor to affirmative action provisions in a federal program (*Adarand v. Mineta*), Bolick said, "I'm inclined to give the administration a pass on this due to the institutional imperative of defending federal statutes and staying the course on prior positions taken in litigation...I don't think this decision says anything about the Bush administration's position on racial preferences."[1086]

Others have been more critical of the Bush administration's record, notably Ward Connerly and Edward Blum, who head the American Civil Rights Institute (ACRI).[1087] Connerly, who was blocked from addressing the 2000 Republican convention for not going along with the "compassionate conservative" program in an effort to avoid too much public discussion of race issues (a motif that continues[1088]), has charged that

> Bush and my good friend John Ashcroft, the attorney general, have seamlessly embraced the issue of "racial profiling" as if it were an epidemic threatening black America. Then we have the decision in support of continued discrimination [i.e., affirmative action policies] in government contracting. When it comes to issues of race and preferences, Bush and a host of other Republican leaders have been drifting tragically leftward for about five years. Mesmerized by the quest for skin-color "diversity," and hoping to "broaden the base" of the party, they have been moving away from the Republican rank-and-file in ways that are fundamentally transforming the party—the party that should carry the banner of Equality for All.[1089]

According to Phil Kent, president of the Southeastern Legal Foundation, Ashcroft appears "adrift," unsure of his political moorings.[1090] Edward Blum— who with Connerly has launched a November 2002 California ballot initiative to end the collection of statistics on race that underpin the very possibility of constructing a factual record for the purpose of ensuring racial and gender fairness[1091]—has charged "the Bush presidential report card is decidedly mixed on the racial preference issue." He gives the administration failing marks for letting stand a Clinton-era *amicus* brief that defended school integration measures in Charlotte, North Carolina, and another in the University of Georgia's system for undergraduate admissions. "Fortunately," writes Blum, "the courts ignored their arguments and ruled for the plaintiffs in each case. The greatest heartbreaker for conservatives, however, was watching Bush-appointed Solicitor General Ted Olson, one of the nation's most articulate defenders of colorblind jurisprudence, defend a race-based federal highway contracting program before the high court in October."[1092]

However, even this ACRI stalwart sees progress in the Bush record. "On the other hand, to their credit," Blum wrote on the eve of the crucial oral argument before the U.S. Court of Appeals for the Sixth Circuit in the University of Michigan cases, "this administration seems less tolerant of racial gerrymandering, even when it may help Republicans, and they seem to disfavor the 'disparate impact' theory, which has been a major litigation club in dozens of discrimination cases. But, going forward, it is critically important for the president to instruct the Justice Department to stand with the plaintiffs in the University of Michigan cases."[1093]

Clearly the right wing is watching closely to see what position the Bush administration will take in the University of Michigan cases, possibly the most important affirmative action case in a generation. But many on the Right feel that undermining the enforcement side of the equation is equally important. For example, "disparate impact" featured prominently in a wish list on anti-civil rights measures produced by Roger Clegg a couple of months after Bush took office. "Are existing regulations under Title VI of the 1964 Civil Rights Act that ban disparate-impact discrimination valid?" Clegg asked. "A number of Supreme Court decisions make clear that this statute—which prohibits racial and ethnic discrimination in federally funded programs and activities—bans only disparate treatment. Yet many federal agency regulations incorporate a disparate-impact approach as well."[1094]

Clegg also suggests other areas of promising action, which would require joint action by administration attorneys and sympathetic judges to overturn. "Can a disparate-impact cause of action be brought under the Age Discrimination in Employment Act and the Fair Housing Act?" he asks. "While the disparate-impact approach has been a part of Title VII for 30 years and now is written into the statute itself, the Supreme Court has never recognized this sort of claim under these two other important civil rights statutes. Indeed, the court has expressly reserved the question—for the ADEA, in *Hazen Paper Co. v. Biggins* (1993), and for the FHA in *Town of Huntington v. NAACP* (1988)—and the lower courts are divided."[1095]

Focusing on the Courts

Bolick's emphasis on the importance of efforts to "wrest the judicial forum" from the mainstream defenders of diversity remedies has been taken up by disappointed hard-liners, precisely because of their dismay with the Bush administration's record. Linda Chavez, head of the Center for Equal Opportunity and unsuccessful Bush nominee for the post of labor secretary, has reacted bitterly to what she sees as the failure of the administration to take on affirmative action. Speaking to an October 10, 2001, meeting of the Labor and Employment Law Practice Group of the Federalist Society, Chavez asserted that guilt about opposing the first civil rights act, and now the politics of attracting Latino voters, which is important to the White House, is the reason the Republican establishment controlling the White House will not move against so-called racial preferences. Objecting to this rationale, Chavez claimed Latinos have "never been as wedded to the concept of racial preference as has the organized Black community." Her remarks echoed a long-standing theme on the Right about shortcomings in the Reagan and first Bush administrations. For example, Clint Bolick accused Bush, Sr., of having lost his nerve for a fight to adequately roll back civil rights protections, and "the administration's loyal allies were left to lick the wounds of betrayal."[1096] "I'm hoping and looking to the courts to bail us out," Chavez told her Federalist Society audience.

However, Blum's comment about "disparate impact" as a possible area in which to work with the Bush administration deserves serious attention. It is in the area of fundamental principles underlying federal enforcement of civil rights that the Right may be looking to the Bush administration to vindicate its support (or at least relative silence) for him during the campaign. But this clearly raises the importance of the issue of right-wing nominations to federal agencies and the judiciary, and particularly how hard Bush fights for his nominees. Here, the question of whether the hard-line opponents of institutional policies to promote diversity will be seated on the federal bench will clearly be crucial. One of the top priorities of right-wing legal groups has been to attract judges into political networks in order to advance their agenda in the law. As the process of judicial elections, particularly at the state level, becomes more politicized (for example, in proposals to permit judges to comment freely on political issues in the course of judicial elections), a new front of political conflict will likely emerge. In March 2001 the Federalist Society sponsored a conference to begin developing strategy on this issue; and a key U.S. Supreme Court case filed by the Minnesota Republican Party regarding free speech and judicial elections was decided in favor of political speech by judicial candidates.[1097]

In the Pipeline: The "Interesting Cases"

Universities will not only be facing suits from right-wing organizations over the specific formulas they use to ensure diversity. Speaking as a member of the show-case panel of the Federalist Society's Civil Rights Practice Group in November 2001, Prop 209 chair Gail Heriot pointed to the need for aggressive litigation to attack what she called the "subtle forms of race preferences." Heriot said, for example, that the provision of scholarship money by donors for such a purpose would present "some interesting legal questions," such as, "can the [University of California] accept such a gift, to what degree can the U.C. participate in the administration of such a scholarship." The Millennium Scholarship Fund,[1098] a program that recently provoked controversy in California, used tax dollars to ask donors for funds for this purpose, so Heriot said its striking down was "a legal no brainer."

"The more interesting cases are those that don't involve a return to facial preferences," Heriot argued, but rather involve

> subtler questions of law and policy. And there are two main such programs at the University of California today. First there's the already implemented 4 percent solution as they call it, in which U.C. commits to admit anyone who graduates in the top 4 percent of a California high school, regardless of SAT score or other factors. Second, there's U.C. President Richard Atkinson's proposal to phase out the SAT ultimately in favor of what he calls a more holistic admissions policy. And on Thursday, the U.C. Regents voted 15 to 4 to authorize U.C. campuses to fashion such a policy if they so choose.

According to Heriot, these plans raise key legal issues: "Are they legal? Can opponents of the plans prevail in litigation? Should they try? Sometimes discretion really is the better part of valor. What effect will they have on the University of California? What effect will they have on education generally?"

Heriot charges that "what's driving this is a desire to admit more blacks, more Hispanics, and more American Indian students, to try to get the numbers a little closer to what they were prior to the passage of 209. Therein, of course, lies the problem. The evidence is overwhelming that the purpose for proposing these programs is to produce an agreeable mix of students from the standpoint of race and ethnicity. And that they would not have been offered but for that result." She concludes, "If it's wrong or illegal to grant preferential treatment to minorities directly, then it's also wrong to do so by indirection. Otherwise all anti-discrimination laws from Prop 209 to Title VII to the equal protection clause of the United States Constitution would be essentially paper tigers, easily avoidable while hiding what's being done."

Bush and the Far Right: Moving toward Common Ground

One of the strongest proponents of a frontal attack on "disparate impact" causes of action and remedies is Brian Jones, former president of the Center for New Black Leadership (CNBL), who was confirmed by the Senate as the Department of Education's general counsel (three days after the September 11 attacks, and in the midst of a storm of congressional sentiment to accommodate Bush), despite the vigorous opposition of civil rights advocates.[1099] Jones, a former vice chair of the Federalist Society's Civil Rights Practice Group, published an article in its newsletter opposing the application of disparate impact under Title VI.[1100] Prior to the April 2001 landmark Supreme Court decision in *Alexander v. Sandoval*,[1101] which held that there is no private right of action to enforce disparate impact regulations under Title VI of the Civil Rights Act of 1964, several right-wing legal groups submitted *amicus* briefs, and claimed a "tremendous win" in the case.[1102] Having supporters like Jones on the inside will enable the Right to set its sights even higher.

Brian Jones is, however, hardly the only, or even most important, veteran opponent of diversity remedies to have moved from the ranks of right-wing policy and litigating organizations into a federal position where their agendas can be put into practice. The Office of White House Counsel has been virtually taken over by Federalist Society activists.[1103] Such connections are not just resume or social gossip material; they form an organic and functioning political symbiosis, producing policy and law at rapid speed. The Federalist Society's National Lawyers Conference this year was a triumphant return of Society veterans at the highest levels of government. Addressing the conference, Vice President Cheney boasted, "There are many members of the Federalist Society in our administration. We know that because they were quizzed about it under oath. We're especially proud to have two of your founders at the Department of Energy—the general counsel, Lee Liberman Otis, and Secretary Spence Abraham."[1104]

Cheney also commented that "in ways too numerous to mention, President Bush and I have counted on the friendship and good counsel of many in this room tonight." Presumably, he was referring not only to the help his audience provided Bush in gaining the presidency ("I'd guess that a year ago, about half of you were down in Florida"), but also to the intense outburst of activity and support Federalist Society members both inside and outside government gave to the administration in crafting the breathtaking array of constitutionally suspect measures related to the attacks of September 11. With amazing rapidity, the Federalist Society produced a spate of White Papers laying out ready-to-hand arguments for defending the administration's positions.[1105] William P. Barr, George Terwilliger, Michael Chertoff, and John Yoo, all of whom have been directly involved in the administration's efforts (Yoo in particular began working on drafting the legal response shortly after the attacks), participated actively at the 2001 National Lawyers Meeting, which took as a special theme "the war on terrorism."

Terwilliger gave a briefing on the legal issues to Society stalwarts at Gibson, Dunn and Crutcher—Solicitor General and Federalist Society leader Ted Olson's former firm. Roger Clegg delivered the practice group luncheon speech on racial profiling and the war on terrorism.

Civil Rights Policy and Right-Wing Personnel

At the Department of Justice, the lead department for enforcement of civil rights law, veteran opponents of diversity remedies hold two of the top jobs where decisions affecting civil rights law will be made. Attorney General Ashcroft is a longtime opponent of affirmative action. His deputy, Larry D. Thompson, who served on the advisory board of the Southeastern Legal Foundation, claimed that Atlanta's affirmative action plan discriminated against white males, and won a key appeals court case on August 27, 2001, against affirmative action practices at the University of Georgia. Ralph Boyd, Bush's head of the Civil Rights Division (whose appointment Clint Bolick called "inspired") recently urged Federalist Society members to be patient in assessing the speed with which the new administration turns to their concerns, due to the press of business created by the September attacks.[1106]

Other cabinet-level officials who will be making decisions on diversity issues are longtime members of right-wing organizations. Gale Norton, the interior secretary who will be dealing with the problem of environmental racism (for example, the practice of placing heavily polluting industrial facilities or dangerous dump sites in poor African American neighborhoods), is a longtime Federalist Society member, and spoke alongside Ashcroft at the 2001 National Lawyers Conference. Elaine Chao, a veteran of the Heritage Foundation, where she was a close colleague of Kay Coles James (former dean of Robertson School of Goverment and now head of the Office of Personnel Management), now heads the Labor Department, which oversees the Office of Federal Contract Compliance Programs (OFCCP). Kay Coles James's husband, Charles James, heads OFCCP.

The Heritage Foundation has a long antipathy to the enforcement activities of OFCCP, and in fact advocates that "Congress should nullify Executive Order 11246, as amended; repeal all affirmative action provisions in federal law; and eliminate the Office of Federal Contract Compliance Programs."[1107] Placing Heritage veteran Chao and Charles James in charge of this agency is analogous to the Reagan administration's placing Clarence Thomas and Clint Bolick at the EEOC. The Labor Department, which has the second-largest legal department in the government, will have its coming battles in employment law and compliance directed by Eugene Scalia (son of Supreme Court Associate Justice Antonin Scalia), who was given a recess appointment by President Bush in January 2002, despite widespread opposition in the Senate.[1108]

But this rapturing of right-wing ringleaders into positions in the Bush administration is not restricted to the top levels of government. It is also happening at the middle levels of departments and agencies—where much of the real action is. Virtually the entire leadership of the Federalist Society's Atlanta chapter has moved to Washington to take up positions in the administration, including several key civil rights posts. Hans A. von Spakovsky, for example, has been hired as a career lawyer in the voting rights section of the Justice Department, along with Hugh Joseph Beard, former general counsel of the Center for Equal Opportunity (until his death in July 2002).[1109] Spakovsky told the *Fulton County Daily Report* that he was going to the DOJ to "work on all election reform issues that came out of the last election."[1110] J. Michael Wiggins, Bush's new deputy assistant attorney general for civil rights, who chaired the Federalist Society's Civil Rights Practice Group's panel at the 2001 national lawyers conference, was on the Atlanta Federalist Society's executive board. Larry D. Thompson is also a former board member of the Atlanta Federalist Society.[1111]

The Bush administration has also taken aim at the U.S. Commission on Civil Rights, long a thorn in the side of the Right. Bush recently appointed Jennifer Cabranes Braceras, who is currently listed as serving on the executive committee of the Civil Rights Practice Group of the Federalist Society, to the Commission[1112]—despite the fact that in an interview she said the panel "doesn't have much to do."[1113] Braceras has forcefully criticized the Clinton administration's enforcement rules for Title IX (key legislation ensuring gender equity in higher education) for allegedly imposing "a vast and rigid quota system."[1114] The Commission went through a period of turmoil as a result of a legal dispute over the Bush administration's successful attempt (as decided by the Washington, D.C., Federal Appeals Court[1115]) to impose Peter Kirsanow—a former chairman of the Center for New Black Leadership—as a member. Joining with longtime Commission member and veteran affirmative action opponent Abigail Thernstrom, Braceras led the charge within the commission to have Kirsanow seated. In coming to Kirsanow's defense, the *Washington Times* pointed to the Center for New Black Leadership's declaration that it "takes exception to a civic order in which past victimization is made the currency of a near-permanent black identity of protest and entitlement."[1116]

Beyond the Judiciary

Whatever gains are being made by the right wing in terms of government appointments, and no matter how much faith Linda Chavez places in the courts to "bail us out," there are those on the Right who argue that more will be needed. Speaking at the November 2001 Federalist Society National Lawyers Conference, Center for Individual Rights lawyer Michael Rosman, contrary to Chavez, claimed that the courts cannot do it on their own, and neither can the battle be won "if Mountains States and the Pacific Legal Foundation and Center for Individual Rights and the Fifth Circuit are out there on their own." Rosman said that there is a lack of political will to mobilize the overwhelming public opinion that allegedly exists to end "racial preferences." "One of the primary functions of a lawsuit," Rosman said, "is public education. It's an extremely important function, or at least it was.... To ultimately eliminate race conscious decision-making what we need are political leaders who are willing to harness the dissatisfaction in this country over preferences and turn it into action. And it will take political courage to do so, because the political minority, as I've said before, has a strong intensity of preference on this issue."

Another area of possible litigation that raises the issue of how right-wing populism may be used in conjunction with litigation is over the use of Scholastic Aptitude Tests (SATs) or other tests for university admissions. Again, speaking before a Federalist Society audience, Rosman also raised the specter of legal action over de-emphasizing or eliminating SAT scores as a criterion of admission to institutions of higher learning. "I think standardized tests can and frequently are overemphasized," he said, "and I have no objection to their de-emphasis if they are de-emphasized because their value as an admissions criterion is diminished in the eyes of university officials through admissions officers. But if they are de-emphasized in order to achieve a racial result, that's pretty much race conscious decision-making. So lawsuits without the political will to enforce the results will often end up only changing the form of race conscious decision-making then, making them less conspicuous."

The immediate outlook is for a "flexible response" by the Right. In looking at the key court cases, Gail Heriot suggested a number of alternative scenarios, depending upon how the Supreme Court handles the University of Michigan and University of Georgia cases. Speaking at the 2001 Federalist Society National Lawyers Convention, Heriot said:

> Two things can happen if the Michigan case reaches the Supreme Court, or if in fact some other racial preference case reaches the Supreme Court in the next couple of years. The court could determine that the University of Michigan's or whoever's practices are fully constitutional, *in which case the spotlight is likely to go back to popular initiatives like Prop 209 and Washington State's I-200* [emphasis added]. Or at the other extreme, of course, the Supreme Court [could write a ruling that] declares the constitution requires no less than that which Californians and Washingtonians have already voluntarily adopted through the initiative process. If that happens, then racial preference supporters will likely employ some of the same strategies that have been employed, legally or illegally depending upon your point of view, to soften the impact of Prop 209 and I-200.

Conclusion

However the political battle over diversity remedies is resolved, it seems that we may be reaching a point of no return in the battle for an inclusive society. Civil rights lawyers appear to agree that the judicial noose is tightening around these remedies.[1117] While some believe that it's time to approach Congress for relief from an increasingly conservative judiciary,[1118] it is worth bearing in mind that there are those on the Right who feel confident enough about their chances in Congress in the wake of the October 2001 *Adarand* non-decision to call for a major effort to ban the consideration of race in public programs.[1119] At the same time, "Almost a half century after the U.S. Supreme Court concluded that Southern school segregation was unconstitutional and 'inherently unequal,'" Harvard professor Gary Orfield reported in a major study in July 2001, "new statistics from the 1998–99 school year show that segregation continued to intensify throughout the 1990s, a period in which there were three major Supreme Court decisions authorizing a return to segregated neighborhood schools and limiting the reach and duration of desegregation orders."[1120] America stands at a crossroads in the battle for social justice. Those blocking the schoolhouse doors of the past now wear the cheerful smiles of Clint Bolick, the judicial robes of the U.S. Fifth Circuit Court of Appeals (among other courts), the earnest demeanors of the victimized white plaintiff, or the up-from-the-bootstraps mantle of Ward Connerly, rather than the tin star of Alabama's Bull Connor or the stern visage of its segregationist governor, George Wallace. The question now is whether or not America can see through the present day's softer-focus and rationalized defenses of exclusionary policies to recover its sense of fairness and justice in time to turn the tide once again.

Figure 5.1. The Challenge to Diversity Policies

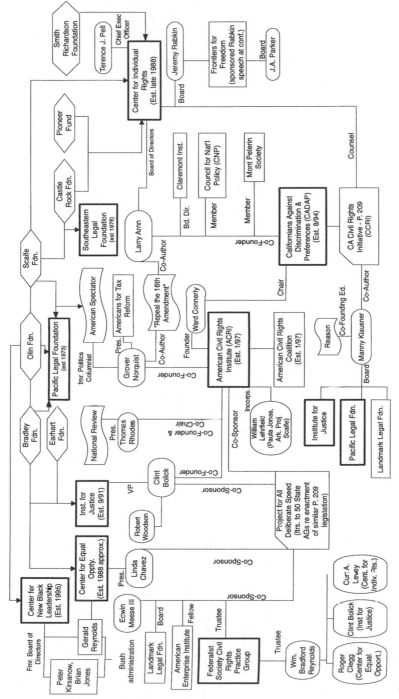

Source: © Institute for Democracy Studies 2002.

Notes

1. *Grutter v. Bollinger*, 137 F. Supp. 2d 821 (E.D. Mich. 2001), *rev'd by, in part, vacated by, in part*, 288 F.3d 732 (6th Cir. Mich. 2002), (challenging affirmative action policies at the University of Michigan School of Law). In a bitterly divided 5-4 decision (May 13, 2002) the U.S. Court of Appeals for the Sixth Circuit decided in favor of the law school, ruling that it "has a compelling state interest in achieving a diverse student body." It is widely expected that the Supreme Court will agree to hear this case in the fall of 2002.

2. Roger Pearson, *Race, Intelligence, and Bias in Academe* (Washington, D.C.: Scott-Townsend Publishers, 1991), 111. Pearson was a member of the editorial board of the Heritage Foundation's *Policy Review* in the late 1970s. See Russ Bellant, *Old Nazis, the New Right, and the Republican Party* (Boston: South End Press, 1991), 61; and Scott and Jon Lee Anderson, *Inside the League* (New York: Dodd, Mead, 1986), 92-93. For further information on Pearson, see below at note 23.

3. "John M. Mitchell Dies at 75; Major Figure in Watergate," *New York Times*, November 10, 1988, A1.

4. Terry Eastland, "Reagan Justice: Combating Excess, Strengthening the Rule of Law," *Policy Review*, 46 (Fall 1988), 16. *Policy Review* was the journal of the Heritage Foundation at the time. The case for diversity was eloquently and authoritatively documented by William G. Bowen and Derek Bok in *The Shape of the River: Long-Term Consequences of Considering Race in College and University Admissions* (Princeton, NJ: Princeton University Press, 1998).

5. Michael Greve, "The Vanity of Diversity," *Weekly Standard*, July 20, 1998, 26.

6. See Lee Cokorinos, "Unfinished Business: The Continuing Assault on Diversity," *IDS Insights*, 3, no. 1 (May 2002).

7. See "Review & Outlook: The Politics of Demonization," *Wall Street Journal*, May 11, 2001, A14.

8. Indeed, Jean Stefancic and Richard Delgado begin to do just this in *No Mercy: How Conservative Think Tanks and Foundations Changed America's Social Agenda* (Philadelphia: Temple University Press, 1996), 154-57.

9. For more information on the Federalist Society and its members, see Lee Cokorinos and Julie Gerchik, *The Federalist Society and the Challenge to a Democratic Jurisprudence*,

briefing paper (New York: Institute for Democracy Studies, January 2001); Julie R. F. Gerchik, "Slouching towards Extremism: The Federalist Society and the Transformation of American Jurisprudence," *IDS Insights,* 1, no. 2 (November 2000), available at www.idsonline.org/publications.html; and Julie R. F. Gerchik, "People Are Policy: Timothy Flanigan, Judicial Selection, and the Office of White House Counsel," *IDS Insights,* 2, no. 1 (September 2001), available at www.idsonline.org/publications.html. Federalist Society annual reports, 2000 and 1997.

10. Adam Clymer, "Bush Aide Accused of Having a Talk Cancelled," *New York Times,* August 21, 2001, A12.

11. In *Metro Broadcasting, Inc. v. FCC,* 497 U.S. 547 (1990), the Court held that remedial affirmative action programs only require "intermediate" scrutiny, meaning that such programs will survive challenge if they serve an "important governmental objective" and that the discriminatory aspects of the program are "substantially related" to achieving those objectives. In overruling *Metro Broadcasting,* the Court in *Adarand v. Pena* effectively eliminated this distinction, requiring application of the more onerous "strict scrutiny" test to all affirmative action programs.

12. In *Grutter v. Bollinger, et al.,* 288 F.3d 732 (6th Cir. 2002), the U.S. Court of Appeals for the Sixth Circuit held that schools may use racial categories to ensure balance in admissions policies because there is a compelling state interest in providing for student body diversity in institutions of higher learning. In *Hopwood v. Texas,* 78 F.3d 932 (5th Cir. 1996), *cert. denied,* 116 S.Ct. 2581 (1996), the U.S. Court of Appeals for the Fifth Circuit banned the use of race as a factor in admissions and scholarships, holding that there is no compelling state interest in diversity.

13. Howard Gleckman et al., "Race in the Workplace: Is Affirmative Action Working?" *Business Week,* July 8, 1991, 50. Cover page quotation cited in Gerald Horne, "Affirmative Action: It's a Black Thing ... Or Is It?" *Extra,* July/August 1992, 21.

14. David Byrd, "Affirmatively Acting," *National Journal* 31, no. 10 (March 6, 1999); and, more recently, see results of survey by Americans for a Fair Chance, "Coalition of Six Leading Civil Rights Groups Rally behind University of Michigan; Say Two-Thirds of Americans Support Affirmative Action in College Admissions," *PR Newswire,* December 6, 2001. Summary at www.law.harvard.edu/civilrights/publications/FCpress3.html.

15. Richard Morin, "Misperceptions Cloud Whites' View of Blacks," *Washington Post,* July 11, 2001, A1.

16. This process and the individuals who drove it is analyzed in detail in Russ Bellant's seminal work, *The Coors Connection: How Coors Family Philanthropy Undermines Democratic Pluralism* (Boston: South End Press, 1991). See also Lee Edwards, *The Power of Ideas: The Heritage Foundation at 25 Years* (Chicago: Jameson Books, Inc., 1998), chapter 1; Stefancic and Delgado, *No Mercy,* 45–82; and Leon Howell, *Funding the War of Ideas: A Report to the United Church Board for Homeland Ministries* (Cleveland: United Church Board for Homeland Ministries, 1995).

17. "Legal Services Foe Is Offered Seat on Board," *Washington Post,* April 8, 1983, A5.

18. "Appointments: Blackburn's Joke," *Newsweek,* November 24, 1975, 95.

19. Edwin J. Feulner, "Welcome," Leadership for America 2000, *Heritage Foundation,* www.heritage.org/leadership/ (December 18, 2001).

20. The seminal research resources on this are, for the 1970s and 1980s, Oliver A. Houck, "With Charity for All," 93 *Yale L.J.* 1415 (1984); Russ Bellant, *The Coors Connection: How Coors Family Philanthropy Undermines Democratic Pluralism* (Boston: South End Press, 1991); and Douglas T. Kendall and Charles P. Lord, *The Takings Project: Using Federal Courts to Attack Community and Environmental Protections* (Washington, DC: Community Rights Counsel, 1998). For the 1990s, see Jean Stefancic and Richard Delgado, *No Mercy: How Conservative Think Tanks and Foundations Changed America's*

Social Agenda (Philadelphia: Temple University Press, 1996).

21. Houck, "With Charity for All," and *Justice for Sale: Shortchanging the Public Interest for Private Gain* (Washington, DC: Alliance for Justice, 1993).

22. U.S. Department of Justice, Supplemental Statement Pursuant to Section 2 of the Foreign Agents Registration Act of 1938, as amended, Registration No. 3730, March 28, 1988 (p. 2, "political propaganda," named foreign principal, "Embassy of South Africa"). Clarence Thomas attended a dinner organized by Parker for the South African ambassador, Pieter Koornhof. Timothy M. Phelps, "Thomas Attended S. Africa Dinner," *Newsday*, July 16, 1991, 7; Jane Mayer and Jill Abramson, *Strange Justice: The Selling of Clarence Thomas* (Boston: Houghton-Mifflin, 1994), 71–74.

23. The World Anti-Communist League, an international right-wing network that has since been renamed the World League for Freedom and Democracy, was described by one of its former members as encompassing "a world of ideological fanaticism, racialism, ignorance and fear which is almost beyond the comprehension of the average American ... a collection of oriental fascists, militarists, right wing terrorists ... death squads, assassins, [and] criminals" (Anderson and Anderson, vii.). Parker served on the board of directors and Inside the League, as treasurer of the American section of the WACL (letterhead, American Council for World Freedom; see also Anderson and Anderson, *Inside the League*, 33). According to the Andersons, the German delegations to WACL conferences in the 1980s were led by Theodor Oberlander, a former Nazi officer who commanded the notorious Ukrainian Nightingale division of the Waffen SS (44-45). The 1978 WACL conference was organized by Roger Pearson, a British racial theorist and organizer who emigrated to the U.S. in 1965 and has played an important role as a leader of the ultra-right. A former organizer of the Northern League, a European white supremacy group that included former Nazi SS officials, Pearson once claimed if an advanced nation did not exterminate, instead of mingling with, an "inferior tribe" it would commit "racial suicide." Russ Bellant, *Old Nazis, the New Right, and the Republican Party*. See also Anderson and Anderson, chapter 8, for an outline of Pearson's activities. (See note 2 above)

24. Eastland, "Reagan Justice," 16. For more discussion on Eastland, see Charles Fried's *Order and Law: Arguing the Reagan Revolution* (New York: Simon & Schuster, 1991). For more on Gary McDowell, see below.

25. Nina Easton, *Gang of Five: Leaders at the Center of the Conservative Crusade* (New York: Simon & Schuster, 2000), 196ff.

26. Michael Isikoff, "Power behind the Thrown Nominee: Activist with Scores to Settle," *Washington Post*, June 6, 1993, A11.

27. Timothy M. Phelps, "The Education of Clarence Thomas: Nominee Still an Enigma; Thomas' Views Forged by Two Black Mentors," *Newsday*, September 8, 1991, 7.

28. Clint Bolick, "A Call to Judicial Action," *Lincoln Review* (Spring 1983), 49–55.

29. Clint Bolick, *Changing Course: Civil Rights at the Crossroads* (New Brunswick, NJ: Transaction Books, 1988), 122–123.

30. *Lincoln Review*, 10, no. 1 (Spring 1990), masthead. On Thomas's relationship to Parker, see more below.

31. Clint Bolick, *Changing Course: Civil Rights at the Crossroads*, 55, 85–86, 105, 113–117. According to Sidney Blumenthal, Murray was discovered by Michael Horowitz, who wrote the seminal study on the need for a radical right national legal movement, which was funded by Richard Mellon Scaife, a major financial supporter of right-wing organizations (see below). See Sidney Blumenthal, *The Rise of the Counter-Establishment: From Conservative Ideology to Political Power* (New York: Times Books, 1986), 294.

32. On Herrnstein's relationship to Jensen, see Roger Pearson, *Race, Intelligence, and Bias in Academe* (Washington, DC: Scott-Townsend Publishers, 1991), 141; and David Layzer, "Science or Superstition," in Russell Jacoby and Naomi Glauberman, *The Bell*

Curve Debate (New York: Times Books, 1995), 656. On Murray's and Herrnstein's book, see Jacoby and Glauberman, passim.

33. Bolick, *Changing Course*, 114–115.

34. Ibid., 143–144.

35. Ibid., 124.

36. For example, Bolick forcefully argues for a restoration of *Lochner*-era jurisprudence seriously limiting labor rights. See Clint Bolick, *Unfinished Business: A Civil Rights Strategy for America's Third Century* (San Francisco: Pacific Research Institute for Public Policy, 1990), 60–69, 72–73, 129–135.

37. For more on the Pioneer Fund and its relationship to the eugenics movement in the United States and Nazi Germany, see Stefan Kuhl, *The Nazi Connection: Eugenics, American Racism, and German National Socialism* (New York: Oxford University Press, 1994, reprinted 2002).

38. Bolick, *Unfinished Business*.

39. Ibid., ix–xiii.

40. Dawn M. Weyrich, "Affirmative Action Called Counterproductive for Blacks," *Washington Times*, March 19, 1990. Paul Weyrich was the first president of the Heritage Foundation, and is currently the president of the Free Congress Foundation. He is on the board of the Campaign for a Color Blind America, along with Federalist Society veteran Daniel Troy (now the new chief counsel of the Food and Drug Administration), Midge Decter, Linda Chavez, and Abigail Thernstrom. See www.equalrights.com/directors.html. Edward Blum of the American Civil Rights Institute (ACRI—see below) is a cochair.

41. During a conversation with veteran right-wing leader Grover Norquist at the February 2001 Conservative Political Action Conference, Robert Dreyfuss of *The Nation* reported that Norquist reached into his pocket and pulled out "a sketched-out timeline starting in 1980 and going to 2040. On it, neatly arrayed in rows, are a dozen to fifteen projects of Norquist's 'center-right coalition,' some nearly completed, others not even to begin for a decade or more. Some, like privatization of Social Security, will take twenty years, he believes. Others, such as the elimination of racial preferences, abolition of affirmative action and even the elimination of racial and ethnic categories in future censuses—a package he lumps together as 'the creation of a color-blind society'—may take longer than that." Robert Dreyfuss, "Grover Norquist: 'Field Marshal' of the Bush Tax Plan," *The Nation*, May 14, 2001, available at www.thenation.com/doc.mhtml?i=20010514&s=dreyfuss, March 29, 2002.

42. Such as the Capital Research Center in Washington, D.C. (see below). According to the conservative magazine *Human Events*, Capital Research Center president and board chair Terrence Scanlon told the Conservative Political Action Conference in February 2001 that with the new Bush administration in power, "for the very first time, we have a chance to go after these groups and defund them." See "Optimism Keynote of Hugely Successful Conference: CPAC 2001 Attracted Largest Number of Participants Ever," *Human Events* website, at www.humanevents.org/articles/02-26-01/CPAC.html (February 27, 2002).

43. Clint Bolick, *The Affirmative Action Fraud* (Washington, D.C.: Cato Institute, 1996), 118.

44. Ibid., 122–128, index.

45. The Law and Economics movement is a broad postwar intellectual and academic school of thought that has sought, by subjecting the law to a critical analysis rooted in neoclassical economics, to undermine arguments for a strong regulatory role for the state in many areas, including anti-discrimination law. The movement has been heavily supported by key funding institutions of the Right, particularly the Olin Foundation.

46. A more recent, but striking, example of this is M. Lester O'Shea, *A Cure Worse Than the Disease: Fighting Discrimination through Government Control* (Tampa: Hallberg Publishing, 1999).

47. David Wiener and Marc Berley, eds., *The Diversity Hoax* (New York: Foundation for Academic Standards and Tradition, 1999).

48. From barely 1 percent in 1960, the number of African Americans in the nation's law schools has grown to 7.5 percent. In less than three decades, the proportion of African Americans earning more than $50,000 rose from 5.8 percent (in 1967) to 13 percent (in 1992). William G. Bowen and Derek Bok, *The Shape of the River: Long-Term Consequences of Considering Race in College and University Admissions* (Princeton, NJ: Princeton University Press, 1998), 10.

49. Gary Orfield, "Schools More Separate: Consequences of a Decade of Resegregation," Civil Rights Project, Harvard University, July 2001, 3.

50. Charles Toutant, "Civil Rights Lawyers Commiserate over Roadblocks Erected by Court Rulings of Last Term Limited Causes of Action, Fee Applications," *New Jersey Law Journal*, October 8, 2001.

51. *Hopwood v. Texas*, 78 F.3d 932 (5th Cir.), *cert. denied*, 116 S.Ct. 2581 (1996). See also, Linda Greenhouse, "Justices Decline Affirmative-Action Case," *New York Times*, July 2, 1996, A12.

52. Peter Schmidt, "U. of Michigan Turns to Scholars to Bolster Its Defense of Affirmative Action," *Chronicle of Higher Education*, April 2, 1999, A38.

53. *Hopwood,* 78 F.3d 932.

54. *Grutter v. Bollinger,* 288 F.3d 732 (6th Cir. 2002). Jacques Steinberg, "Court Says Law School May Consider Race in Admissions," *New York Times*, May 15, 2002, A16. Tony Mauro, "Powell's Bakke Opinion Tested in Michigan Admissions Case," *Fulton County Daily Report*, December 13, 2001.

55. Elizabeth Kassab, "U. Michigan Hopes to Avoid Changing Admission Policies in Upcoming Court Cases," *Michigan Daily* (via University Wire), October 17, 2001.

56. Evelyn Nieves, "Civil Rights Groups Suing Berkeley over Admissions Policy," *New York Times*, February 3, 1999, A9. In the first freshman class at UCLA to be enrolled under Proposition 209, 160 out of 3,775 students were African American (down from 230 in 1997). Fifteen were Native American (compared to 40 in 1997). Chicanos and Latinos accounted for 485 (590 enrolled the previous year). "UCLA Enrollment Figures Show Fewer Under-Represented Minorities Enrolled as Freshmen for Fall 1998," UCLA Press Release, November 4, 1998 (at www.uclanews.ucla.edu/docs/DDC499.html [March 10, 1999]).

57. Piper Fogg, "University of California Admits More Minority Students," *Chronicle of Higher Education*, April 19, 2002, 26.

58. Amie Parnes, "Enrollment Data Feed Rift on Florida Policy," *Boston Globe*, September 9, 2001, A19. See also Gary Orfield and Edward Miller, eds., *Chilling Admissions: The Affirmative Action Crisis and the Search for Alternatives* (Cambridge, MA: The Civil Rights Project, Harvard University).

59. For the text of the order see the EEOC website at www.eeoc.gov/35th/thelaw/eo-10925.html, June 12, 2002. Section 301 states that government contractors "will take affirmative action to ensure that applicants are employed, and that employees are treated during employment, without regard to their race, creed, color, or national origin."

60. "Johnson overwhelmed Goldwater by nearly sixteen million votes." Taylor Branch, *Pillar of Fire: America in the King Years, 1963-65* (New York: Touchstone, 1998), 522.

61. "Lasting 534 hours, the 1964 filibuster filled 63,000 pages of the Congressional Record, with an estimated ten million words." Ibid., 336.

62. *New York Times*, November 5, 1964, 1. Quoted in Branch, *Pillar of Fire*, 695.

63. Branch, *Pillar of Fire*, 522.

64. Ibid., 340.

65. Harold H. Martin, "George Wallace Shakes Up the Political Scene," *Saturday Evening Post*, May 9, 1964, 87. Quoted in Branch, *Pillar of Fire*, 340.

66. In the last speech of the Senate's 10-million-word filibuster against the Civil Rights Act, Senator Robert Byrd of West Virginia turned to Scripture. Conceding that the Good Samaritan parable might have some relevance to civil rights, he addressed Jesus' command to love one's neighbor as oneself. "But the Scriptural admonition does not say that we may not *choose* our neighbor!" bellowed Byrd. "It does not admonish that we shall not build a wall betwixt us and our neighbor." Branch, *Pillar of Fire*, 336.

67. The supposed right to private racial segregation is a hardy perennial, and bridges both traditional segregationist and current libertarian thinking. For an example of the latter, see Richard Epstein, "Unexplored Tributaries," *Reason* (February 1999), 61–67. Epstein argues that "*our core national commitment should be* to a rule of law that creates zones of private authority where individuals may form voluntary associations that reflect the aspirations of their members and not those of the population at large." Emphasis added.

68. Branch, *Pillar of Fire*, 521.

69. Miguel Bustillo, "Ban on Gathering Racial Data on 2004 Ballot," *Los Angeles Times*, July 16, 2002, part 2, 7.

70. On the creation and early days of the right-wing media machine, see John Saloma III, *Ominous Politics: The New Conservative Labyrinth* (New York: Hill and Wang, 1984), chapter 9.

71. *The World & I* is a monthly publication of the *Washington Times*, which is owned by News World Communications, a company founded by Unification Church leader Sun Myung Moon. See the masthead, at www.worldandi.com/about.shtml, February 27, 2002. Also, David Stout, "Helen Thomas, Washington Fixture, Resigns as U.P.I. Reporter," *New York Times*, May 17, 2000, A18.

72. Lee Edwards, *The Power of Ideas*, chapter 1. The business plan for what was to become the Heritage Foundation was drawn up, according to Edwards, by Weyrich's mentor, J. Frederic (Fritz) Rench, a Wisconsin businessman and Republican activist.

73. Houck, "With Charity for All." Houck reports "when asked in one interview about his relationship with Peter Fluor, Dan Burt, Capital's president, responded, 'Peter is a personal friend, which is why he is on the board.'"

74. Alan Crawford, *Thunder on the Right* (New York: Pantheon Books, 1980), 10–14. This battle took place within the Schuchman Foundation and also extended to a sharp fight for political control of the fledgling American Legislative Exchange Council, the key umbrella organization for state-level legislative activity of the right wing. See also Edwards, *The Power of Ideas*.

75. John Saloma III, *Ominous Politics: The New Conservative Labyrinth* (New York: Hill and Wang, 1984), 120 and chapter 10, passim.

76. Sidney Blumenthal, "Quest for Lasting Power: A New Generation Is Being Nurtured to Carry the Banner for the Right," *Washington Post*, September 25, 1985, p. A1.

77. During this period, Calabresi (1978) and McIntosh (1979) alternately served as president of the Yale Political Union; Keisler as speaker; and Liberman as chair of the Rules Committee. Nina Easton, *Gang of Five: Leaders at the Center of the Conservative Crusade* (New York: Simon & Schuster, 2000), 54–55.

78. Eliminating affirmative action was part of the Republican Party platform in 1980. See Terry Eastland, *Energy in the Executive: The Case for the Strong Presidency* (New York: Free Press, 1992), 179. In writing this influential book, Eastland was assisted by Steven G. Calabresi of the Federalist Society, Michael Carvin of the Center for Individual Rights, Roger Clegg of the Center for Equal Opportunity, Charles Cooper of Cooper and Carvin (a major anti-affirmative action lawyer—see below), Theodore Olson, Kenneth W. Starr, and others. Eastland wrote the book while a fellow at the National Legal Center for the Public Interest (on whose board of directors Joseph Coors, NLCPI president emeritus, sits) and while in residence at the Ethics and Public Policy Center. Eastland is still on the academic

advisory board of the NLCPI. The Bradley and Olin Foundations backed the book, along with the Ethics and Public Policy Center. Eastland, acknowledgments, 383–384; NLCPI website at www.nlcpi.org/lead.htm (December 30, 2001); Foundation Center Grants Database, 1997.

79. Cribb emphasized that "the movement inhabits the party to advance its own ideals." Sidney Blumenthal, "A Vanguard for the Right; Activists Promote a New Establishment," *Washington Post*, September 22, 1985, A1.

80. Institute for Justice, "IJ's Financials: The Cost of Justice," IJ website, at www.ij.org/publications/liberty/1996/l_11_96_j.html (December 30, 2001).

81. Al Kamen, "Liberals Uneasy over High Court Review of Discrimination Laws," *Washington Post*, May 1, 1988, A4.

82. Michael J. Sniffen, "Washington Dateline: Reagan Urged to End Affirmative Action," *Associated Press*, November 12, 1980.

83. Turner Rose, "'Miranda' under Attack," *Washington Post*, November 25, 1986, A21.

84. Meese had also worked as vice president for Rohr Industries, and in 1977 he became director of the Center of Criminal Justice Policy and Management at the University of California-San Diego Law School. "A Brief Look at Subjects of the Shift," *New York Times*, January 23, 1984, A16.

85. Lou Cannon and Bill McAllister, "Meese Announces Resignation, Says Probe 'Vindicated' Him; GOP Sheds a Political Liability," *Washington Post*, July 6, 1988, A1.

86. On the CNP see, generally, Bellant, *The Coors Connection*; and National Education Association, *The Real Story behind Paycheck Protection* (Washington, DC: 1998), 18.

87. Dobson addressed the CNP on national strategy on February 7, 1998. "Dr. James Dobson at CNP," audiotape distributed by the US Taxpayers Party, tape no. AA932.

88. Biography of James McClellan, at www.Yorktownuniversity.com, June 13, 2002.

89. Charles Fried, *Order and Law: Arguing the Reagan Revolution* (New York: Simon & Schuster, 1991), 105–106.

90. Douglas S. Kmiec, *The Attorney General's Lawyer: Inside the Meese Justice Department* (New York: Praeger, 1992), 153.

91. Fried, *Order and Law*, 35

92. Sidney Blumenthal, "The Right's Quest for Law from a Mythical Past," *Washington Post*, November, 3, 1985, C1.

93. Bruce Fein, "Demeaning True Diversity," September 4, 2001, *Washington Times*, A12.

94. Ruth Marcus, "Conservatives in Civil War over Eastland Firing," *Washington Post*, May 18, 1988, A1.

95. Terry Eastland is the nephew of Senator James O. Eastland of Mississippi, the wealthy cotton planter whose opposition to civil rights legislation was virtually unparalleled in congressional history. According to Marjorie Hunter, the major civil rights bills of the 1960s only became law through maneuvers that allowed them to bypass the Senate Judiciary Committee, which Eastland chaired for twenty-two years. Eastland also served as chairman of the Internal Security Committee, which tracked subversive groups and the threat of "communism." Allan Brownfeld, who would later serve on Reagan's EEOC transition team, was special assistant to the Internal Security Committee from 1967 to 1969. Larry Speakes, who became White House chief spokesman under Reagan, also served as Eastland's chief spokesman for a time. Marjorie Hunter, "James O. Eastland Is Dead at 81: Leading Senate Foe of Integration," *New York Times*, February 20, 1986, D23.

96. Eastland has proposed, in the pages of the *Spectator*, a constitutional amendment that would allow Congress to overturn Supreme Court rulings, past or present. Such an amendment, the idea for which originated with Robert Bork, would enable Congress to overturn such key landmark decisions as *Brown v. Board of Education* and *Roe v. Wade*.

Terry Eastland, "Deactivate the Courts: How Congress Can Lead a Conservative Counterattack," *American Spectator*, March 1997.

97. Terry Eastland, "The Court's Decision Not to Decide," *Washington Times*, December 5, 2001, A16.

98. Funded by the Archer Daniels Midland Foundation, Earhart Foundation, Olin Foundation, and Starr Foundation. Foundation Center Grants Database, 1997. Stratton is the author, together with Paul Craig Roberts, of the 1997 book *The New Color Line: How Quotas and Privileges Destroy Democracy*, published by the right-wing Regnery publishing house. Roberts, now a *Washington Times* columnist, was on the editorial advisory board of *Modern Age*. This conservative intellectual journal had a number of prominent right-wing figures on its editorial advisory board who are mentioned in this book, such as John P. East and James McClellan. Henry Regnery was associate editor. *Modern Age*, masthead, vol. 26, nos. 3–4, Summer/Fall 1982.

99. "The Passage of Proposition 209," *Ethics and Public Policy Newsletter*, no. 57, Winter 1997 (at www.eppc.org/newsletters/newsw97.html).

100. His mother is Nancy Du Pont. His father, William Reynolds, was the chief patent attorney at Du Pont.

101. As of 1995, Reynolds protégé Charles Cooper was a partner at Shaw, Pittman, Potts & Trowbridge. Cf. "The Goldwater Institute and the Federalist Society: Federalism and Judicial Mandates" (edited transcripts from the panel discussions held in Phoenix, Arizona on November 3 and 4, 1995), 28 *Ariz. S. L. J.* 17 (1996). Cooper went on to found his own law firm, Cooper & Carvin (with anti-affirmative action lawyer Michael Carvin), which has now become Cooper & Kirk. See www.cooperkirk.com/bio_cooper.html (December 19, 2001). For more on Cooper, see below.

102. Bell is now on the board of directors of the National Legal Center for the Public Interest. See www.nlcpi.org/lead.htm (December 20, 2001).

103. Robert Pear, "Senate Committee Rejects Reynolds for Justice Post," *New York Times*, June 28, 1985, A1.

104. Juan Williams, "In His Mind but Not His Heart," *Washington Post*, January 10, 1988, W10.

105. Federalist Society for Law and Public Policy website, at www.fed-soc.org/boardofdirectors.htm (December 20, 2001).

106. *Southern Partisan*, February 7, 2002, 2.

107. Ronald Brownstein, "A More Forceful Tone," *National Journal*, May 18, 1985, 1142.

108. For an inside account, see the discussion by Reagan's solicitor general (1985–1989), Charles Fried, *Order and Law: Arguing the Reagan Revolution* (New York: Simon & Schuster, 1991), 30–31. Reynolds, according to Fried, had been considered for the solicitor general's post, but was considered too controversial.

109. Sarah Scaife Foundation IRS Form 990, 1999, 30. Richard Mellon Scaife is also a longtime member of the Heritage Foundation's Board of Trustees.

110. See Aaron Freiwald, "Justice in American Samoa: From Insider to Islander: Rocky Rees' Exotic Journey," *Legal Times*, March 28, 1988, 1; Tom Castleton, "U.S. Claims Court Crusader Puts Property Rights Up Front," *Connecticut Law Tribune*, August 31, 1992/September 7, 1992, 22. Rees currently serves as an aide to Rep. Christopher Smith (R-NJ), and heads the Human Rights and Immigration subcommittee of the Federalist Society's International and National Security Practice Group. See www.fedsoc.org/Publications/practicegroupnewsletters/internationalnews/contacts.htm (December 17, 2001).

111. Sidney Blumenthal, "The Right's Quest for Law from a Mythical Past," *Washington Post*, November 3, 1985, C1. McDowell now heads the Institute for United States Studies at the University of London. See www.sas.ac.uk/iuss/about_Gary McDowell.htm (December 17, 2001).

112. East committed suicide in 1983, but not before introducing legislation designed to eliminate federal court powers of desegregation as well as nullify the entire legal legacy of desegregation beginning with *Brown v. Board of Education.* John Shattuck and David Landau, "The Brown Decision—To the Junkpile?" *New York Times,* February 14, 1982, section 4, 19.

113. Sidney Blumenthal, "Quest for Lasting Power: A New Generation Is Being Nurtured to Carry the Banner for the Right," *Washington Post,* September 25, 1985, A1.

114. McClellan served as an editorial advisor to Pearson's *Journal of Social, Political and Economic Studies.* See Bellant, *The Coors Connection,* 39, 112, n. 116.

115. Agreement dated February 5, 1977, between Jay Parker Associates, Inc., and the Republic of Transkei.

116. Anderson and Anderson, *Inside the League,* 233.

117. Jane Mayer and Jill Abramson, *Strange Justice: The Selling of Clarence Thomas* (Boston: Houghton Mifflin, 1994), 71–74.

118. Clarence Thomas, speaking before the Third Annual Lincoln Day Colloquium Dinner, February 9, 1999, Mayflower Hotel, Washington, D.C. Audio available at www.claremont.org.lincoln_day3_av.cfm, March 10, 1999.

119. EEOC transition team document, "EEOC Transition Categories," 1980; James Conaway, "Young and Restless on the Right; The Under-30 Conservative Movement: Rooting for Reagan & Challenging the '60s Generation," *Washington Post,* January 25, 1985, C1; Ron Nixon, "The Content of Their Character," *Ethnic News Watch,* June 30, 1995, 3, no. 2: 29; *Human Events,* June 6, 1987.

120. Robert Safian, "Civil Right, Conservative Style," *American Lawyer,* May 1989, 129.

121. Patrick McGuigan, at the time legal director of Paul Weyrich's Free Congress Foundation, weighed in as well. Mayer and Abramson, *Strange Justice,* 153–154. On Bolick's devotion to Ayn Rand (imitating her, he wore a dollar sign around his neck), see Easton, *Gang of Five,* 104.

122. Eastland, *Energy in the Executive,* chapters 10–12. Among William French Smith's clients when he was in private practice in California before coming to Washington was J. Simon Fluor, who was instrumental in setting up the Pacific Legal Foundation. Oliver A. Houck, "With Charity for All," *Yale Law Journal* 93 (July 1984).

123. As an instance of such equivocation, Douglas Kmiec, head of the Office of Legal Counsel in the Meese Justice Department singles out the administration's position on the landmark 1988 *Croson* case, developed by Charles Fried, that under certain circumstances race could be used by a city to address discrimination in contracting. Kmiec, *The Attorney General's Lawyer,* 172-175.

124. Fried, *Order and Law,* 105–106.

125. "If there's any single person responsible for my being in the administration it's Bill Bennett," Chavez (now head of the Center for Equal Opportunity [CEO]), told the *Washington Post.* Phil McCombes, "The Civil Rights Struggles of Linda Chavez," *Washington Post,* January 30, 1984, A1.

126. The title of chapter 11 of Terry Eastland's *Energy in the Executive,* discussing the key civil rights cases of the Reagan administrations.

127. Eastland, *Energy in the Executive,* 167–170.

128. Fried, *Order and Law,* 89–132.

129. *Williams v. New Orleans S.S. Ass'n,* 688 F.2d 412 (5th Cir. 1982), *cert. denied,* 460 U.S. 1038 (1983).

130. *Firefighters Local Union No. 1784 v. Stotts,* 467 U.S. 561 (1984).

131. *Wygant v. Jackson Bd. of Educ.,* 476 U.S. 267 (1986).

132. *Local 28 of Sheet Metal Workers Int'l Ass'n v. EEOC,* 478 U.S. 421 (1986). See

Kmiec, *The Attorney General's Lawyer,* 178, n. 80.

133. *Richmond v. J.A. Croson Co.*, 488 U.S. 469 (1989).

134. However, Justice O'Connor wrote in a separate opinion in *Richmond v. Croson* that "it is beyond dispute that any public entity, state or federal, has a compelling interest in assuring that public dollars, drawn from the tax contributions of all citizens, do not serve to finance the evil of private prejudice." In the 1995 *Adarand* decision, O'Connor built upon this by stating that "we wish to dispel the notion that strict [constitutional] scrutiny is strict in theory, but fatal in fact." See Linda Greenhouse, "Justices to Revisit Affirmative Action in a Test Case for Bush," *New York Times*, March 27, 2001, A15.

135. Terry Eastland specifically mentions Labor Department anti-discrimination regulations, and the 1971 *Griggs* and 1979 *Weber* Supreme Court decisions. Terry Eastland, *Ending Affirmative Action: The Case for Colorblind Justice* (New York: Basic Books, 1997), 53-54 and 93-103. *Weber* permitted a voluntary affirmative action plan in a steel company's in-plant craft training program. *United Steelworkers of America v. Weber*, 443 U.S. 193 (1979). The *Griggs* ruling held that the 1964 Civil Rights Act prohibited practices that are fair in form but discriminatory in effect as well as practices that are overtly discriminatory. *Griggs v. Duke Power Co.*, 401 U.S. 424 (1971).

136. Charles Fried, *Order and Law*, 43-44.

137. Sidney Blumenthal, "The Right's Quest for Law from a Mythical Past," *Washington Post,* November 3, 1985, C1. As Blumenthal notes, Meese recognized the need to soften his rhetoric in the wake of the controversy over his speech. Douglas Kmiec's review of the matter in *The Attorney General's Lawyer: Inside the Meese Justice Department* (New York: Praeger, 1992), chapter 2, focuses on the role of natural law as it relates to original intent.

138. Stuart Taylor, Jr., "Meese and the Supreme Court: He Deals with Critics by Softening His Remarks," *New York Times*, November 19, 1986, A16.

139. Philip Hager, "Stevens Assails Meese on Interpreting Constitution," *Los Angeles Times*, October 26, 1985.

140. Burt Solomon, "Meese Sets Ambitious Agenda That Challenges Fundamental Legal Beliefs," *National Journal*, November 23, 1985, 2640.

141. Blumenthal, "The Right's Quest for Law from a Mythical Past."

142. Ibid. See also Harry V. Jaffa, "The Deepening Crisis: Defending the Cause of Human Freedom," Claremont Institute website, at www.claremont.org/publications/jaffafreedom.cfm, June 13, 2002.

143. See, for instance, the eulogies of the leading neo-confederate intellectual M. E. Bradford by Cribb and McClellan, which can be found in the Spring 1994 issue of the *Intercollegiate Review*, published by the Intercollegiate Studies Association. T. Kenneth Cribb, Jr., "Not in Memoriam, but in Affirmation: M.E. Bradford" (35-36); and James McClellan, "Defending the High Ground: The Legacy of M. E. Bradford" (37-48). For Jaffa's description of McClellan, see Harry V. Jaffa, "The Deepening Crisis: Defending the Cause of Human Freedom," Claremont Institute website at www.claremont.org/publications/jaffafreedom.cfm, June 13, 2002.

144. Kmiec, *The Attorney General's Lawyer*, 155.

145. *Regents of Univ. of Cal. v. Bakke,* 438 U.S. 912 (1978) (Blackmun, J., concurring in the judgment in part and dissenting). See also Linda Greenhouse, "Justice Blackmun, Author of Abortion Right, Dies," *New York Times,* March 5, 1999, A1.

146. The magnum opus of the law and economics movement vis-à-vis anti-discrimination law is Richard A. Epstein, *Forbidden Grounds: The Case against Employment Discrimination Laws* (Cambridge, MA: Harvard University Press, 1992; reprinted 1995). Epstein's research was funded by the Olin Foundation, and he "benefited enormously" (xv) in preparing the manuscript from discussions with, among others, Michael W. McConnell,

who has been nominated by the George W. Bush administration to be U.S. circuit judge for the Tenth Circuit. Epstein argues that "there is no adequate theoretical foundation or practical justification for the employment discrimination laws" (xii). Epstein, a University of Chicago law professor (and interim dean), is a frequent speaker at Federalist Society events.

147. For a discussion of the impact of the legal right on environmental issues, see Douglas T. Kendall and Charles P. Lord, *The Takings Project: Using Federal Courts to Attack Community and Environmental Protections* (Washington, DC: Community Rights Counsel, 1998). Many of the points raised by Kendall and Lord bear striking similarity to the recent history of the anti-affirmative action groups considered here.

148. Barry Bearak, "Ward Connerly: Between Black and White—A Special Report. Questions of Race Run Deep for Foe of Preferences," *New York Times*, July 27, 1997, 1.

149. For example, Bearak (ibid.) cites Prop 209 campaign internal memos showing that the white male leaders of the campaign "had a calculated preference for women and minorities in top positions." For an account of such racially based recruiting in the campaign against affirmative action in Washington State, see Timothy Egan, "Blacks Recruited by 'Rights' Drive to End Preferences," *New York Times*, December 17, 1997, A18. On Connerly's recruitment, see also Sam Gideon Anson, "Indecent Proposal: The Selling of CCRI: How Proposition 209 Evolved from Crusade to Wedge Issue," *LA Weekly*, November 1, 1996, 34.

150. ACRI *Egalitarian*, December 1998, 6.

151. ACRI and ACRI websites at www.acri.org (December 12, 2001).

152. Lynde and Harry Bradley Foundation, *2000 Annual Report*, 11, at www.bradley fdn.org/00ar/00part2.pdf.

153. Lynde and Harry Bradley Foundation, 1998 IRS Form 990, 369–370.

154. John M. Olin Foundation, IRS Form 990s for 2000, 1999, 1998.

155. Sarah Scaife Foundation, IRS Form 990s for 2000, 1999, 1998.

156. Donner Foundation, 1998 IRS Form 990.

157. David S. Broder, "For 2000, an Issue of Race; Michigan Targeted in Drive against Affirmative Action," *Washington Post*, January 23, 1999, A1; Bill Duryea, "He Champions the Cause against Affirmative Action?" *St. Petersburg Times*, February 7, 1999, 1A.

158. Ward Connerly, "Don't Box Me In: An End to Racial Checkoffs," *National Review*, April 16, 2001. The policy groundwork for this initiative was laid at a panel of the Civil Rights Practice Group of the Federalist Society in November 2000. Participants included Blum, Linda Chavez of CEO, Diana Furchgott-Roth of the American Enterprise Institute and Independent Women's Forum (now chief of staff for the White House Council of Economic Advisers), and Roger Clegg. The proceedings have been published by the Federalist Society, in "Civil Rights: The Use and Misuse of Statistics in Civil Rights Litigation," *Engage,* 2 (November 2001): 21–31.

159. Miguel Bustillo, "Ban on Gathering Racial Data on 2004 Ballot," *Los Angeles Times*, July 16, 2002, part 2, 7.

160. Wood, who is white, has been the executive director of the California Association of Scholars since July 1992. He is known for claiming that he is a victim of reverse discrimination, alleging that he was turned down for a tenured position as a philosophy professor in favor of a woman. NBC's *Dateline* researched the story and concluded that of the five philosophy positions in the Bay Area, four went to white men and the fifth position is held by a woman, an officer of the American Philosophical Association. [*Dateline*, "Affirmative Action," January 23, 1996, Josh Mankiewicz reporting]. In 1992, Wood was hired by Glynn Custred to be the executive director of the California Association of Scholars (CAS), one of the conservative movement's campus organizing projects. CAS became known for its two-year campaign to block the adoption of a policy statement by the Western Association of Schools and Colleges that called for preparing students to live and work in a multiethnic, heterogeneous society.

161. Custred, the founder of CAS, is a professor of anthropology at California State University, Hayward. Custred is secretary of CAS, and serves on its board of directors along with Gail Heriot (one of three statewide cochairs for the California Civil Rights Initiative campaign) [CAS website, www.calscholars.org/board.html (February 10, 1999)].

162. *Coalition for Econ. Equity v. Wilson*, 122 F.3d 718 (9th Cir. 1997). CADAP was defendant-intervenor/appellant.

163. At www.calscholars.org/board.html, and www.calscholars.org/mission.html (December 12, 2001). Bradford P. Wilson, executive director of the National Association of Scholars, spent three years as research associate to Chief Justice William Rehnquist [www.nas.org/newsletters/update/spring97/page3.htm]. He is currently leading the charge to restrict what can be taught in Black Studies programs across the country under the guise of establishing "standards." Andrea Simakis, "Black Studies Finds Secure Spot at Colleges," *Plain Dealer* (Cleveland, OH), February 7, 1999, 1A. Ward Connerly has also set his sights on restricting Black Studies programs. John H. Bunzel, "Education: Are Ethnic Studies Separate or Equal?" *Los Angeles Times*, November 8, 1998, M2.

164. London currently serves as president of the Indianapolis-based Hudson Institute, one of the first of the conservative think tanks, and is the John M. Olin University Professor of Humanities at New York University. See www.hudson.org/learn/index.cfm?fuseaction=staff_bio&eid=LondHerb, July 15, 2002.

165. Stefancic and Delgado, *No Mercy,* 124-28. Quote on 125.

166. Ronald Roach, "National Association of Scholars Cheer CUNY Changes, Decry Affirmative Action during Conference; City University of New York," *Black Issues in Higher Education*, February 1, 2001. For a contrasting view, see Bowen and Bok, *Shape of the River.*

167. Ward Connerly, *Creating Equal: My Fight against Race Preferences* (San Francisco: Encounter Books, 2000), 61.

168. Brief for *Amicus Curiae* National Association of Scholars in Support of Reversal in Nos. 01-1333, 01-1418, *Gratz v. Bollinger*, 277 F.3d 803 (6th Cir. 2001) (Nos. 01-1333, 01-1418). The brief was prepared by Brice M. Clagett, Oscar M. Garibaldi, and Keith A. Noreika of Covington & Burling, Washington, D.C., attorneys for *Amicus Curiae* National Association of Scholars. Noreika is director of programs for the Federalist Society's Civil Rights Practice Group. See www.fed-soc.org/Publications/practicegroupnewsletters/civil-rights/contacts.htm (December 12, 2001).

169. Sherman is an associate professor of mathematics and statistics at SUNY Albany, and former assistant to Linda Chavez at the Civil Rights Commission from 1984 to 1985. He has been vice president of the New York chapter of the NAS since 1993. ["Malcolm Jay Sherman," *Who's Who in the East,* 27th edition, 26th edition; *Who's Who in America,* 55th edition.]

170. Thomas Wood and Malcolm Sherman, "Is Campus Racial Diversity Correlated with Educational Benefits," National Association of Scholars, at www.nas.org, and www.calscholars.org, March 28, 2002. For a comprehensive presentation of the case for promoting diversity in institutions of higher education, see "The Compelling Need for Diversity in Higher Education," a collection of expert reports prepared for the *Gratz* and *Grutter* lawsuits by, among others, Mellon Foundation president William Bowen, Columbia University history professor Eric Foner, and University of Michigan psychology professor Patricia Gurin. The reports can be found at www.umich.edu/~urel/admissions/legal/expert/index.html.

171. Gurin's report can be found at www.umich.edu/~urel/admissions/legal/expert/gurintoc.html (December 13, 2001).

172. Roger Clegg, "Case Closed? No Matter How Courts Decide Litigation on Racial Preferences at Universities, Only Schools Can Stop the Practice," *Legal Times*, December

17, 2001. Clegg also praises two other reports, one by CEO attacking affirmative action practices at the University of Washington School of Medicine, and a second commissioned by the Connecticut Association of Scholars, an NAS affiliate, asserting that faculty at that state's institutions of higher education oppose affirmative action. See www.nas.org/affiliates/connecticut/conn_surv_apr00.html.

173. Arnn left the presidency of Claremont in June 2000 to take over the scandal-besieged Hillsdale College in Michigan. Hillsdale, a right-wing fundamentalist university preaching traditional mores, was rocked by the resignation of its president, George Roche III, amid a sex scandal. Julia Duin, "Hillsdale Head Aims to Restore Its Values; Sex Scandal Rocked College Last Year," *Washington Times*, October 20, 2000, A2.

174. On February 9, 1999, Jaffa received the Henry Salvatori award at the same Claremont Institute "Lincoln Day" gala event in Washington, D.C., at which Clarence Thomas paid tribute to Jay Parker (see above). Michael Joyce, then head of the Bradley Foundation, served as dinner chairman and gave a stirring speech honoring Jaffa for, among other things, setting the record straight by critiquing American Progressivism's attempt to claim Abraham Lincoln as one of its own. This was followed by a keynote address by Clarence Thomas essentially calling on the far right to scrupulously observe the rule of law, as Lincoln had, while it set about radically transforming the country [C-Span, February 9, 1999].

175. Connerly, *Creating Equal*, 164–165.

176. Edwin Meese and John C. Eastman, "The Death Throes of Preference; Historic Chance to End Legalized Prejudice," *Washington Times*, August 10, 2001, A21.

177. Ahmanson's wife, Roberta Green Ahmanson, is also on the board, along with Harry Jaffa, TV game show host Pat Sajak, and Thomas L. Phillips (chair of Phillips International, Inc., and a member of the Council for National Policy). Claremont website, www.claremont.org/directors.cfm (December 31, 2001).

178. California Secretary of State report, "November 5, 1996 General Election Proposition 209: Prohibition against Discrimination or Preferential Treatment by State and Other Public Entities. Vote: Yes 54.55 No 45.45," at Secretary of State's website, www.ss.ca.gov/prd/bmc96/prop209.htm (December 31, 2001). See also Connerly, *Creating Equal*, 167.

179. Dobson, head of the $100 million Colorado Springs-based Focus on the Family organization, is one of the top leaders of the American Christian Right. CRI is headed by Michael Bowman, a former aide to state senator Ray Haynes (R-Riverside), a leading opponent of abortion rights in California. Haynes is on the board of directors of the American Legislative Exchange Council (see above) and was assisted in his state senate race by a $512,000 contribution from multimillionaire state senator Rob Hurtt [Dan Morain, "Bankrolling Their Beliefs," *Los Angeles Times*, July 8, 1996, A1]. In the late 1980s, James Dobson attracted the support of Hurtt, a partner of Howard Ahmanson's in funding the far right in California. Between 1987 and 1989, Hurtt gave Dobson's organization $250,000. Hurtt cofounded the Capitol Resource Institute with Ahmanson.

180. On Rushdoony's relationship to Ahmanson, see Frederick Clarkson, *Eternal Hostility: The Struggle between Theocracy and Democracy* (Monroe, Maine: Common Courage Press, 1997), 113–115; and Dan Morain, "2 Wealthy Conservatives Use Think Tanks to Push Goals—Politics: Ahmanson Heir, Sen. Hurtt Give Millions to Tax-Exempt Groups. Critics Question Legitimacy of Research," *Los Angeles Times*, July 8, 1996, A1.

181. Rushdoony has written that "the white man is being systematically indoctrinated into believing that he is guilty of enslaving and abusing the Negro," despite the fact that slavery in the United States was "generally benevolent." For Rushdoony, "slavery is not intrinsically evil," but rather "a legitimate way of life." Rousas J. Rushdoony, *Politics of Guilt and Pity* (Fairfax, VA: Thoburn Press, 1978), 19–20, 24, 29. Rushdoony is the author of *The*

Institutes of Biblical Law (Phillipsburg, NJ: Presbyterian and Reformed Publishing Company, 1973). In it, he rails against "the heresy of democracy" (100). For more background on Rushdoony and the intersection between the Christian Right and the White Supremacist Movement, see Sara Diamond, *Roads to Dominion: Right-Wing Movements and Political Power in the United States* (New York: Guilford Press, 1995).

182. Joe Gelman, "A Closer Inspection of Connerly's 209 Role," *Daily News of Los Angeles*, August 3, 1997.

183. Connerly, *Creating Equal*, 79, 82, 88–96.

184. Ibid., and Amy Wallace, "He's Either Mr. Right or Mr. Wrong: What Drives Ward Connerly in His Crusade to End Affirmative Action?" *Los Angeles Times Magazine*, March 31, 1996, 12.

185. Connerly, *Creating Equal*, 101.

186. B. Drummond Ayres, Jr., "Fighting Affirmative Action, He Finds His Race an Issue," *New York Times,* April 18, 1996, A1.

187. The businessman was John Davies, Jr. John Jacobs, "The Poor Minorities Quota?" *Sacramento Bee*, February 25, 1993, B8. Davies is also chairman of the tax-exempt California Governor's Foundation, of which Connerly served as president. Dana Wilkie, "Wilson Talks Austerity, Lives Prosperity, Thanks to Foundation," *San Diego Union-Tribune*, July 11, 1994, A3; Regents of the University of California website, profile of Connerly at www.ucop.edu/regents/regbios/connerly.html (March 14, 1999).

188. Connerly singles out as especially important the support he received from Sally Pipes of the Pacific Research Institute (PRI). Pipes testified in favor of the measure. Connerly, *Creating Equal*, 152.

189. The opening paragraph of Prop 209 reads as follows: "The state shall not discriminate against, or grant preferential treatment to, any individual or group on the basis of race, sex, color, ethnicity, or national origin in the operation of public employment, public education, or public contracting." See vote96.ss.ca.gov/Vote96/html/BP/209text.htm.

190. Anson, "Indecent Proposal."

191. Lynde and Harry Bradley Foundation, *Annual Report*, 1997, 11; Sarah Scaife Foundation, 1997 IRS Form 990.

192. ACRI, "Connerly Forms New National Civil Rights Group: 'American Civil Rights Institute'," News Release, January 15, 1997 (www.acri.org/news/nr0115.html).

193. All figures from California Secretary of State report, "November 5, 1996 General Election Proposition 209: Prohibition against Discrimination or Preferential Treatment By State and Other Public Entities. Vote: Yes 54.55 No 45.45," at Secretary of State's website, www.ss.ca.gov/prd/bmc96/prop209.htm (March 4, 2002).

194. George Skelton, "Capitol Journal; Elections '96; A Sober End to the GOP's Revolution," *Los Angeles Times*, November 7, 1996, A3.

195. Blaine Harden, "Dole Backs California Proposition," *Chicago Sun-Times*, October 29, 1996, 8.

196. The California Republican Party gave almost exactly this amount to support Prop 209—$997,034, California Secretary of State report.

197. Trevor W. Coleman, "Affirmative Action Wars: A Conservative and Well-Financed Army Is on the March, as Civil Rights Activists Struggle for Dollars and Direction," *Emerge*, March 1998, 34.

198. Figures from California Secretary of State report.

199. Coleman, "Affirmative Action Wars."

200. California Secretary of State report.

201. Ibid.

202. In 1991, Kohler was nominated by then-Governor Tommy Thompson to the University of Wisconsin System Board of Regents, but the state Senate turned him down.

Kohler's nomination became controversial when his writings about a trip to South Africa revealed his view that "giving black citizens the right to vote would be a 'disaster' and that most of them were in 'the Stone Age,'" Matt Pommer, "Rejected Kohler Still Trying," *Capital Times* (Madison, WI), November 2, 1998, 3A.

203. Coleman, "Affirmative Action Wars."

204. Ibid.

205. Ayres, Jr., "Fighting Affirmative Action, He Finds His Race an Issue."

206. Connerly, *Creating Equal*, 277. According to Barbara Miner, a Milwaukee journalist who has written extensively on the Bradley Foundation, Joyce also funded David Brock to turn his hit piece on Anita Hill in the *American Spectator* magazine into a book, under Joyce's tutelage. From 1986 to 1999, Bradley granted the *American Spectator* $1.4 million.Barbara Miner, "Michael Joyce: Gone but Not Forgotten," *Milwaukee Shepherd-Express*, July 12, 2001 (www.shepherd-express.com/shepherd/22/28/cover_story.html). For more on the key role that Joyce has played for a generation in reshaping social policy from the political Right, see Lew Daly, "Charitable Choice: The Architecture of a Social Policy Revolution," *IDS Insights* 2 no. 1 (September 2001), at www.idsonline.org/art/Insights_Vol02Iss01.pdf.

207. The head of the Pope Foundation, James Arthur Pope, is on the "Donors Working Group" of the American Council of Trustees and Alumni (ACTA) along with Federalist Society board of visitors member C. Boyden Gray. Ward Connerly is also on the ACTA Trustees Council. ACTA made headlines in fall 2001 by issuing a report widely considered an attack on the diversity of views that can be expressed on university campuses regarding the September 11 terrorist attacks. See ACTA website, at www.goacta.org/advisorycommittees.htm; and Stuart Eskenazi, "Academic Freedom under Attack since Sept. 11, Some Professors Say," *Seattle Times*, December 25, 2001. The John M. Olin Foundation gave ACTA $100,000 in 2000, Olin 2000 IRS form 990.

208. Connerly, *Creating Equal*, 278.

209. Barry Bearak, "Between Black and White," *New York Times,* July 27, 1997, A1.

210. Ibid.

211. Ibid.

212. Ibid.

213. Connerly, *Creating Equal*, 22–24.

214. Bearak, "Between Black and White."

215. Connerly, *Creating Equal*, 98.

216. Suzanne Espinosa Solis, "Affirmative Action Critic Used His Minority Status: UC Regent Got No-Bid State Contracts," *San Francisco Chronicle*, May 8, 1995, A1.

217. Ibid.

218. Suzanne Espinosa Solis, "UC Regent Fights Law That Helped Him," *San Francisco Chronicle*, May 8, 1995, A1.

219. Theodore Cross, "Embarrassing Gaffe for a Man Who Has Dedicated His Life to the Defeat of Affirmative Action," *Journal of Blacks in Higher Education,* no. 22 (Winter 1998/1999): 38.

220. The foundation, among other things, paid the lease on former Governor Wilson's Los Angeles condominium. John Davies, the chairman of the foundation, is the man Wilson appointed in 1992 to sit on the Board of Regents, preceding Connerly. Davies also operates a blind trust in Wilson's name. Robert B. Gunnison, "Wilson's Use of Luxury Condo Doesn't Break Law, FPPC Says," *San Francisco Chronicle,* September 28, 1994, A19.

221. Thomas D. Elias, "Connerly Targets Ethnic Studies," *Washington Times*, July 5, 1998, A1.

222. On October 30, 2001, Connerly joined a press conference with the Center for Equal Opportunity and the Mountain States Legal Foundation to support the white male

plaintiff in the *Adarand v. Mineta* case. Center for Equal Opportunity press release, October 28, 2001.

223. A kick-off press conference at the Washington Court Hotel, Washington, D.C., featured Ward Connerly, Clint Bolick, Roger Clegg, and Edwin Meese, among others. Lyle Denniston, "Affirmative Action Foes Mobilizing in 50 States; Persuasion, Publicity, Lawsuits Planned to Prod State Attorneys General," *Baltimore Sun*, March 12, 1998, p. 14A; News Release, "Event: Press Conference on Affirmative Action," *FNS Daybook*, March 11, 1998.

224. ACRI received *amicus* brief support from the Institute for Justice when Proposition 209 was under consideration by the Ninth Circuit Court of Appeals. Institute for Justice, press release, January 31, 1997, "Connerly and Institute for Justice Urge Appeals Court to Lift Proposition 209/CCRI Injunction," at IJ website, www.acri.org/news/ifj01 31.html (December 21, 2001).

225. "Galvanizing the Grassroots against Racial Preferences," *Liberty & Law* 7, no. 1 (March 1998). *Liberty & Law* is the IJ newsletter, at www.ij.org.

226. For more information on the Independent Women's Forum, see Lee Cokorinos, *Antifeminist Organizations: Institutionalizing the Backlash*, briefing paper (New York: Institute for Democracy Studies, March 2000).

227. Ruben Navarrette, Jr., "Preference Foe in State to Back Bill," *Arizona Republic*, February 6, 1998, B3; plus correction, *Arizona Republic*, March 13, 1998, A2.

228. Ralph Z. Hallow, "Connerly, Others Form Alternative Race Panel," *Washington Times*, April 30, 1998, A1. See also *Hoover Institution Newsletter* (Summer 1998), at www-hoover.stanford.edu/pubaffairs/newsletter/98summer/newsbriefs.html.

229. Cris Rapp, "Ward Connerly Says... '[Al Gore] is a hateful man and I don't often use terms like that.' " Interview of Connerly by Rapp for *National Review Online*, April 17, 2000, at www.nationalreview.com/interrogatory/interrogatory041700.html (December 18, 2001).

230. Connerly, *Creating Equal*, 7, 13–15.

231. According to Connerly, Thomas Rhodes "saw the importance of Prop 209 right away and started opening doors for me. One of the people I met through Dusty was Bill Kristol, editor of the *Weekly Standard* and a commentator for ABC-TV." Rhodes also accompanied Connerly to a crucial meeting where he won the support of Rupert Murdoch, who agreed to donate $1 million to the California GOP, which supported Prop 209. Connerly, *Creating Equal*, 169–170.

232. John J. Miller, "Goodbye, Mr. Olin: When Conservative Funds Dry Up," *National Review*, June 11, 2001. On November 21, 2001, the board selected Michael W. Grebe to succeed Joyce. Grebe was a member of the Bradley Board, and is the CEO of Foley & Lardner, a large Milwaukee law firm. He will take up his duties upon his retirement from Foley & Lardner in July 2002. Bradley Foundation Press Release, November 21, 2001 (www.bradleyfdn.org/pr1101.html).

233. "Memo to: Our Readers From: WFB Re: Thomas L. Rhodes," *National Review*, December 14, 1992, 19.

234. Masthead, *National Review*, February 22, 1999.

235. The Empire Foundation was created by Change-NY, a lobbying group formed by millionaire business executive and former New York Republican gubernatorial candidate Lewis E. Lehrman, and Herbert London, a dean of New York University and former Conservative Party gubernatorial candidate. Susan Heller Anderson, "Chronicle," *New York Times*, June 17, 1991, p. B4. London and Lehrman were also cofounders of the National Association of Scholars. Alisa Solomon with Deirdre Hussey, "Enemies of Public Education," *The Village Voice: Education Supplement*, April 21, 1998, 2.

236. ACRI press release, January 15, 1997, at www.acri.org/news/nr0115.html. Financier Lew Lehrman's Lehrman Institute is listed as a substantial funder of the Empire Foundation. Empire Foundation for Public Policy Research 1999 IRS Form 990.

237. "Memo to: Our Readers From: WFB Re: Thomas L. Rhodes," *National Review*.

238. "Why the South Must Prevail," *National Review*, 4 August 24, 1957, 149. See also Richard M. Weaver, "Integration Is Communization," *National Review*, 4 July 13, 1957, 67–68. Cited in George H. Nash, *The Conservative Intellectual Movement in America since 1945* (Wilmington, DE: Intercollegiate Studies Institute, 1996), 185–186.

239. Roger Clegg, "Diversity Nonsense," *National Review*, January 21, 2002.

240. Campaign for a Color-Blind America, press release, October 15, 2000, at www.equalrights.com/acri-ccba.html.

241. Julie Mason, "Prop. A Leader Leaves Job, Says City Official Interfered; Blum Claims Attempt Made to Silence Him," *Houston Chronicle*, July 10, 1998, A1.

242. Campaign for a Color-Blind America, press release, October 15, 2000, at www.equalrights.com/acri-ccba.html.

243. ACRI media release, "Lawsuit Settled, Ending Florida Race-Based School Policy: Connerly-Led Organization Unveils Major Legal Push in Florida and Beyond," September 12, 2000, at www.fcri.org/press-release_09-13-00.htm. Edward Blum, "The Myth of Affirmative Access; Administration's Moment of Truth on Racial Quotas," *Washington Times*, December 5, 2001, A19.

244. ACRI media release, November 5, 2001, at www.acri.org/news/miami_dade.htm.

245. Dawn M. Weyrich, "Analysts Predict Civil Rights Bill Would Cost Billions in Productivity," *Washington Times*, July 12, 1990, A5.

246. CEO website, www.ceousa.org (March 12, 1999).

247. Testimony, June 15, 1995, Linda Chavez, president, Center for Equal Opportunity, before the Senate Committee on Labor and Human Resources, "Affirmative Action in Employment: Federal Contractor Requirements."

248. Ninety-five percent of top corporate jobs in the U.S. are held by white males. Federal Glass Ceiling Commission, *Good for Business: Making Full Use of the Nation's Human Capital* (March 1995).

249. Brief *Amicus Curiae* of Pacific Legal Foundation, American Civil Rights Institute, and Center for Equal Opportunity in Support of Petitioner, *Adarand Constructors, Inc. v. Mineta*, 534 U.S. 103 (2001) (No. 00-730). The brief was prepared by John H. Findley, Counsel of Record; Sharon L. Browne, Pacific Legal Foundation, Counsel for Amici Curiae Pacific Legal Foundation, American Civil Rights Institute, and Center for Equal Opportunity. For more on Sharon Browne, see section on Pacific Legal Foundation.

250. Roger Clegg, "Dismissed!" *National Review*, November 28, 2001.

251. This *amicus* brief is posted on the website of the Federalist Society, at www.fed-soc.org/Publications/practicegroupnewsletters/PG%20Links/grutter.htm, July 11, 2002.

252. See Roger Clegg, "Hi-Voltage Shocks the Left: A Golden Blow to Preference Advocates in California," *National Review Online*, December 5, 2000, at www.nationalreview.com/comment/comment120500e.shtml.

253. Linda Chavez, "High Court Wise on Civil Rights," letter to the editor, *New York Times*, August 16, 1989, A22.

254. Dawn M. Weyrich "Analysts Predict Civil Rights Bill Would Cost Billions in Productivity," *Washington Times*, July 12, 1990, A5.

255. "Linda Chavez Founds Think Tank on Race and Ethnicity," *PR Newswire*, February 21, 1995.

256. Geoffrey S. Underwood, "In the Tanks: Ego Tanks," *United Press International*, March 14, 2001.

257. "National ID Card Ineffective and Intrusive, Study Says," *M2 PRESSWIRE*, September 8, 1995.

258. Among other things, Chavez is a weekly syndicated columnist and appears regularly on such shows as NBC's *McLaughlin Group* and CNN's *Crossfire*.

259. CEO website, www.ceousa.org/multic.html.

260. CEO was, at first, essentially a vehicle for Chavez and her group's position on immigration. Deregulationists in most respects (although Chavez favors increased regulation of, for example, abortion clinics; see *American Feminist*, the journal of Feminists for Life, Winter 1998, 12), CEO opposes new restrictions on immigration, an issue that divided Republicans deeply in 1995. A debate on reducing legal immigration led by Alan Simpson and Lamar Smith was opposed by Majority Leader Dick Armey (R-Texas) in the House and Orrin Hatch (R-Utah) in the Senate. Pat Buchanan and the *National Review* (pro-curbs) lined up against the *Wall Street Journal*, the libertarian *Reason*, the National Association of Manufacturers, Chavez, and CEO. The free marketers favor fewer restrictions on immigration for reasons having to do with access to cheap labor, reduction in the power of some government agencies (CEO has called for the abolition of the Immigration and Naturalization Service; see "Abolish the INS," www.ceousa.org/ins.html), and for electoral reasons. Bob Dole received a smaller proportion of the Hispanic vote than any Republican presidential candidate in twenty-five years, bemoaned Linda Chavez, "and that is bad news for the G.O.P." See Linda Chavez, "The Hispanic Political Tide," *New York Times*, November 18, 1996. CEO attacks welfare for immigrants, illegal immigration, and the institutions (such as bilingual teaching) that "impede assimilation." For more on this discussion, see Linda Chavez, "What to do about Immigration," *Commentary*, March 1995, 29; and Ramesh Ponnuru, "Debating Rights; Debates within Republican Party," *National Review*, December 11, 1995. 76.

261. Under the auspices of Massachusetts public records law, the center wrote to each of the state's thirteen four-year public undergraduate schools asking them to provide information about their freshman classes. Darrell S. Pressley, "Bay State Colleges Could Face Affirmative Action Challenge," *Boston Herald*, November 3, 1998, 1.

262. For a critique of the CEO report, see the letter to the editor by Dr. Jordan Cohen, president of the Association of American Medical Colleges, *Washington Times*, September 8, 2001, A11.

263. Robert Lerner and Althea K. Nagai, "A Critique of the Expert Report of Patricia Gurin in *Gratz v. Bollinger*," prepared for the Center for Equal Opportunity, May 7, 2001.

264. James Q. Wilson, "Proposition 209; When a 'Factor' Becomes a Quota System? For the Record," *Los Angeles Times*, October 20, 1996, M1.

265. Marsha King, "Study: UW, WSU Favor Black Applicants." *Seattle Times*, September 16, 1998, B1.

266. Jennifer A. Galloway, "Data Sought on Race as Admission Factor: UW Group, Think Tank, Oppose Preferences," *Wisconsin State Journal*, April 17, 1998, 3C.

267. "School Applicant Records Not Available for Study," *National Law Journal*, September 17, 2001, B8.

268. Stephan Thernstrom and Abigail Thernstrom, *America in Black and White: One Nation, Indivisible* (New York: Simon & Schuster, 1997). For a caustic review of this book, see G.V. [Gore Vidal], "Bad History: G.V. Picks the Worst History Book of the Year," *The Nation*, April 20, 1998, 11–15.

269. Darrell S. Pressley, "Bay State Colleges Could Face Affirmative Action Challenge," *Boston Herald*, November 3, 1998, 1.

270. Olin Foundation annual reports, 1996, 1997.

271. Abigail Thernstrom spoke at the group's annual conference in New Orleans in 1997. See Cary Nelson, "Listening with a Long Spoon," *Social Text*, Winter 1998.

272. CEO website,www.ceousa.org/taxman.html (March 14, 1999).

273. Ibid.

274. The parents used an increasingly popular argument that existing bilingual education programs violate the Fourteenth Amendment of the U.S. Constitution and the Equal Educational Opportunities Act, as well as Title VI of the Civil Rights Act of 1964

[www.ceousa.org/multied.html].

275. PLF has represented Pete Wilson and Ward Connerly against opponents of Proposition 209, and the California State Board of Education and its board members in defense of Proposition 227 (in the latter case, PLF drew for its argument on a CEO study). For more, see www.pacificlegal.org/cases1/htm.

276. CEO claims that recent Supreme Court decisions related to affirmative action amount to a declaration that all such programs are "presumptively unconstitutional." The cases it points to are *Adarand Constructors, Inc. v. Pena*, 515 U.S. 200 (1995) and *City of Richmond v. Croson*, 488 U.S. 469 (1989). As noted above, despite the 2001 Supreme Court decision not to rule further at that time on the *Adarand* case, CEO counsel Roger Clegg considers the issue still open.

277. Sean Scully, "Foes of Race Preferences Take Fight to State Officials," *Washington Times*, March 12, 1998, A6.

278. Federalist Society National Lawyers Convention, Mayflower Hotel, Washington, D.C., November 12, 1998.

279. CEO website, www.ceousa.org/memo2.html (February 22, 1999).

280. CEO website, www.ceousa.org/html/redist.html (December 12, 2001). Blum and Clegg also joined with Bolick shortly afterward to write an article pressuring Attorney General Ashcroft to withdraw a brief in the University of Georgia case prepared by Bill Lann Lee (Ashcroft didn't; see below). Edward Blum, Clint Bolick, and Roger Clegg, "Gut-Check Time for Ashcroft," *National Review*, May 18, 2001. See also Edward Blum and Roger Clegg, "Don't Repeat Past Mistakes: Keep Race out of Redistricting," CEO website, www.ceousa.org/html/redistarticle2.htm.

281. Federalist Society National Lawyers Convention, Mayflower Hotel, Washington, D.C., November 12, 1998. Prop 209 advocate Ward Connerly also got involved in the I-200 battle. He protested outside a US Bank office in Bellevue, Washington, and announced that ACRI would withdraw $600,000—all its funds on deposit—from a US Bank branch in Sacramento because of its position against Washington State's anti-affirmative action Proposition I-200. "Connerly Joins I-200 Supporters" *Seattle Times*, August 10, 1998 B2.

282. Sean Scully, "White House Gets Warning on Lee: Hatch Position Spurred by Set-Aside Policies at Justice," *Washington Times*, February 17, 1999, A1.

283. Citizens' Initiative on Race and Ethnicity website, www.cire.org/commission_members.html.

284. EOF 1999 IRS Form 990.

285. Rosalie Porter, *Forked Tongue: The Politics of Bilingual Education* (New York: Basic Books, 1990).

286. The registered agent for the Institute for Research in English Acquisition and Development was Gary Imhoff, who coauthored with Gerda Bikales, executive director of U.S. English, a monograph warning of what they saw as the dangers of a lack of Hispanic assimilation in the U.S. For more on Chavez's relationship with U.S. English, see below. U.S. English press release, *PR Newswire*, August 19, 1985; and District of Columbia Department of Consumer and Regulatory Affairs, Corporate Record, Research in English Acquisition and Development, Inc., Incorporation Record, No. 892427, filed June 29, 1989.

287. CEO website, www.ceousa.org/memo2.html (February 25, 1999).

288. Judy Keen, "Buchanan Banking on Simplicity," *USA Today*, February 21, 1996, 4A. While she was at the White House, Linda Chavez reported directly to Buchanan. "Cabinet Councils Restructured," *Facts on File World News Digest*, April 19, 1985, 282, D3.

289. See www.avemarialaw.edu; and Peggy Walsh-Sarnecki, "Domino's Pizza Founder Spending Millions to Create Catholic Law School," *Detroit Free Press*, April 8, 1999.

290. Heritage Foundation annual reports, 1985, 1997. Also on the Heritage board is Thomas L. Rhodes, who sits on Ward Connerly's ACRI board.

291. Reason Foundation, *Annual Report*, 1981, 1982.

292. *Justice for Sale: Shortchanging the Public Interest for Private Gain* (Washington, D.C.: Alliance for Justice, 1993).

293. Mayer and Abramson, *Strange Justice*, 193.

294. Larry Arnn, "Manifesto for Culture Warriors of the Right," *Washington Times*, November 19, 1995, B4.

295. John Olin Foundation, 2000 IRS Form 990, 11.

296. In 1995, Olin awarded EOF $300,000 for "programs at the Center for Equal Opportunity under the direction of Linda Chavez." It was paid out over two years. In 1996 the foundation authorized another grant in the same amount, paid half in 1996 and half in 1997. John M. Olin Foundation, Inc., annual reports, 1995, 1996, 1997.

297. Sarah Scaife Foundation, IRS Form 990s, 1995–2000.

298. Claude R. Lambe Charitable Foundation, 1998 IRS Form 990.

299. Robert Pear, "Rights Aide Asserts the Right to Speak Her Mind," *New York Times*, June 11, 1984, A24.

300. CEO biographical profiles. From CEO promotional packet, distributed January 28, 1999, Washington, D.C.; see also Don Kowet, "She Would Bring Back Melting Pot; Multicultural Gurus Can't Abide Lessons Life Taught Linda Chavez," *Washington Times*, January 9, 1992, E1.

301. CEO website, www.ceousa.org (January 28, 1999).

302. Catholic League website, www.catholicleague.org (March 4, 2002). Also on the advisory board are other opponents of affirmative action, such as Dinesh D'Souza and Alan Keyes.

303. Ron Hutcheson, "Chavez Ends Cabinet Bid; Labor Pick Pulls Out amid Furor over Immigrant," *Miami Herald*, January 10, 2001, p. A1.

304. Michael Finn, "Affirmative Action Creates Inequality, Linda Chavez Tells Audience at UTC," *Chattanooga Times/Chattanooga Free Press*, November 2, 2001, B1.

305. Macarena Hernandez, "Conservative and Hispanic, Linda Chavez Carves Out Leadership Niche," *New York Times*, August 19, 1998 A28.

306. Linda Chavez, *Out of the Barrio: Toward a New Politics of Hispanic Assimilation* (New York: Basic Books, 1991).

307. Linda Chavez biographical note, CEO website, www.ceousa.org/staff.html (March 14, 1999).

308. As one of the few Latina graduate teaching assistants at UCLA, Chavez assigned an Anglo author's writings on the roots of a Mexican dialect and failed her students who objected on political grounds and refused to complete reading. "They wanted to come in and rap about their experiences. I thought they should read the books," she said. Michel McQueen, "GOP's Chavez goes Against the Grain," *Washington Post*, October 29, 1986, A1.

309. Pear, "Rights Aide Asserts the Right to Speak Her Mind."

310. From *Who's Who in Finance and Industry*, 29th edition; *Who's Who in America*, 50th edition, 49th edition.

311. Jay Horning, "Chavez Adept at Shedding Stereotypes," *St. Petersburg Times*, April 24, 1994, 18A. On Shanker, see Merrill Sheils et al., "Teaching in English—Plus," *Newsweek*, February 7, 1977, 64.

312. "If there's any single person responsible for my being in the administration it's Bill Bennett," Chavez told the *Washington Post*. Phil McCombs, "The Civil Struggles of Linda Chavez," *Washington Post*, January 30, 1984, A1.

313. W. Dale Nelson, "Another Ex-Democrat in the White House," *Record* (Bergen,

NJ), April 28, 1985. The membership of the panel was later enlarged from six to eight by Congress, with conservatives retaining control.

314. Larry Margasak, "Commission Appears Headed on New Course," *Associated Press,* January 15, 1984.

315. "Prepared Testimony of Linda Chavez, President, Center for Equal Opportunity, before the House Education and the Workforce Committee Subcommittee on Oversight and Investigations, Subject—'Policies and Enforcement Activities of the Office for Civil Rights at the Department of Education,'" *Federal News Service,* June 22, 1999.

316. Juan Williams, "Power to Aid Blacks Discounted," *Washington Post,* January 9, 1984, A1.

317. "I don't see how you can explain traversing the course she has traversed other than by sheer personal ambition," said William Blakey, formerly her supervisor as assistant secretary of Health, Education, and Welfare in charge of legislation on education. W. Dale Nelson, "Another Ex-Democrat in White House," *Record* (Bergen, NJ), April 28, 1985, A35. See also Nick Thimmesch, "Linda Chavez, Her Political Changes," *New York City Tribune,* April 16, 1985.

318. Larry Margasak, "Commission Angry at Funding Cut Off Suggestion," *Associated Press,* March 15, 1984.

319. McQueen, "GOP's Chavez Goes against the Grain."

320. Phil McCombs, "The Civil Struggles of Linda Chavez," *Washington Post,* January 30, 1984, B1.

321. Sidney Blumenthal, "The Conservative Elite: Activists Promote a New Establishment," *Washington Post,* September 22, 1985, A1.

322. Michel McQueen, "Chavez Backs Reagan's Steadfastness at Summit: Sanctions against South Africa Opposed," *Washington Post,* October 14, 1986, B1.

323. Michel McQueen, "Chavez: A Master Persuader" *Washington Post,* August, 17,1986, D1.

324. Editorial, "Campaign Mudslinging," *Journal of Commerce,* October 31, 1986, 19A.

325. Hernandez, "Conservative and Hispanic, Linda Chavez Carves Out Leadership Niche."

326. "Selected Experience in the Life of Linda Chavez," *Associated Press,* November 21, 1998.

327. James W. Crawford, *Hold Your Tongue, Bilingualism and the Politics of English Only* (Boston: Addison-Wesley, 1992).

328. Ibid.

329. John Sedgwick, "Inside the Pioneer Fund," in Russell Jacoby and Naomi Glauberman, eds., *The Bell Curve: History, Documents, Opinions* (New York: Times Books, 1995), 144-161. Susan Ferriss, "Fair: Mounting Campaign to Keep Immigrants Out; Group's Stated Aim to Cap Population Walks Fine Line of Bigotry, Critics Say," *San Francisco Examiner,* December 12, 1993, A1. "Both Sides Air Ads on Prop. 187," *Los Angeles Times,* November 6, 1994, A35.

330. ProEnglish website, at www.proenglish.org/board/tanton.html, March 13, 2002. See also "ProEnglish Sues President Bush to Overturn Order Mandating Multilingual Government Services," *U.S. Newswire,* March 13, 2002.

331. During the 1980s, Cordelia Scaife May donated at least $5.8 million through her Pittsburgh-based Laurel Foundation to U.S. English, the Federation for American Immigration Reform (FAIR)—an anti-immigration group founded by Tanton—and a network of organizations linked to him. By 1986, according to federal tax documents, she had given U.S. English $650,000—more than 10 percent of its total expenditures. The Pioneer Fund gave FAIR $680,000 between 1982 and 1989. For more information, see Crawford, *Hold Your Tongue,* chapter 6, "Hispanophobia" (available at ourworld.compuserve.com

/homepages/JWCrawford/HYTCH6.htm).

332. Larry Lopez, "Former Reagan Aide Linda Chavez Quits U.S. English Group," Associated Press, October 17, 1988. Zita Arocha, "Dispute Fuels Campaign against 'Official English': Foes Say Memo Shows Racism's Behind Plan," *Washington Post*, November 6, 1988, A20. Published in the *Arizona Republic* in October 1988, the private memo explained that unless something was done, the U.S. would face a Hispanic takeover: "Will the present majority peaceably hand over its political power to a group that is simply more fertile? . . . As Whites see their power and control over their lives declining will they simply go quietly into the night?" Crawford, *Hold Your Tongue*, chapter 6.

333. Julie Amparano and Ruben Navarrette Jr., "Official English Tossed: Arizona Law 1st in Nation Overturned," *Arizona Republic*, April 29, 1998, A1.

334. Don Kowet, "She Would Bring Back Melting Pot," *Washington Times*, January 9, 1992, E1.

335. Ron Unz, the author of Proposition 227, had funded Chavez's Center generously. See Amy Wallace, "Unlikely Path Led to Wilson Foes' Far-Right Challenge: Politics," *Los Angeles Times*, May 8, 1994, A1.

336. Frederick R. Lynch, "The Civil Rights Initiative Is in Danger of Sinking," *Los Angeles Times*, December 19, 1995, B9.

337. Kowet, "She Would Bring Back Melting Pot."

338. The Institute for Religious Values' advisory board includes Jeane Kirkpatrick, Diane Knippers (head of the right-wing Institute on Religion and Democracy), Barbara Ledeen (formerly of the Independent Women's Forum), and Nina Shea of Freedom House. Institute for Religious Values letterhead, June 2, 1998.

339. Darryl Fears, "A Deepening Divide on U.S. Civil Rights Panel; Controversy over Appointment Highlights Historical Disagreements over Commission's Role," *Washington Post*, December 18, 2001, A3.

340. Christopher Edley, a Harvard Law professor who has served as a consultant to President Clinton's race initiative and is also on the U.S. Civil Rights Commission, has called Thernstrom's book "a crime against humanity." Jason Zengerle, "The Gatekeeper," *New Republic*, March 22, 1999, 14. Thernstrom was highly critical of the Clinton initiative.

341. Thernstrom and Thernstrom, *America in Black and White*, acknowledgments.

342. "Voting Rights: New Battlefields," *The Economist* (London), April 7, 1979, 51

343. For which Terry Eastland praised her. See Terry Eastland, "Supreme Court Wronged on Rights Decisions: The Media Distort Effort for Equality," *San Diego Union-Tribune*, October 8, 1989, C4.

344. Michael A. Fletcher, "Scholars Offer Optimism about Racial Progress," *Detroit News*, November 2, 1997 (at www.detnews.com/1997/outlook/9711/14/11020007.htm).

345. Abigail Thernstrom, "Bilingual Mis-education," *New Republic*, April 18, 1981, 16.

346. Independent Women's Forum website, www.iwf.org/about/nab.shtml (December 15, 2001).

347. Wisconsin Federalist Society website, www.execpc.com/~fedsoc/fedmk.html (December 15, 2001).

348. *Marquis Who's Who in American Education*, 5th ed.

349. Like the *Dartmouth Review*, the *Michigan Review* takes its name from the *National Review*. Tracing the progress of conservatism at the University of Michigan, Jonathan Chait notes, "In the 1990s the *Review* gradually adopted libertarianism as a credo, which has made it simultaneously more radical and more socially tolerant. In the past year it repeatedly attacked Newt Gingrich as a 'statist,' while a December article praised the Michigan Militia." Jonathan Chait, "Backfire on Campus," *American Prospect* (Summer 1995).

350. "New Bradley Fellows," *Policy Review*, June 1996.

351. *National Review* website, www.nationalreview.com/masthead/masthead-

miller.shtml (November 29, 2001).

352. Maria Puente, "Prop. 187: Just the Beginning/Battle Shifts to Congress, but GOP Remains Divided," *USA Today*, November 15, 1994, 2A.

353. Equal Opportunity Foundation, IRS Form 990, 1999.

354. On Sun Myung Moon's relationship with the *Washington Times*, see Frederick Clarkson, *Eternal Hostility* (Monroe, Maine: Common Courage Press, 1997), 45–77. Starr's review is Roger Starr, "E. Pluribus Unum: The Dangers of Multiculturalism," *Washington Times*, July 5, 1998.

355. John J. Miller, "The Chavez Debacle: A Personal Account," *National Review*, February 5, 2001.

356. Jonathan Chait, "Backfire on Campus," *American Prospect* (Summer 1995).

357. Christopher Conte, "President Seeks to Soften Two Provisions of Welfare Law," *St. Petersburg Times*, December 27, 1996.

358. Susan Kaufmann, "Immigration Forum Tackles Dual Citizenship, Other Touchy Subjects," *Arkansas Democrat-Gazette*, April 19, 1998.

359. Freedom House website, www.freedomhouse.org/aboutfh/offstaff.htm, March 28, 2002.

360. "Anti-Communists; the Cold War Is Thawing; What Will They Do Now?" *Washington Times*, September 13, 1989, E1.

361. Arch Puddington, "Finding the 'Right' in Human Rights," *Washington Times*, December 16, 1998, A23.

362. Arch Puddington, "Is Labor Back? Trouble in the AFL-CIO," *Commentary*, Vol. 106, no. 1 (July 1998): 39.

363. Arch Puddington, "The War on the War on Crime; Shooting of Amadou Diallo by NYC Police Officers Engenders Protest against Alleged Police Misconduct," *Commentary*, May 1, 1999.

364. Arch Puddington, "Is Affirmative Action on the Way Out? Should It Be?" *Commentary*, March 1998.

365. Michael Massing, "Trotsky's Orphans: From Bolshevism to Reaganism; Social Democrats, USA," *New Republic*, June 22, 1987, 18.

366. U.S. Commission on Civil Rights, press release, *PR Newswire*, December 3, 1984.

367. Jones's official biography on the DOE website helpfully notes that he "served as Deputy Legal Affairs Secretary to California Governor Pete Wilson and as Counsel to the United States Senate Judiciary Committee in Washington, D.C., where he worked on nominations, constitutional law and civil rights issues for then-Chairman Orrin Hatch (R-UT)." At www.ed.gov/offices/OGC/jones.html, March 29, 2002.

368. Center for New Black Leadership website, www.cnbl.org/html/jones.html (March 15, 1999).

369. Ibid.

370. Federalist Society, *Civil Rights News* 1, no. 2 (Spring 1997): 2.

371. A sense of Project 21's level of commitment to minority communities can be gleaned by looking at the online op-eds they produce. For example: Rejecting "the implication" that "businesses impose themselves on relatively powerless communities," Project 21 head David Almasi condemns the Environmental Protection Agency for making an effort to contain one of the worst instances of potential environmental racism in the country—by denying a permit to the Shintech Corporation to build a chemical plant over the objections of the local minority community in Romeville, Louisiana; and David Almasi, "Civil Rights Commission Needs to Assess the Economic Impact of Environmental Justice Policies," a New Visions Commentary paper published January 2002 by the National Center for Public Policy Research, at www.nationalcenter.org/P21NVAlmasiEJ102.html. The National Center for Public Policy Research, incorporated in 1983, is supported by many of the same right-

wing foundations that have funded anti-affirmative action work: the Bradley Foundation, Scaife's Carthage Foundation, and Joseph Coors's Castle Rock Foundation, as well as the J.M. and Randolph Foundations. Foundation Center Grants Database, 1997.

372. G. Pascal Zachary, "Leader of California Proposition 209 Is Bringing Campaign to Other States," *Wall Street Journal*, January 14, 1997.

373. "Wilson Appoints Frick to Office of Administrative Law, Jones as Deputy Legal Affairs Secretary," *Metropolitan News-Enterprise* (Sacramento, CA) January 9, 1998, 3.

374. David Grann, "Robespierre of the Right: What I Ate at the Revolution: Paul Weyrich," *New Republic,* October 27, 1997, 20.

375. Federalist Society website, www.fed-soc.org/Publications/practicegroupnewsletters/civilrights/contacts.htm (December 19, 2001).

376. Kmiec, *The Attorney General's Lawyer,* 83.

377. The National Legal Center was set up by right-wing beer magnate Joseph Coors. It donated $50,000, and Coors donated $25,000 to set up the Mountain States Legal Foundation, where Chip Mellor and Clint Bolick of the Institute for Justice got started. Bellant, *The Coors Connection,* 85.

378. Brief Amici Curiae of the Independent Women's Forum and the Center for Equal Opportunity in Support of Respondent, *Piscataway Township Board of Education v. Taxman,* 522 U.S. 1010 (1997) (No. 96–679). Anita Blair sat on the Virginia Military Institute board while that institution was litigating against admission of women.

379. "Testimony of Roger Clegg," House Judiciary Subcommittee on the Constitution, February 25, 1998, *Federal Document Clearing House Congressional Testimony,* February 25, 1998.

380. "Disparate impact" is "a theory or category of employment discrimination. Disparate impact discrimination may be found when a contractor's use of a facially neutral selection standard (e.g., a test, an interview, a degree requirement) disqualifies members of a particular race or gender group at a significantly higher rate than others and is not justified by business necessity or job relatedness. An intent to discriminate is not necessary to this type of employment discrimination. The disparate impact theory may be used to analyze both objective and subjective selection standards." Glossary of terms produced by the Office of Equal Opportunity Affairs, University of South Florida, at www.usf.edu/eoa/homepage/glossary1.htm.

381. Roger Clegg, "Reading the Tea Leaves of the Supreme Court," *Fulton County Daily Report,* May 8, 2001.

382. Roger Clegg, "Alternatives to Race Preferences," *Washington Times,* June 3, 1998, 18.

383. Susan Baer, "Buchanan Leads with His Right on Home Front," *Baltimore Sun,* February 21, 1992.

384. Jorge Amselle, "Federal Goals and Timetables," letter in *Washington Post,* August 19, 1995.

385. CEO website, www.ceousa.org/staff.html (March 13, 1998).

386. CEO website, www.ceousa.org/html/staff.html (January 2, 2002).

387. Jorge Amselle, "Bye-bye to Bilingual Ed?" *The World and I,* March 1, 2000.

388. See, for example, Jorge Amselle, "The Blob on the Border," *Weekly Standard,* February 19, 1996, "Misremember the Alamo!" *Weekly Standard,* October 20, 1997, "Adios Bilingual Ed," *Policy Review,* November/December 1997.

389. *Testimony of Jorge Amselle, Communications Director, Center for Equal Opportunity, Before the Senate Committee on Labor and Human Resources,* April 29, 1996.

390. See, for example, Marnie S. Shaul, "Public Education: Meeting the Needs of Students with Limited English Proficiency," General Accounting Office report, February 23, 2001. Rosalie Porter, a member of the EOF board, is also cited.

391. Jorge Amselle, "Bilingual Education a Failed Fad," *Denver Post*, February 23, 1998.

392. David S. Broder, "Convention 1980: The Republicans in Detroit: Convention Moving to Let Delegates Vote 'Conscience,'" *Washington Post*, July 13, 1980, A14.

393. CEO website, www.ceousa.org/html/staff.html, January 2, 2002.

394. Ellen Nakashima and Thomas B. Edsall, "Ashcroft Personnel Moves Irk Career Justice Lawyers," *Washington Post*, March 15, 2002, A5.

395. Beard's professional career is outlined in an opinion of the U.S. Tax Court, *Beard v. Commissioner*, 69 T.C.M. (CCH) 1768 (1995) (requiring Beard to pay back taxes and penalties for a dispute with the IRS over his 1988-1990 tax returns).

396. *Arrington v. Taylor*, 380 F.Supp. 1348 (M.D. N.C. 1974), *aff'd*, 529 F2d 567 (4th Cir. 1975), *cert. denied*, 424 U.S. 913 (1976). Other interesting cases litigated by Beard include *Uzzell v. Friday*, 625. F.2d. 1117 (4th Cir. 1980), *cert. denied*, 446 U.S. 951 (1980) (challenging U.N.C. regulations requiring at least two blacks and two women on the eighteen-seat student government); *Poovery v. Edminsten*, 526 F.Supp. 759 (E.D. N.C. 1981) (representing member of state legislature challenging minority position on U.N.C. board of directors); *Swann v. Charlotte-Mecklenburg Bd. of Educ.*, 501 F.2d. 383 (4th Cir. 1974) (challenging minority quotas in a gifted children program); *Galda v. Bloustein*, 516 F. Supp. 1142 (D. N.J. 1981) (arguing a class action suit brought by Rutgers students opposing the use of school money to support the Public Interest Research Group).

397. Marjorie Hunter, "Bell Plans to Ease Some Rules for Education of the Handicapped," *New York Times*, September 30, 1982, A1.

398. *MacNeil-Lehrer News Hour* (September 8, 1982), Transcript #1813.

399. Coauthoring a brief with Reynolds, Charles J. Cooper, and Michael A. Carvin unsuccessfully attempting to end a court-supervised desegregation plan in the Denver public schools. *Keyes v. School Dist. Number 1*, 609 F. Supp. 1491 (D. Colo. 1985), *cert. denied*, 498 U.S. 1082 (1991).

400. *Beard v. The North Carolina State Bar*, 357 S.E.2d. 694 (1987).

401. Beard cowrote an *amicus curiae* brief for EOF in *Podberesky v. Kirwan*, 38 F.3d. 147, *reh'g, en banc, denied*, 46 F.3d. 5 (4th Cir. 1994), *cert. denied*, 514 U.S. 1128 (1995) (overturning University of Maryland scholarship program for African-Americans).

402. Anne Groer, "Despite Cold, 35,000 March in D.C. to Protest Abortion," *Orlando Sentinel*, January 22, 1994, A13.

403. At the anniversary dinner in 2001 at which Beard received the award, a letter by one of the leaders of the extreme militant wing of the anti-abortion movement, Fr. Frank A. Pavone, was read out. The letter is reprinted in the anniversary edition of the organization's newsletter, *PLAGAL Memorandum*, no. 40 (August 2001) at www.plagal.org/news/plagal40.html (February 14, 2002). For more on Frank Pavone and the important role of his organization, see Lee Cokorinos and Gillian Kane, *Priests for Life: A New Era in Antiabortion Activism*, briefing paper (New York: Institute for Democracy Studies, April 2001); and Gillian Kane, "Priests for Life: A New Stage of Antiabortion Activism," *IDS Insights*, 1, no. 2 (November 2000) at www.idsonline.org/art/Insights_Vol01Iss02.pdf.

404. Ibid.

405. Lou Chibbaro, Jr., "Affirmative Action Splits Log Cabin," *Washington Blade*, August 21, 1998.

406. "Mitch's Place: Conservative Think Tank Creates a Niche," *Minneapolis Star-Tribune*, June 28, 1995.

407. www.cnbl/mission.org (March 4, 1999).

408. Lynde and Harry Bradley Foundation, *2000 Annual Report*. CNBL has also been supported by the right-wing DeVos Foundation [DeVos IRS Form 990, 1998].

409. *The Real Story behind Paycheck Protection: The Hidden Link between Anti-*

worker and Anti-public Education Initiatives, (Washington, D.C.: National Education Association, 1998); online at www.nea.org/publiced/paycheck/.

410. Center for New Black Leadership website at www.cnbl/mission.org (March 4, 1999).

411. The J.M. Foundation's president emeritus, Jeremiah Milbank, Jr., is a former member of Reagan's "kitchen cabinet," and was, along with J. William Middendorf II, one of the two financial angels who saved the Draft Goldwater campaign in 1962. See Lee Edwards, "The Unforgettable Candidate," *National Review,* July 6, 1998. His son, Jeremiah Milbank III, is now president of the J.M. Foundation, which has funded both CNBL and the Center of the American Experiment, the Goldwater Institute in Phoenix, the Heritage Foundation, and the Landmark Legal Foundation. J.M. Foundation, 1998 IRS Form 990. The Olin Foundation granted $50,000 to CNBL in 1997, 1997 IRS Form 990, and $20,000 to the Center of the American Experiment in 1998, Olin Foundation website, schedule of 1998 grants, at www.jmof.org/grants/1998c.htm.

412. Donner Foundation, 1998 IRS Form 990.

413. Jonathan Broder, "The Attack Judge," Salon.com, July 21, 1998; Mayer and Abramson, *Strange Justice,* 154, 326; and Trish Wilson Antonucci, "The Independent Women's Forum: An Overview," *Women Leaders Online,* at www.wlo.org (December 16, 1997).

414. The founder of the right-wing Institute for Justice, Clint Bolick (who worked for Clarence Thomas and played a key role in his confirmation) described relations between the evangelical right and libertarians during the Thomas confirmation battle as "the most harmonious I'd ever seen." Mayer and Abramson, *Strange Justice,* 198.

415. For an analysis of the growth of antifeminist organizations, see Lee Cokorinos, *Antifeminist Organizations: Institutionalizing the Backlash,* briefing paper (New York: Institute for Democracy Studies, March 2000).

416. Lynde and Harry Bradley Foundation, *2000 Annual Report,* 26. Bradley granted the IWF $80,000 in 1998 (Bradley 1988 IRS Form 990).

417. W.H. Brady 2000 IRS Form 990. IWF was the biggest grant recipient on the Brady Foundation's grants list.

418. That year the Randolph Foundation also granted $70,000 to Ward Connerly's American Civil Rights Institute. Randolph Foundation 1999 IRS Form 990.

419. Sarah Scaife Foundation 1999 IRS Form 990.

420. Ironically, Laurence Silberman implemented affirmative actions programs while serving in Nixon's Labor Department, a subject he rather ruefully recounted to a meeting of the Labor Practice Group of the Federalist Society in October 2001.

421. Independent Women's Forum Board of Directors list, IWF website, www.iwf.org/about/board.shtml (December 27, 2001).

422. Ibid.

423. Donner Foundation 1998 IRS Form 990. On February 6, 2002, Louise Oliver was appointed president of GOPAC, the organization formerly headed by Newt Gingrich that was caught up in a funding scandal.

424. Heather Richardson Higgins is a powerhouse of the far right. She is also a trustee of the Randolph Foundation (along with James Q. Wilson and R. Randolph Richardson); a board member of the W.H. Brady Foundation (at which Elizabeth B. Lurie, a former director of IWF, serves as president and treasurer); on the executive committee of the Hoover Institution (along with Richard Mellon Scaife—see www-hoover.stanford.edu/main/board-ovr.html#officers); and previously an advisory board member of the right-wing Donner Foundation's New Leadership Fellows Project. She is also first vice president of the Women's National Republican Club, and served as a member of Newt Gingrich's strategy team. See biographical sketch, Progress and Freedom Foundation website, www.pff.org/as-

pen96/higgins.html (December 27, 2001). In 1996, *Roll Call* reported that Higgins, at the time head of the massive Smith Richardson Foundation, gave money to the Progress and Freedom Foundation to finance Gingrich's controversial college course, and that she co-hosted a show with Gingrich on Paul Weyrich's National Empowerment Television. Juliet Eilperin, "Conservative Foundation Is Latest Lightning Rod in Hill Ethics Battle," *Roll Call*, May, 9, 1996. For more on Higgins and Weyrich, see Leon Howell, "Funding the War of Ideas: Conservative Foundations," *Christian Century*, July 19, 1995.

425. Nancy Pfotenhauer biography at IWF website, at http://www.iwf.org/news /010301.shtml.

426. Margot Slade and Katherine Roberts, "Ideas & Trends; Civil Liberties on Campus," *New York Times*, July 22, 1984, section 4, 22. See also Ishmael Reed, "Unequal Rights for Haters," Salon.com, January 23, 1999; Margaret Carlson, "Only in My Backyard," *Time*, April 21, 1997, 32; John Milne, "Knowing All the Right People," *Boston Globe*, April 19, 1992, A21; and Alexander Cockburn and Ken Silverstein, *Counterpunch* (September 1995). According to Reed, Ingraham worked at *Dartmouth Review* while its editor, Dinesh D'Souza, "presided over a regular column written in Ebonics, which used to split his readers' sides."

427. Anita Blair and Kathryn Balmforth, "Beijing Plus Five: Deconstructing the UN Conference on Women," *Ex Femina*, April 2000. *Ex Femina* is published by the Independent Women's Forum.

428. George Archibald, "Women Riled by 'Gender' Agenda," *Washington Times*, July 24, 1995, A1.

429. Capital Research Center advisory board member Linda Chavez also weighed in with Ingraham and Satel, attacking feminists for criticizing Promise Keepers' view of "man as head of his household." Hernandez, "Conservative and Hispanic, Linda Chavez Carves Out Leadership Niche."

430. See Patrick Reilly, "National Organization for Women: Campaign for Power and Control Harms American Business and Society," Capital Research Center, November 1997, at www.capitalresearch.org:80/trends/ot-1197.html (March 30, 1999). For more on the emerging links between secular right-wing antifeminist groups, including the Independent Women's Forum, and the religious right, see Lee Cokorinos, "Promise Keepers, Southern Baptists, and Antifeminist Groups Join Forces: 'Hard' and 'Soft' Patriarchy: The New Antifeminist Alliance," *PK Watch*, no. 3 (1999).

431. Earhart Foundation 2000 IRS Form 990.

432. Intercollegiate Studies Institute, letterhead, August 14, 1998.

433. Sarah Scaife Foundation website, www.scaife.com/sarah01.html (April 7, 1999).

434. Sarah Scaife Foundation IRS Form 990s, 1993–1999.

435. Barbara Ledeen's husband, Reagan-era National Security Council consultant Michael Ledeen, played a central role in the Iran-Contra scandal. See Lawrence E. Walsh, *Firewall: The Iran-Contra Conspiracy and Cover-Up* (New York: W.W. Norton, 1997), 37, 39, 42–43, 191. Michael Ledeen, a colleague of Charles Murray at the American Enterprise Institute, said of Murray's *The Bell Curve* (see above), "never has such a moderate book attracted such an immoderate response." Charles Murray, "*The Bell Curve* and Its Critics; Social Consequences of Intelligence," *Commentary*, May 1995, p. 23.

436. Geoffrey S. Underwood, "In the Tanks: Lessons from IWF Rumble," *United Press International*, May 18, 2001.

437. Toby Harnden, "'We Won't Be Victims Any More:' An Influential Group of Post Feminist, Republican Women Has a Powerful Voice in the Bush Administration," *Daily Telegraph* (London), July 25, 2001, 17.

438. Leslie Alan Horvitz, "Public-Interest Law Center Fights Political Correctness," *Insight*, November 6, 1995, 16.

439. Michael A. Carvin, a CIR board member, directed the American Legal Foundation before CIR was established. See Francis J. Flaherty, "Right-Wing Firms Pick Up Steam; A Growing Force in Public Interest Work," *National Law Journal*, May 23, 1983, 1.

440. Judi Hasson, "Top Smith Aide Goes into Private Practice," *U.P.I.*, October 25, 1984.

441. Indeed, Olson was on the receiving end of a subpoena from independent prosecutor Alexia Morrison, who was investigating the illegalities of the Iran-Contra scandal. Olson unsuccessfully challenged the Independent Prosecutor statute. *Morrison v. Olson*, 487 U.S. 654 (1988).

442. David L. Wilson, "Washington's Movers and Shakers: Rightists," *National Journal*, February 25, 1989, 488. *Marquis Who's Who in American Law*, 4th edition.

443. At OLC, Cooper also worked on Robert Bork's confirmation hearings.

444. See www.ff.org/leadership/board2.html (March 29, 1999).

445. Michael Greve curriculum vitae, at AEI website, www.aei.org/scholars/greve.htm (December 28, 2001); Idris M. Diaz, "Mischief Makers: The Men behind All Those Anti-Affirmative Action Lawsuits," *Black Issues in Higher Education*, December 25, 1997, 14.

446. David L. Wilson, "People; Washington's Movers and Shakers; Rightists" *National Journal*, 21, no. 8, 488. Michael Greve curriculum vitae, at AEI website.

447. An indication of this trend, discussed above and below, is evident in Clint Bolick's decision in 1988 to leave the Department of Justice's Civil Rights Division and launch a new organization, the Landmark Center for Civil Rights.

448. Susan Dominus, "Attacking Affirmative Action," *American Lawyer*, May 1996, 35.

449. *Grutter v. Bollinger*, 137 F. Supp. 2d 821 (E.D. Mich. 2001), *rev'd by, in part, vacated by, in part*, 288 F.3d 732 (6th Cir. Mich. 2002).

450. CIR Fall 2000 docket report, at www.cir-usa.org/articles/winter2000_dr.pdf, March 28, 2002.

451. CIR, *Annual Report*, 1996–1997.

452. See Curt Levey (director of Legal and Public Affairs at the Center for Individual Rights), "Diversity on Trial," *National Review*, June 11, 2001; and Mary Beth Marklein, "Students Turning to the Right: Colleges Are Catching the Latest Wave of Conservatism," *USA Today*, February 23, 1999, 6D. Because *Hopwood* was decided on the Circuit level, it is not binding to the rest of the states. Thus, CIR "shops" for plaintiffs in various states with experiences similar to that of *Hopwood* in order to move forward with its goal of eradicating affirmative action.

453. Pioneer Fund website, www.pioneerfund.org/, March 27, 2002. See also Adam Shatz, "The Thernstroms in Black and White; The Story of How Two Dedicated Civil Rights Activists Became the First Couple of the Crusade against Racial Preferences," *American Prospect*, March 12-March 26, 2001. Regarding CIR's acceptance of Pioneer Fund money, Greve told *Detroit Free Press* columnist Trevor Coleman, "Our acceptance of their funds does not by any stretch of the imagination constitute an endorsement of their views." Institute for the Study of Academic Racism website, www.ferris.edu/isar/Institut/CIR/freep/coleman.htm (December 28, 2001).

454. Bob Herbert, "In America; Affront to Black People," *New York Times*, February 12, 1996, A15. See also John Sedgwick, "Inside the Pioneer Fund," in Jacoby and Glauberman, eds., *The Bell Curve*, 144–161.

455. Tim Kelsey and Trevor Rowe, "Academics 'Were Funded by Racist American Trust,'" *The Independent*, March 4, 1990, 4; Tim Kelsey, "Ulster University Took Grant from Fund Backing Whites," *The Independent*, January 9, 1994, 2; Alfredo J. Estrada, "Divided over a Common Language," *Washington Post*, October 4, 1992, X4; James J. Heckman et al., "IQ, Race, and Heredity; Reactions to Charles Murray's '*The Bell Curve* and Its Critics'"; letter to the editor," *Commentary*, August 1995, 15.

456. CIR represented Gottfredson and Michael Levin in their disputes with universities.

457. On his website, Rushton states, "I consistently find that East Asians and their descendants average a larger brain size, greater intelligence, more sexual restraint, slower rates of maturation, and a greater law abidingness and social organization than do Europeans and their descendants who average higher scores on these dimensions than do Africans and their decendants. To explain this pattern I propose a gene-based evolutionary theory. My book, *Race, Evolution and Behavior,* reviews the theory and many of the data sets." See www.ssc. uwo.ca/psychology/faculty/rushton.html, September 13, 2002. Also, see Barry Mehler, "Race Science and the Pioneer Fund" at www.ferris.edu/isar/Institut/pioneer/search.htm, September 13, 2002.

458. Famous for his attack on Head Start in the *Harvard Education Review*. In that article Jensen wrote, "Is there a danger that current welfare policies, unaided by eugenic foresight, could lead to the genetic enslavement of a substantial segment of our population?" Arthur R. Jensen, "How Much Can We Boost IQ and Scholastic Achievement?" *Harvard Education Review,* 39, no. 1 (1969), 95. See also Barry Mehler, "The Roots of the I.Q. Debate: Eugenics and Social Control," at www.ferris.edu/isar/archives/mehler/IQ.htm (March 4, 2002).

459. CIR website, www.cir-usa.org/bios.html (December 28, 2001).

460. CIR 2001 IRS Form 990.

461. Jonathan Tilove, "Divided They Stand; Affirmative Action; GOP Pulls Back on Delicate Issue," *Atlanta Journal and Constitution,* March 3, 1996, C2.

462. Cynthia Barnett, "Broad Takes on Tough Issue," *News and Observer* (Raleigh, NC), December 8, 1997, A1.

463. Michael Greve, "Segregation, 90s Style, and How to Fight It," *Weekly Standard,* December 25, 1995, 31.

464. Frances Grandy Taylor, "Ruling on College Admissions May Eventually Be Felt in State," *Hartford Courant,* April 7, 1996, C1.

465. Diaz, "Mischief Makers."

466. Rochelle L. Stanfield, "The Wedge Issue," *National Journal,* April 1, 1995, 790.

467. Rochelle L. Stanfield, "Too Hot to Touch," *National Journal,* May 4, 1996, 986.

468. In 1990, CIR legally assisted Michael Levin, a tenured professor of philosophy at the City University of New York. Levin had claimed in a series of articles, among other things, that, "It has been amply confirmed over the last several decades that, on average, (B)lacks are significantly less intelligent than (W)hites." When CUNY officials took steps to revoke Levin's tenure, and created "shadow" sections of his courses to shield students who were offended by his views, CIR sued on Levin's behalf. A federal appeals court eventually held that the university had violated Levin's right of free speech and proscribed any further action against him. Diaz, "Mischief Makers."

469. Diaz, "Mischief Makers."

470. CIR 2001 IRS Form 990. See its Winter 2000 Docket Report, at www.cir-usa.org/articles/winter2000_dr.pdf.

471. David Segal, "Putting Affirmative Action on Trial; D.C. Public Interest Law Firm Scores Victories in War on Preferences," *Washington Post,* February 20, 1998, A1.

472. *Coalition for Econ. Equity v. Wilson.* 122 F.3d 692 (9th Cir. 1997), *stay denied,* 521 U.S. 1141 (1997), *cert. denied,* 522 U.S. 963 (1997).

473. *R.A.V. v. City of St. Paul,* 505 U.S. 377 (1992).

474. These materials can be found on CIR's website, at www.cir-usa.org/recent_cases/michigan.html.

475. John Schwartz, "FCC Unveils New Rules on Hiring; Broadcasters Must Have Outreach Program for Women, Minorities," *Washington Post,* January 21, 2000, E1. Pat Robertson and Jay Sekulow's American Center for Law and Justice also weighed in with an

amicus brief supporting the Lutheran Church-Missouri Synod position. *Lutheran Church-Missouri Synod v. FCC,* 332 U.S. App. DC 165 (1998).

476. David Segal, "Putting Affirmative Action on Trial; DC Public Interest Law Firm Scores Victories in War on Preferences," *Washington Post,* February 20, 1998, A1.

477. CIR has also been active in taking on the rights of Native Americans. CIR defended a professor in the education department at the University of Alaska who had been charged with arguing before the local Chamber of Commerce that university professors were under "equity pressure" to graduate native students who were often inadequately trained for teaching careers. Michael S. Greve and Joseph A. Shea, "Feds PC Crusade Imperils Academic Freedom," *Connecticut Law Tribune,* February 15, 1993, 20.

478. Kolbo persuaded Maslon, Edelman's chair, the prominent appellate lawyer David Herr, to join him in working with CIR on the case. Carter, "On a Roll(Back)."

479. *Brzonkala v. Morrison,* 528 U.S. 1044 (1999). Jan Vertefeuille, "Testing the Legal Limits: A Federal Judge in Roanoke Is Being Asked to Decide the Constitutionality of the Violence Against Women Act," *Times & World News* (Roanoke, VA), March 24, 1996, p. A1; and Laurence Hammack, "Judge Dismisses Suit against Tech's Morrison in Student Rape Case," *Virginian-Pilot* (Norfolk, VA), July 30, 1996, B1.

480. Brooke A. Masters, "Appeals Court Rejects Part of Gender-Violence Act: U.S. Law Ruled Invalid in Virginia Rape Suit," *Washington Post,* March 6, 1999, A1.

481. *Rosenberger v. Rector & Visitors of the University of Virginia,* 515 U.S. 819 (1995). Dennis Cauchon and Tony Mauro, "Case May Redraw Church-State Lines," *USA Today,* February 27, 1995, A2.

482. W. John Moore, "A Little Group Makes Big Law," *National Journal,* November 15, 1997, 2323.

483. Leslie Alan Horvitz, "Public-Interest Law Center Fights Political Correctness," *Insight,* November 6, 1995, 16.

484. Jay Mathews, "Use of Testers to Fight Bias Stirs Backlash," *Washington Post,* December 14, 1992, E1. In this case they also received assistance from Kirkland and Ellis.

485. Elsa C. Arnett, "Labor Decisions Seen as Next Battleground," *News and Observer* (Raleigh, NC), November 22, 1997, A18.

486. Anne Kornhauser, "The Right versus the Correct: Free-Market Firm Sees Campuses as Fertile Battleground," *Legal Times,* April 29, 1991, 1; Paul Feldman, "Group's Funding of Immigration Measure Assailed," *Los Angeles Times,* September 10, 1994, B3.

487. Available at www.cir-usa.org/handbook.html.

488. Ethan Bronner, "Conservatives Open Drive against Affirmative Action," *New York Times,* January 26, 1999, A10.

489. This principle, "private citizens' rights to deal *or not deal* with other private citizens" (emphasis added) was articulated on the CIR website for some time (for example, at www.wdn.com/cir/cr-aa.htm on February 20, 1998), then subsequently rephrased to read "'private citizens' right to deal with other private citizens without government scrutiny"(at www.wdn.com/cir/cr-aa.htm on March 30, 1999; document source information indicates the document was changed on March 5, 1999).

490. Linda Himelstein, "'It Has Been a Nightmare'; Ruefully, Maguire Readies His Legal Defense," *American Lawyer Newspapers Group Inc.,* April 22, 1991, 12.

491. Saundra Torry, "Affirmative Action a Flash Point at GU; Law Students Jam Meeting to Decry Article as Racist," *Washington Post,* April 17, 1991, D1.

492. *Hurley v. Irish-American Gay, Lesbian and Bisexual Group,* 515 U.S. 557 (1995).

493. Roger K. Newman, "Public-Interest Firms Crop Up on the Right; Suits with Agendas," *National Law Journal,* August 26, 1996, A1.

494. Stephen Goode, "Conservative Legal Eagles Fight for Individual Rights," *Insight,* January 11, 1999, 21.

495. Kornhauser, "The Right versus the Correct."

496. Davidson Goldin, "Law Center Wages a Fight against Political Correctness," *New York Times*, August 13, 1995, A28.

497. Diaz, "Mischief Makers."

498. Randolph Foundation IRS Form 990.

499. Olin Foundation, 2000 IRS Form 990.

500. Lynde and Harry Bradley Foundation 2000 *Annual Report*.

501. Sarah Scaife Foundation, 2000 IRS Form 990.

502. CIR, 2000 IRS Form 990. See also Goode, "Conservative Legal Eagles Fight for Individual Rights."

503. Carter, "On a Roll(Back),"

504. Goldin, "Law Center Wages a Fight against Political Correctness."

505. Wilson, "Washington's Movers and Shakers; Rightists."

506. Diaz, "Mischief Makers."

507. Federal Document Clearing House, Congressional Testimony, July 19, 1994, Senate Environment/Clean Water, Fisheries and Wildlife Endangered Species Act Reauthorization.

508. Michael S. Greve, *The Demise of Environmentalism in American Law* (Washington, D.C.: AEI Press, 1996), vii. Greve thanks two noted affirmative action opponents for reviewing the manuscript—Richard A. Epstein and Michael Rosman (of CIR), as well as Leonard Leo, now vice president of the Federalist Society in charge of its Lawyers Division. Publication of the book was made possible by the Paul F. Oreffice Fund for Legal and Governmental Studies at AEI. Paul Oreffice (1927–1983) was chair of the board of the Dow chemical company.

509. CIR website, www.wdn.com/cir/bios.htm (March 18, 1999), McDonald profile.

510. Diaz, "Mischief Makers."

511. CIR website, www.wdn.com/cir/ (March 18, 1999), McDonald profile.

512. David Crook, "ABC Hit with a Second 'Slanting' Complaint," *Los Angeles Times*, January 15, 1985, part 6, 1; "'We're Not Novices,' Says ALF; ABC Again Targeted in Fairness Doctrine Complaint," *Communications Daily*, January 15, 1985, 1; Eleanor Randolph, "FCC Permits U.S. to File against Media; Complaint CIA Filed about ABC Rejected," *Washington Post*, July 13, 1985, A1.

513. CIR website, www.wdn.com/cir/ (February 23, 1999); Institute for the Study of Academic Racism website, ibid.

514. Along with Michael Rosman of the Center for Individual Rights and Manuel S. Klausner of Los Angeles. See *Coalition for Econ. Equity v. Wilson*, 122 F.3d. 692 (9th Cir. 1997).

515. *Lee v. Weisman*, 505 U.S. 577 (1992).

516. *FEC v. NRA. Political Victory Fund*, 513 U.S. 88 (1994).

517. *DOC v. United States House of Representatives*, 525 U.S. 316 (1999).

518. Martindale-Hubbell website, lawyers.martindale.com (March 18, 1999).

519. David Segal, "Putting Affirmative Action on Trial; DC Public Interest Law Firm Scores Victories in War on Preferences," *Washington Post*, February 20, 1998 A1.

520. CIR website, www.wdn.com/cir/ (February 23, 1999).

521. CIR website, www.cir-usa.org/bios.html (December 29, 2001).

522. Emily Barker et al., "The Public Sector 45," *American Lawyer*, January 1997/February 1997, 64ff.

523. *Columbia Union College v. Clarke*, 159 F.3d. 151 (4th Cir. 1998).

524. CIR website, www.cir-usa.org/bios.html (December 29, 2001).

525. Mellor was the former head of the Pacific Research Institute, which received $150,000 from the Sarah Scaife Foundation and $75,000 from the Bradley Foundation in

2000. Sarah Scaife Foundation 2000 IRS Form 990; Bradley Foundation 2000 *Annual Report.*

526. Clint Bolick, *The Affirmative Action Fraud* (Washington, D.C.: Cato Institute, 1996).

527. Steven A. Holmes, "Political Right's Point Man on Race." *New York Times,* November 15, 1997, 24.

528. Leslie Wayne, "Pulling the Wraps off Koch Industries," *New York Times,* November 20, 1994, C1.

529. Cato Institute website, www.cato.org/about/timeline.html; www.cato.org/people/people.html#boarddir.

530. Reason Foundation letterhead, 1997.

531. Institute for Justice website, www.instituteforjustice.org (November 19, 1997).

532. Institute for Justice IRS Form 990s, 1997-1998, 2000-2001.

533. David H. Koch Charitable Foundation IRS Form 990s. 1999, 2000.

534. Charles G. Koch Charitable Foundation 2000 IRS Form 990.

535. Institute for Justice, 1999 IRS Form 990 (through June 2000). Also, Chip Mellor, "The Magnificent Seven: IJ's Board of Directors," *Liberty & Law* (Institute for Justice), 8, no. 1 (February 1999): 4–5.

536. Foundation Center Grants Database, 1997.

537. Philanthropy Roundtable, 1999 IRS Form 990.

538. Institute for Justice, "IJ's Financials: The Cost of Justice," IJ website, www.instituteforjustice.org/ (July 31, 1997). The Institute for Justice "absolutely won't take gay rights cases," says Clint Bolick. "Our support there is really divided. We won't take something that won't sell in the public arena." Roger K. Newman, "Public-Interest Firms Crop Up on the Right: Suits with Agendas," *National Law Journal*, August 26, 1996, A1.

539. Federalist Society Civil Rights Practice Group webpage, practice group executive committee contact information, at www.fed-soc.org/Publications/practicegroupnewsletters/civilrights/contacts.htm (December 24, 2001).

540. Richard Morin and Claudia Deane, "The Ideas Industry," *Washington Post*, July 24, 2001, A19.

541. Bolick, *The Affirmative Action Fraud*, 42.

542. Nancy E. Roman, "Senate, House to Mull Ban on Preferences," *Washington Times,* June 18, 1997, A1.

543. Stefancic and Delgado, *No Mercy*, 46.

544. Nina J. Easton, "Welcome to the Clint Bolick Revolution," *Los Angeles Times Magazine*, April 20, 1997, 12.

545. See above. The Denver-based Mountain States Legal Foundation was underwritten by conservative western businessmen and first led by James Watt, former Reagan administration secretary of the interior. Watt was the most controversial member of Reagan's first cabinet (every major conservation group and forty members of Congress called for his resignation). Like Reagan, Watt was bent on reducing federal government power and driven by a conservative Christian zeal. As his friend Wyoming Senator Alan Simpson attested, he was "convinced he has God on his side."Kurt Anderson, "Always Right and Ready to Fight; with James Watt in Charge, the Interior Department Means Business," *Time,* August, 23, 1982, 26. Watt once described his affirmative action appointments to an advisory panel on coal leasing: They included "a black, a woman, two Jews and a cripple." "News and Views: The Apostle of Racial Cleansing in Higher Education," editorial, *Journal of Blacks in Higher Education,* January 31, 1998.

546. Landmark Legal Foundation vigorously challenged Kansas City's court-ordered school desegregation effort on behalf of some taxpayers in the mid-1990s. Landmark Legal Foundation press release, "Landmark Legal Foundation to Assist Taxpayers in

Desegregation Follow-up," *PR Newswire*, September 6, 1995. This issue figured prominently in the contested confirmation of John Ashcroft for attorney general in January 2001, who Landmark Legal's Mark Levin vigorously defended.

547. Jerry Seper, "Probe of Civil Rights Panelist Urged; Wilson's Refusal to Vacate Office Violates Federal Law, Legal Group Says," *Washington Times*, December 20, 2001, A4.

548. Deirdre Davidson, "Conservative Groups to Push Bush," *Legal Times*, January 8, 2001, 12.

549. *United Press International*, September 8, 1982.

550. See David Kennedy's account of how Chip Mellor and Clint Bolick approached him in 1986 for support to start IJ in IJ's newsletter, *Liberty and Law*, 10, no. 2 (March 2001), at www.ij.org/publications/liberty/2001/10%5F2%5F01%5Fc.asp (December 12, 2001).

551. "Human Faces, Cutting Edge Cases," IJ leaflet, 1999.

552. Institute for Justice website, www.instituteforjustice.org (January 20, 1998). For a discussion of libertarianism and the trends within it, see Jean Hardisty, "Libertarianism and Civil Society: The Romance of Free Market Capitalism," *Public Eye* (Spring 1998.)

553. Institute for Justice website, www2.ij.org/profile/body.shtml, March 28, 2002.

554. Talk hosted by the Manhattan Institute at the Harvard Club, New York, January 27, 1999.

555. *Jackson. v. Benson*, 578 N.W. 2d 602 (Wis. 1998).

556. Andrea Billups, "Decision Puts Vouchers on Track to High Court," *Washington Times*, March 2, 2001, A4.

557. Vanessa Blum, "National," *Legal Times*, July 1, 2002, 8.

558. Rick Garnett, "Future Church-State Battles Loom," *Wall Street Journal*, July 1, 2002, A15. On Bush's "faith-based initiative," see Lewis C. Daly, "Charitable Choice: The Architecture of a Social Policy Revolution," *IDS Insights*, 2, no. 1 (September 2001), at www.idsonline.org/art/Insights_Vol02Iss01.pdf.

559. Tony Mauro, "Court Seems Ready to Uphold Voucher Program," *Legal Times*, February 25, 2002, 11. The Institute for Justice's brief in the original Ohio case is available at its website, www.ij.org/PDF_folder/ohio_choice/USSC_IJ_school_choice.pdf.

560. Terence Moran, "When Clarence Thomas Defied a Judge," *Legal Times*, August 19, 1991, 1. Al Kamen, John M. Goshko, and John E. Yang, "Talking Points," *Washington Post*, May 10, 1990, A29.

561. "Institute for Justice: Consent Decree Allows Teen Challenge to Continue Faith-based Healing," *The Insider*, December/January 1996. *The Insider* is published by the Heritage Foundation. For more on Teen Challenge, see Rob Boston, "Is Faith-Based Better? Critics Ask to See the Proof," *Church and State*, April 2001, at www.au.org/churchstate/cs4012.htm (January 3, 2002).

562. Gregory Stanford, "School Choice Victory Could Prove Hollow," *Milwaukee Journal Sentinel*, June 14, 1998, 1. The Bradley Foundation also paid a share of Starr's legal fees, his job as Whitewater independent counsel notwithstanding. See editorial, "Starring as 'The Partisan,'" *Capital Times* (Madison, WI), November 20, 1998, 12a; Matt Pommer, "Gov Mum on Retaining Starr," *Capital Times* (Madison, WI), June 15, 1998, 3A; and Farai Chideya and Carole Simpson, "Kenneth Starr's Other Jobs," *ABC World News Sunday*, March 1, 1998 [transcript].

563. For a critique of the W-2 program, see the report issued by the Interfaith Conference of Greater Milwaukee, the Center for Economic Development at the University of Wisconsin-Milwaukee, and the Institute for Wisconsin's Future, "Passing the Buck: W-2 and Emergency Services in Milwaukee," December 23, 2001. The report can be found at www.wisconsinsfuture.org/Low%20Wage%20Workers/Passing%20the%20Buck.pdf.

564. Institute for Justice, "Welfare: Right or Blight ? The Legal Battle over Reform," *Litigation Backgrounder*, at www.ij.org/cases/civil/newjerseybk.shtml, July 3, 2002.

565. *Ricketts v. City of New York,* 97 N.Y.2d 639 (2001).

566. Slaughter-House Cases, 83 U.S. (16 Wall) 36 (1873).

567. Institute for Justice, *Litigation Backgrounder*, July 31, 1997, p. 11.

568. Institute for Justice website, www.ij.org/clients/vans/body.shtml.

569. *Brazier Construction co., et al. v. Robert Reich et al.,* No 93-2318 (D.DC)

570. For example, Douglas W. Kmiec, former Pepperdine Law School professor (now dean of Catholic University Law School), formerly of the Office of Legal Counsel under Attorney General Edwin Meese (1985–1989.) See above.

571. Institute for Justice website, www.ij.org/HAN_folder/caj.html (April 2, 1999).

572. The network's title recalls a book, *Human Action*, by one of the key ideologues of an unregulated free market, Ludwig Von Mises.

573. Clint Bolick, "Meet the New Activists," *Liberty and Law,* 6, no. 5 (June 1997), at www.ij.org/Publication_folder/liberty/1997/1_11_97.

574. Lynde and Harry Bradley Foundation, 2000 *Annual Report*. In 1999 it gave $180,000 to IJ; in 1998, $120,000, according to Bradley IRS Form 990s for those years.

575. John M. Olin Foundation, 2000 IRS Form 990. Olin also gave IJ $225,000 in 1999, and $225,000 in 1998 (1999 and 1998 Olin IRS Form 990s).

576. $25,000 in 1999 (Jacqueline Hume Foundation, 1999 IRS Form 990).

577. Sarah Scaife Foundation 2000 IRS Form 990. This foundation also gave IJ $100,000 in 1999, and $75,000 in 1998, according to Scaife 990s for those years.

578. W. Dale Nelson, "Conservatives Complain Bush Hasn't Developed Civil Rights Agenda," *Associated Press*, September 28, 1989.

579. Fellow members include Michael Greve of AEI, Robert Bork (who serves on the policy board of the anti-affirmative action American Civil Rights Union/ACRU along with Linda Chavez and William Bradford Reynolds), former Congressman Bob Barr, Steven Calabresi of the Federalist Society, Kenneth Cribb, C. Boyden Gray, Edwin Meese (who is a director of the ACRU), DC Court of Appeals judge David Sentelle, Phyllis Schlafly, Prof. Richard A. Epstein (see above), and others. The chairman of the board of directors is Adam B. Ross. *Texas Review of Law and Politics,* www.trolp.org/main_pgs/bd_directors/about.htm (January 3, 2002). R. Alex Acosta, who has gone into the Ashcroft Justice Department, was on their steering committee. So was R. Ted Cruz (a former clerk of Judge J. Michael Luttig, widely tipped for a possible Supreme Court appointment by the Bush administration), who was active in the Federalist Society's Religious Liberties Practice Group, and is now director of the Office of Policy Planning of the Federal Trade Commission at the tender age of thirty. Alexandra Starr, "The Way We Live Now: 10-14-01: Phenomenon; The Politics of Love," *New York Times,* October 14, 2001, 34.

580. Ralph Z. Hallow, "Connerly, Others Form Alternative Race Panel," *Washington Times*, April 30, 1998, A1.

581. Clint Bolick, *Changing Course: Civil Rights at the Crossroads.*

582. Clint Bolick, *Unfinished Business: A Civil Rights Strategy for America's Third Century* (San Francisco, Pacific Research Institute, 1991).

583. Clint Bolick, *Grassroots Tyranny: The Limits of Federalism* (Washington, D.C.: Cato Institute, 1993).

584. Clint Bolick, *The Affirmative Action Fraud* (Washington, D.C.: Cato Institute, 1996).

585. Clint Bolick, *Transformation: The Promise and Politics of Empowerment* (Oakland, CA: Institute for Contemporary Studies, 1998).

586. For a rather hagiographic biographical sketch of Bolick, see Easton, *Gang of Five*, 89–110 and passim. See also Steven A. Holmes, "Political Right's Point Man on Race," *New York Times,* November 15, 1997, A24.

587. Bellant, *Old Nazis, the New Right, and the Republican Party,* 104, note 227. This

refers to the Fall 1984 issue of the *Journal of Social, Political and Economic Studies.*

588. Clint Bolick, "Cable Television: An Unnatural Monopoly," *Policy Analysis* no. 34 (Cato: March 13, 1984).

589. *Communications Daily,* March 12, 1984, 6.

590. Douglas Kmiec also knew Bolick when both of them worked at the Reagan Justice Department. Emily Barker et al., "The Public Sector 45," *American Lawyer,* January 1997/February 1997, 64ff.

591. Robert Safian, "Civil Rights, Conservative Style," *American Lawyer* May 1989, 129.

592. W. Dale Nelson, "Conservatives Complain Bush Hasn't Developed Civil Rights Agenda," *Associated Press*, September 28, 1989.

593. Peter Griggs and Daviryne D. McNeill, "Brown v. Barry" *Legal Times*, April 3, 1989, 17.

594. Dawn M. Weyrich, "Short List Rumored for Top Rights Post," *Washington Times,* November 15, 1989.

595. *Inside Washington,* October 7, 1989, 2445.

596. Clint Bolick, "The Supreme Court and Civil Rights: A Challenge for George Bush," *Heritage Foundation Backgrounder,* September 28, 1989.

597. Barker et al., "The Public Sector 45" 64.

598. Safian, "Civil Rights, Conservative Style," 129.

599. Mayer and Abramson, *Strange Justice*, 178.

600. Safian, "Civil Rights, Conservative Style," 129.

601. Bolick later turned up the heat on another critic of Clarence Thomas, during the judge's hearings for nomination to the Supreme Court in 1992. When Angela Wright, another former employee of Thomas at EEOC came forward with a story to corroborate the pattern of sexual harassment suggested by Anita Hill, Thomas's former aide Phyllis Berry and Clint Bolick worked together to push negative stories about Wright into the media. They cast Wright as a slighted admirer of Thomas and a homophobe—allegations she complained were fabrications, but the onslaught was enough to force her out of town. Wright's story "could have killed Clarence Thomas," Ricky Silberman told Mayer and Abramson later. Mayer and Jill, *Strange Justice*, 326.

602. Michael Isikoff, "Power behind the Thrown Nominee: Activist with Scores to Settle," *Washington Post,* June 6, 1993, A11.

603. Michael Isikoff, "Power Behind the Thrown Nominee: Activist with a Score to Settle," *Washington Post,* June 6, 1993, A11.

604. William Powers, "The Dynamics of Personal Destruction," *National Journal*, January 20, 2001. With Guinier's confirmation hearings still at least a month away, minds were already being made up. Orrin Hatch, a conservative senator from Utah, was quoted in the *New York Times* as saying, "She is an architect of a theory of racial preferences that if enacted would push America down the road of racial balkanization." Within a month of the nomination, the American media were telling the public that Guinier was dangerous. For more, see *Contemporary Black Biography*, 1994, vol. 7.

605. Clint Bolick, "Civil Rights Nominee, Quota Clone," *Wall Street Journal,* February 2, 1994.

606. Roger Clegg and Clint Bolick, *Defying the Rule of Law: A Report on the Tenure of Bill Lann Lee, "Acting" Assistant Attorney General for Civil Rights,* February 1999, at Institute for Justice website, www.ij.org/media/lann_lee/bll2.shtml, July 12, 2002. CEO and IJ held a joint press conference on their report at the National Press Club. *Federal News Service*, February 16, 1999.

607. Clint Bolick, appearing on National Public Radio's *Morning Edition,* March 23, 2001. Transcript.

608. Steven A. Holmes, "Political Right's Point Man on Race," *New York Times*,

November 16, 1997, A24.

609. "Editorial," *The Nation*, March 22, 1999, 4.

610. *Institute for Justice*, www.ij.org/staff/mellor.shtml (December 20, 2001).

611. *Inside Energy/with Federal Lands*, January 9, 1984, 5.

612. See Bellant, *The Coors Connection*, 84–90.

613. On Watt's background, see Andersen, "Always Right and Ready to Fight," *Time*, August 23, 1982, 26; and Bellant, *The Coors Connection*, 84–90.

614. Andersen, "Always Right and Ready to Fight."

615. Hodel served as energy secretary from 1982–1985. He was appointed president of the Christian Coalition in 1997, after the departure of Ralph Reed, and subsequently resigned from his Christian Coalition post. Hodel, a member of the Council for National Policy (see above), is former chairman of the Independence Institute, a Colorado-based group producing research to support the movement for private and charter schools and against gun control. Jeff Coors, president of the Coors Foundation, is a member of the board. Hodel also sits on the board of a number of oil and gas marketing companies. For more, see National Education Association, "The Real Story behind Paycheck Protection," (Washington, D.C., September 1998).

616. *Inside Energy,* June 4, 1984.

617. *United Press International*, Regional News (Carson City), September 17, 1985.

618. *Institute for Justice*, www.instituteforjustice.org (June 2, 1998).

619. The Pacific Institute for Public Policy Research was established in 1979 by Anthony Fisher, who also helped establish the Institute for Economic Affairs in London, the Manhattan Institute in New York, the Fraser Institute in Vancouver, B.C., and the National Center for Policy Analysis in Texas. Richard M. Harnett, "Government without Taxes," *United Press International*, September 3, 1986.

620. In 1984 it changed its name to the Pacific Research Institute. The Institute provided testimony before California's Board of Regents on behalf of the California Civil Rights Initiative (Proposition 209). Its funding comes from the Lilly Endowment, the David Koch Charitable Foundation, Charles G. Koch Charitable Foundation, John M. Olin Foundation, Philip M. McKenna Foundation, Earhart, and others. National Education Association, "The Real Story behind Paycheck Protection," 67.

621. San Francisco: Pacific Research Institute, 1986.

622. Mack attempts to show that the need to take care of the poor and to provide essential services such as roads and water are fallacies. Harnett, "Government without Taxes," *United Press International*, September 3, 1986.

623. Ibid.

624. Other officers and trustees of the Earhart Foundation include Dennis L. Bark (chair), Earl I. Heenan, Antony T. Sullivan (secretary and director of programs), Kathleen B. Mason (treasurer), Thomas J. Bray, Ann K. Irish, Paul W. McCracken, Ingrid Merikoski (assistant secretary/program officer), John H. Moore, Robert L. Queller; and Richard A. Ware. Earhart Foundation 2000 IRS Form 990.

625. Biographical data obtained from *Marquis Who's Who in America 1995* (49th edition), vol. 1, 1981.

626. Ann Sweeney, "Richard Earhart, Businessman," *Detroit News*, June 20, 1995, Obituaries.

627. Foundation Center Grants Database, 1997.

628. Jeff Barker, "Judges on Junkets: Conservatives Fund Seminars; 5-Day Getaways at Montana Resorts Focus on 'Takings,'" *Arizona Republic*, May 10, 1988, A1.

629. "The Goldwater Institute and the Federalist Society: Federalism and Judicial Mandates" (transcripts), *Arizona State Law Journal*, Spring 1996.

630. CRC, www2.crcmich.org (March 3, 1999).

631. *Martindale-Hubbell*, lawyers.martindale.com/marhub (March 3, 1999).

632. Ibid., April 5, 1999.

633. Ibid.

634. *Harvey*, 878 F.2d 1235 (10th Cir. 1989), *cert. denied*, 493 U.S. 1074 (1990).

635. *Unified School Dist. v. Epperson*, 583 F.2d 1118 (10th Cir. 1978). *McCarthy v. Burkholder*, 448 F. Supp. 41 (D. Kan. 1978).

636. Robert A. Levy, "The ABA's Public-Financing Scheme," *National Review*, August 9, 2001.

637. On July 16, 1997, he testified against the government's proposed tobacco settlement before the Senate Judiciary Committee (cf. Cato Institute, www.cato.org [March 8, 1999]). On Microsoft, see Bob Levy, "Microsoft Is No Monopoly," *USA Today*, January 14, 1999, 14A.

638. Stephen M. Ryan, "Troops Start to Gather for Microsoft Legal Battle," *Government Computer News*, October 19, 1998, 19.

639. George Mason University website, www.gmu.edu/news (March 9, 1999).

640. Lee Cokorinos and Julie Gerchik, *The Federalist Society and the Challenge to a Democratic Jurisprudence*, briefing paper (New York: Institute for Democracy Studies, January 2001).

641. Julie R. F. Gerchik, "People Are Policy: Timothy Flanigan, Judicial Selection, and the Office of White House Counsel," *IDS Insights*, 2, no. 1 (September 2001), available at www.idsonline.org/publications.html.

642. Federalist Society annual reports, 2000 ànd 1997.

643. Longtime conservative activist Frank Fahrenkopf, Jr. (who is also on the board of directors of the International Republican Institute) is on the Wiegand Foundation board of trustees. E. L. Wiegand Foundation 2000 IRS Form 990.

644. Wiegand Foundation 1998 IRS Form 990 (covering 11/1/98–10/31/99). Wiegand granted the Federalist Society $120,000 in the fiscal year ending October 31, 1998 for the practice groups. The same year it also gave the Institute for Justice over $30,000 for office equipment, Wiegand 1997 IRS Form 990.

645. Federalist Society, *2000 Annual Report*, 26.

646. Charles J. Cooper and Brian W. Jones, "From the Chairman and Editor," *Civil Rights News*, 1, no. 1 (Fall 1996): 2.

647. Federalist Society, Civil Rights Practice Group webpage, www.fed-soc.org/Publications/practicegroupnewsletters/civilrights/civilrights.htm (December 24, 2001).

648. Federalist Society, Civil Rights Practice Group executive committee contact information list, www.fed-soc.org/Publications/practicegroupnewsletters/civilrights/civilrights.htm (December 24, 2001).

649. Vanessa Blum, "When Client Loyalty Trumps Political Fervor: Choosing Electoral Sides Is a Given at Many DC Law Firms, but Conflicts Have Kept Some on the Sidelines in Florida," *Legal Times*, November 27, 2000, 17.

650. Cooper bio at Cooper and Kirk website, www.cooperkirk.com/bio_cooper.html (December 24, 2001). The Judicial Conference of the U.S. is a body of twenty-seven federal judges composed of the chief justice of the United States, who serves as the presiding officer; the chief judges of the thirteen courts of appeal; the chief judge of the Court of International Trade; and twelve district judges from the regional circuits who are chosen by the judges of their circuit to serve terms of three years. The Judicial Conference meets twice yearly to consider policy issues affecting the federal courts, to make recommendations to Congress on legislation affecting the judicial system, to propose amendments to the federal rules of practice and procedure, and to consider the administrative problems of the courts. See www.uscourts.gov/understanding_courts/89914.htm.

651. Martindale-Hubbell website, lawyers.martindale.com (March 4, 1999).

652. Ibid.

653. Among the Supreme Court opinions Rehnquist authored during Cooper's term as clerk was a scathing dissent in a case permitting a voluntary affirmative action plan in a steel company's in-plant craft training program, *United Steelworkers v. Weber*, 443 U.S. 193 (1979).

654. Robert Pear, "Study Urges Fight for States' Power," *New York Times*, November 9, 1986, 1.

655. Kmiec, *The Attorney General's Lawyer*, 153. Kmiec was Cooper's deputy and successor as head of the Office of Legal Counsel in the Justice Department.

656. Aaron Freiwald, "Ten Years of Upheaval: William Bradford Reynolds," *American Lawyer*, March 1989, 147.

657. Federalist Society, Civil Rights Practice Group executive committee list, www.fed-soc.org/Publications/practicegroupnewsletters/civilrights/civilrights.htm (December 24, 2001.)

658. Jake Tapper, *Down and Dirty: The Plot to Steal the Presidency* (Boston: Little, Brown, 2001), 467–476. Also, Petition for Writ of Certiorari on Behalf of Petitioner George W. Bush, *Bush v. Palm Beach Co. Canvassing Bd., et al.*

659. Jeffrey Toobin, *Too Close to Call: The Thirty-Six Day Battle to Decide the 2000 Election* (New York: Random House, 2001), 95-96.

660. *Lamprecht v. FCC*, No. 92-1586, *1994 U.S. App. LEXIS 13757 (DC Cir. Feb. 9, 1994).* "Promoting Diversity for Diversity's Sake," *Legal Times,* July 15, 1991, 10.

661. *Harding v. Gray*, 9 F.3d 150 (DC Cir. 1993).

662. Robert Ruth, "OSU to Drop Minority Set-Aside Program," *Columbus Dispatch*, March 27, 1996, 1A.

663. *Board of Educ. v. Grumet,* 512 U.S. 687, 689 (1994). *Amicus* briefs in the case also were filed by, among others, Pat Robertson's American Center for Law and Justice (by its chief counsel, Jay Sekulow), and the Christian Legal Society (by Michael McConnell, who was nominated by President George W. Bush for a seat on the Federal 10th Circuit Court of Appeals).

664. *DOC v. United States House of Representatives*, 525 U.S. 316 (1999).

665. Kmiec, *The Attorney General's Lawyer*, 83. Also, see Clegg's biography at the CEO website, www.ceousa.org/html/staff.html, July 12, 2002.

666. Julie R. F. Gerchik, "People Are Policy: Timothy Flanigan, Judicial Selection, and the Office of White House Counsel," *IDS Insights,* 2, no. 1 (September 2001), available at www.idsonline.org/publications.html.

667. Gail Heriot, "The Truth about Preferences," *Weekly Standard*, July 21, 1997, 13; Eugene Volokh, "The California Civil Rights Initiative: An Interpretive Guide," *U.C.L.A. Law Review,* no. 44 (1997): 1335–1403, at 1367 n. 101.

668. *Foster v. Love*, 522 U.S. 67 (1997).

669. *Jordahl v. Democratic Party*, 122 F.3d 192 (4th Cir. 1997), *cert. denied*, 522 U.S. 1077 (1998).

670. Nelson Lund, "The Second Amendment, Political Liberty, and the Right to Self-Preservation," 39 *Ala. L. Rev.* 103 (1987).

671. Tom Wood, "How Honest Is the Debate over the California Civil Rights Initiative," *Civil Rights News* 1, no. 1 (Fall 1996); Hans Bader, "The California Civil Rights Initiative Goes to Court," *Civil Rights News* 1, no. 2 (Spring 1997); Ward Connerly, "The American Civil Rights Institute: Taking C.C.R.I. to the National Stage," *Civil Rights News* 1, no. 2 (Spring 1997).

672. Federalist Society Civil Rights Practice Group webpage, www.fed-soc.org /Publications/practicegroupnewsletters/civilrights/news2001.htm (December 24, 2001).

673. Clint Bolick, "Fighting a Left Turn on Rights: The Battle against the Bill Lann Lee

Nomination," *Civil Rights News* 2, no. 1 (Spring 1998).

674. Federalist Society Civil Rights Practice Group webpage, www.fed-soc.org /Publications/practicegroupnewsletters/civilrights/contacts.htm, December 24, 2001.

675. At the November 1998 Federalist Society National Lawyers Convention, the Civil Rights Practice Group presented panels on "The Americans with Disabilities Act: A New Litigation Explosion?" and "State Civil Rights Initiatives: Where Do We Go from Here?"

676. This is the same Lewis Powell who, ironically, as an associate justice of the Supreme Court would later provide the controlling opinion in the precedent-setting affirmative action case, *Bakke v. Regents of the University of California,* which the Pacific Legal Foundation and others have been seeking to overturn ever since.

677. Oliver A. Houck, "With Charity for All," 93 *Yale L.J.* 1415 (1984).

678. Ibid.

679. Ibid.

680. Ibid.

681. Ibid.

682. Ibid.

683. Lisa Baertlein, "Enlisting in Property Rights Fight; A California-based Legal Foundation with a Broad Conservative Agenda Is Setting up Shop in South Florida to Help Landowners Fight Government Actions That Impinge on Land Use," *Broward Daily Business Review,* April 11, 1997, A5.

684. Houck, "With Charity for All."

685. Joseph F. Garcia, "Rightist Conspiracy? Maybe Not; a Better Word Would Be 'Industry': A Fortune Has Funded Many Conservative Obsessions. Clinton May Simply Be the Latest Scapegoat." *Philadelphia Inquirer,* March 7, 1998, A11.

686. Pacific Legal was in good company; other early Scaife grantees included the Heritage Foundation and later the American Enterprise Institute. Robert G. Kaiser and Ira Chinoy, "How Scaife's Money Powered a Movement," *Washington Post,* May 2, 1999, A1.

687. *Alliance for Justice,* "Justice for Sale," 1993, 12.

688. James W. Singer, "Liberal Public Interest Law Firms Face Budgetary, Ideological Challenges," *National Journal,* 11, no. 49 (December 8, 1979): 2052.

689. Meese has been a fellow at the Hoover Institute and the Heritage Foundation, past president of the Right's Council for National Policy, and has served on the boards of Capital Research Center, Landmark Legal Foundation, and the Federalist Society.

690. "Pacific Legal Foundation," *National Heritage 2020,* www.supportnh2020. com/plf.shtml (December 1, 2001); Mike Feinsilber, "Business-Backed Public Law Firms Accused of Spurning IRS Curbs," *Associated Press,* November 20, 1984.

691. Mary Thornton, "Reagan Wants Conservatives to Direct Legal Services," *Washington Post,* November 21, 1981, A8.

692. Pacific Legal Foundation, www.pacificlegal.org (December 5, 2001).

693. David Wagner, "When Conservatives Lay Down the Law," *Insight on the News,* August 10, 1998, 31.

694. Garcia, "Rightist Conspiracy?" *Philadelphia Inquirer,* March 7, 1998, p. A11.

695. In addition to designing Reagan's communications strategy for both his successful 1980 and 1984 presidential campaigns, Deaver & Hannaford also did publicity for the Institute for Contemporary Studies, a conservative think tank.

696. This office was opened in order to battle against the Public Access Shoreline decision by the Hawaii Supreme Court, which required all land use decisions to take into account the right traditionally recognized in Hawaii of people to hunt and gather.

697. "Frequently Asked Questions," Pacific Legal Foundation, www.pacificlegal. org/miscell/plf-ques.htm (November 13, 2001); James W. Singer, "Liberal Public Interest Law Firms Face Budgetary, Ideological Challenges.," *The National Journal* 11, no. 49

(December 8, 1979): 2052.

698. Houck, "With Charity for All."

699. Ibid.

700. In *California Teachers Ass'n v. Davis*, 64 F. Supp. 2d 945 (C.D. Cal. 1999), *aff'd*, 263 F.3d 888 (9th Cir. 2001), *amended by* 271 F. 3d 1141 (9th Cir. 2001), PLF intervened on behalf of parents and the Center for Equal Opportunity. Although the question arose in the context of an English-only policy, PLF's *amicus* brief in *Sandoval v. Hagan*, 268 F.3d 1065 (11th Cir. 2001) involved a fundamental challenge to the scope of disparate impact theory as applied to Title VI of the Civil Rights Act of 1964. Pacific Legal Foundation, *Action Report: Supreme Court Rejects Private Challenge to Alabama English-Only Policy* (April 27, 2001), available at www.pacificlegal.org/actionreport/2001/ar4-27a.htm. In yet another precedent-setting case, the Supreme Court held that a lawsuit based on disparate impact theory may not be brought by private parties under Title VI of the Civil Rights Act. Pacific Legal Foundation, *Federal Judge Upholds Parental Enforcement Provision of English Immersion Initiative (Proposition 227)* (September. 15, 1999) available at www.pacific legal.org/press_releases/pr-cta.htm (September 15, 1999); Baertlein, "Enlisting in Property Rights Fight."

701. "Pac-Legal-Foundation; Right to Challenge Affirmative Action Plan Upheld," *Business Wire,* June 12, 1989.

702. *Associated Gen. Contractors v. Secretary of Commerce of United States Dep't of Commerce,* 459 F. Supp. 766 (C.D. Cal. 1978), *vacated,* 438 U.S. 909 (1998).

703. Houck, "With Charity for All."

704. Kaiser and Chinoy, "How Scaife's Money Powered a Movement."

705. The Fifth Amendment states, in part, "nor shall private property be taken for public use without just compensation."

706. David Helvarg, "Legal Assault on the Environment: 'Property Rights' Movement" *The Nation,* 260, no. 4 (January 30, 1995): 126.

707. Douglas Kendall and Charles P. Lord, "The Takings Project: A Critical Analysis and Assessment of the Progress So Far," 25 *B.C. Envtl. Aff. L. Rev.* 509, Spring 1998.

708. "Frequently Asked Questions," www.pacificlegal.org/miscell/plf-ques.htm (November 13, 2001).

709. Ibid.

710. "Special Projects," www.pacificlegal.org/index/projects.htm (December 10, 2001).

711. "Regents' Risky Vote," *Orange County Register,* May 23, 2001, commentary.

712. "Race and Sex Preferences Continue Despite Proposition 209; Pacific Legal Foundation Discloses Violators and Unveils Whistle-Blower Project," www.pacific legal.org/press_releases/prendb.htm (May 8, 2001).

713. "Q&A on Operation End Bias, PLF's Campaign to Enforce Proposition 209," www.pacificlegal.org/endbias/209qa.htm (November 2001).

714. "PLF Unleashes Operation End Bias; Becomes *de facto* Enforcer of Prop. 209," www.pacificlegal.org/actionreport/ar5-17c.htm (May 17, 2001).

715. Harold Johnson [PLF attorney], "Governments Cling to Policies of Racial Bias," *Daily News of Los Angeles,* May 20, 2001, V1.

716. "PLF Unleashes Operation End Bias; Becomes *de facto* Enforcer of Prop. 209."

717. www.endbias.org.

718. "Race and Sex Preferences Continue Despite Proposition 209."

719. "A.G. Gets Failing Grade for Prop. 209 Enforcement; PLF Calls for End to Racially Divisive Programs," www.pacificlegal.org/endbias/pr_5thanv.htm (November 5, 2001).

720. "Race and Sex Preferences Continue Despite Proposition 209."

721. Ibid.

722. "PLF's Proposition 209 Cases," www.pacificlegal.org/endbias/209cases.htm (November 2001).

723. *Regents of the University of California v. Bakke,* 438 U.S. 265 (1978).

724. Mary Thornton, "Reagan Wants Conservatives to Direct Legal Services," *Washington Post,* November 21, 1981, A8.

725. "Pacific Legal Foundation Sues Sacramento Municipal Utility District for Violating Antibias Initiative—Proposition 209," www.pacificlegal.org/press_releases/pr-smud.htm (June 20, 2000).

726. "Q&A on Operation End Bias."

727. "A.G. Gets Failing Grade for Prop. 209 Enforcement."

728. Ibid.

729. Ibid.

730. "Pacific Legal Foundation Charges That Los Angeles County Imposes Illegal Race and Sex Preferences, Violating Proposition 209," www.pacificlegal.org/press_ releases/prla.htm (May 8, 2001). See also County of Los Angeles, Office of Affirmative Action Compliance (OAAC) website, oaac.co.la.ca.us/construcontr.htm (March 12, 2002).

731. "Pacific Legal Foundation Says East Bay Municipal Utility District Imposes Illegal Race and Sex Preferences, Violating Proposition 209," www.pacificlegal.org /press_releases/prembud.htm (May 8, 2001).

732. *Hi-Voltage Wire Works, Inc. v. City of San Jose,* 24 Cal 4th 537 (2000).

733. "Proposition 209 Vindicated in Landmark Test Case," www.pacificlegal.org /press_releases/pr-209wi.htm (November 13, 2001).

734. "Pacific Legal Foundation Sues City and County of San Francisco for Violating Proposition 209 in Awarding Public Contracts," www.pacificlegal.org/press_releases/pr-crl.htm (September 12, 2000).

735. *Cheresnik v. City and County of S. F.,* 248 F.3d 1170 (9th Cir. 2001).

736. "Pacific Legal Foundation Sues City and County of San Francisco Charging S.F. Airport's Employment Rules Violate Proposition 209," www.pacificlegal.org/press_re-leases/pr-chres.htm (September 7, 1999).

737. "Pacific Legal Foundation Sues Sacramento Municipal Utility District for Violating Antibias Initiative—Proposition 209," www.pacificlegal.org/press_releases/pr-smud.htm (June 20, 2000).

738. Pacific Legal Foundation press release, "Pacific Legal Foundation Scores Victory in Prop 209 Challenge; SMUD's Race- and Gender-Based Preference Ruled Illegal," January 11, 2002, www.pacificlegal.org/press_releases/pr-smudvictory.htm.

739. *Connerly v. State Personnel Bd.,* 92 Cal. App. 4th 16 (Cal. App. 31 Dist., 2001).

740. "PLF Applauds Appellate Court Ruling against Race Preferences in Hiring by State Government and Community Colleges," www.pacificlegal.org/press_release/pr-con-nerly-win.htm (September 4, 2001).

741. *Katuria Smith, et. al. v. Univ. of Wash. Law Sch.,* 532 U.S. 1051 (2001).

742. *Regents of the Univ. of Cal. v. Bakke,* 438 U.S. 912 (1978).

743. "Diversity' Not a Compelling Interest Justifying Race Preferences," www.pacifi-clegal.org/actionreport/ar4-27b.htm (May 17, 2001).

744. *Smith,* 532 U.S. 1051.

745. "Gilroy Unified School District's Race and Gender Balancing Policies Come under Fire; PLF Files Prop. 209 Action," www.pacificlegal.org/press_releases/pr-gilroy.htm (November 9, 2001).

746. Ibid.

747. "Program for Judicial Awareness," www.pacificlegal.org/miscell/pjashort.htm (October 30, 2001).

748. Ibid.

749. "$9,500 to Be Awarded for Graduate Writing Excellence," www.pacificlegal.org/miscell/pjatopics.htm (October 30, 2001).

750. Ibid.

751. Baertlein, "Enlisting in Property Rights Fight."

752. "Frequently Asked Questions."

753. Kendall and Lord, "The Takings Project."

754. Robert P. King, "California Property Rights Crusaders Move in on Florida Growth Laws," *Palm Beach Post,* May 29, 1997, 1A.

755. *Palazzolo v. Rhode Island,* 533 U.S. 606 (2001).

756. "Mission," www.pacificlegal.org/miscell/mission.htm (November 13, 2001).

757. *Nollan et al. v. California Coastal Commission,* 483 U.S. 825 (1987). "Pacific Legal Foundation," *Media Transparency,* www.mediatransparency.org/search_results /info_on_any_recipient.asp?760 (December 4, 2001).

758. Kaiser and Chinoy, "How Scaife's Money Powered a Movement."

759. James W. Singer, "Liberal Public Interest Law Firms Face Budgetary, Ideological Challenges," *National Journal,* 11, no. 49 (December 8, 1979): 2052; Nancy Blodgett, "The Ralph Naders of the Right," *American Bar Association Journal,* 70, no. 71 (May 1984).

760. Wallace Turner, "Possible Chief for Law Unit Stirs Concern," *New York Times,* November 20, 1981, A25.

761. "Property Rights Law Firm Opens Hawaii Office, Eyes Florida," *A Clear View: Clearinghouse on Environmental Advocacy and Research,* www.ewg.org/pub/home /clear/view/CV_Vol4_No7.html#U1 (May 6, 1996).

762. Lisa Baertlein, "Property Rights Group Presses Fund-raising Effort," *Broward Daily Business Review,* April 23, 1997, A1.

763. Baertlein, "Enlisting in Property Rights Fight."

764. King, "California Property Rights Crusaders Move In."

765. "'Little Guy' Is a Front," *Palm Beach Post,* July 15, 1997, 1A.

766. Baertlein, "Property Rights Group Presses Fund-raising Effort."

767. Pacific Legal Foundation, IRS Form 990, calendar year 2000, 1.

768. Ibid., 1.

769. "Pacific Legal Foundation," *Media Transparency,* www.mediatransparency.org/ search_results/info_on_any_recipient.asp?760 (December 4, 2001).

770. "History of the Takings Project; Creating the Courts, Packing the Benches, Greasing the Wheels," *Community Rights Counsel,* www.communityrights.org/history.html (December 8, 2001).

771. Sarah Scaife Foundation 1999 IRS Form 990.

772. John M. Olin Foundation 1999 IRS Form 990.

773. John M. Olin Foundation 2000 IRS Form 990.

774. Castle Rock Foundation 1998 IRS Form 990.

775. Castle Rock Foundation 1999 IRS Form 990.

776. Weyerhaeuser Company Foundation 1999 IRS Form 990.

777. Weyerhaeuser Company Foundation 2000 IRS Form 990.

778. "M.J. Murdock Charitable Trust – Grants Awarded 2000," www.murdock-trust.org/grants_awarded/education2000.html (December 6, 2001).

779. "Pacific Legal Foundation Changes Leadership," *Business Wire,* January 18, 1995.

780. Ibid.

781. Turner, "Possible Chief for Law Unit Stirs Concern."

782. Ibid.

783. Mary Thornton, "Reagan Wants Conservatives to Direct Legal Services," *Washington Post,* November 21, 1981, A8.

784. Michael Fumento, "Leaders and Success: Pacific Legal's Zumbrun; He's Fighting a Lonely Battle to Bolster Property Rights," *Investor's Business Daily,* 1992, reproduced at www.fumento.com/zumbrun.html, March 29, 2002.

785. Turner, "Possible Chief for Law Unit Stirs Concern."

786. Ibid.

787. Stuart Taylor, Jr., "Collusion Request Laid to Law Firm," *New York Times,* October 13, 1981, B8.

788. Ibid. At the time, William "Chip" Mellor of the Institute for Justice was still an attorney for Mountain States Legal Foundation, and represented Mountain States in this lawsuit.

789. Irvin Molotsky, "Reagan Chooses Lawyer as Chief of Legal Aid Agency for the Poor," *New York Times,* January 1, 1982, 8. Olson's writings have been published by the Cato Institute and the American Enterprise Institute (see his biography at www.wjopc.com/aboutus/wjo.html [February 26, 2002]). He has also served as tax counsel to the Protect the Family Foundation, Charles E. Shepard, "Aiding 'Rescue' May Cost Benefactor Tax Status; Nonprofit Group Helped Pay Protesters' Debt," *Washington Post,* November 24, 1991, A21. PFF is run by right-winger Larry Pratt, who founded English First, a spin-off of U.S. English, which is one of the key groups involved in the English Only movement, Stefancic and Delgado, *No Mercy,* 15–17. Larry Pratt is currently executive director of Gun Owners of America.

790. "William J. Olson, P.C.," *Martindale-Hubbell Law Directory,* 2001.

791. Eric Grant, also a past Pacific Legal Foundation attorney, was the chairman of the Land Use Regulation Subcommittee of the Environmental Law Practice Group of the Federalist Society in 1998 and 1999 and has written for its newsletter. In addition, James Burling, one of PLF's top property rights attorneys, has written several articles for the Environmental Law Practice Group newsletter.

792. Pacific Legal Foundation 2000 IRS Form 990.

793. Ibid.

794. McCarthy was a member of Ronald Reagan's 1980–1981 presidential transition team. In 1981, he became a consultant for the White House's Office of Policy Development. Since 1988, McCarthy has served on the Pepperdine University School of Law Board of Visitors. "Robert E. McCarthy," *Martindale-Hubbell Law Directory,* 2001.

795. Ronald Brownstein and Nina Easton, *Reagan's Ruling Class: Portraits of the President's Top One Hundred Officials* (New York: Pantheon Books, 1983), 427–428.

796. Nancy Blodgett, "The Ralph Naders of the Right," *ABA Journal,* 70 (May, 1984).

797. "W. Glenn Campbell," Hoover Institution, www-hoover.stanford.edu/bios/campbell.html (December 10, 2001).

798. "Contact List for Editors and Reporters," www.pacficlegal.org/miscell/media.htm (November 13, 2001).

799. "Pacific Legal Foundation Changes Leadership."

800. "Contact List for Editors and Reporters."

801. Established in 1974, the Lincoln Institute of Land Policy is a nonprofit educational institution. The Institute describes its purpose as "to study and teach about land policy, including land economics and land taxation. A major portion of the Institute's support comes from the Lincoln Foundation, established in 1947 by Cleveland industrialist John C. Lincoln." "Lincoln Institute home," www.lincolninst.edu/main.html (December 4, 2001).

802. "Pacific Legal Foundation Changes Leadership."

803. Robert K. Best, "The Supreme Court Becomes Serious about Takings Law: The *First Church, Keystone* and *Irving* Cases (Part 1)"; *Zoning and Planning Law Report,* 10, no. 135 (1987). Robert K. Best, "The Supreme Court Becomes Serious about Takings Law: *Nollan* Sets New Rules for Exactions (Part 2)," *Zoning and Planning Law Report,* 10, no.

153 (1987).

804. Robert K. Best et al., "Evolution and Thumbnail Sketch of Takings Law," SB14 ALI-ABA 1, 5 (1996).

805. Robert K. Best, "All Dressed Up but Where Do We Go?" C997 A.L.I.-A.B.A. 223 (1995).

806. *Nollan v. California Coastal Comm'n*, 483 U.S. 825 (1987).

807. "Unique Public Issue Law Firm Formed," *Business Wire*, June 17, 1991.

808. After leaving PLF, Corry was recruited by extreme conservative Rep. Charles Canady (R-Fla.) to work on the staff of the U.S. House of Representatives Judiciary Committee's subcommittee on the Constitution, focusing on civil rights and affirmative action issues. *Roll Call* reported that Canady chose him based on the reputation he gained in conservative circles for his legal work in dismantling California's affirmative action programs. Damon Chappie, "Panel Counsel Arrested on Gun Charges Judiciary Staffer Accused of Aiming Rifle at Car," *Roll Call*, August 6, 1998. Corry was sentenced to thirty-five days in jail after pleading guilty to assault and possession of a firearm. John McCaslin, "Inside the Beltway," *Washington Times*, October 23, 1998, A6.

809. "Robert John Corry, Jr.," *Martindale-Hubbell Law Directory*, 2001.

810. Maura Dolan, "Giving the Right Its Day in Court; Taking on Liberals on Their Own Turf, the Pacific Legal Foundation Emerges as a Potent Public Interest Advocate. A Favorite Target; Big Government," *Los Angeles Times*, February 8, 1996, A1.

811. "Robert John Corry, Jr.," *Martindale-Hubbell Law Directory*.

812. At issue in this case was whether a redistricting plan that takes into account voters' race is constitutional in compliance with the Voting Rights Act.

813. At issue in this case was whether Amendment 2 to Colorado's state constitution, prohibiting any governmental protection to a class of people based on sexual orientation, should be subjected to strict scrutiny under the Fourteenth Amendment.

814. Along with briefs filed by Charles Cooper; Jay Sekulow and Keith Fournier of the American Center for Law and Justice Family Life Project; Steven McFarland of the Christian Legal Society; David Myers and Wendell Bird of Concerned Women for America; Michael Carvin and Robert Bork for Equal Rights Not Special Rights, Inc.; and Melissa Wells-Petry for Family Research Council.

815. At issue in this case was whether a state university that excluded a student publication from receiving student activity funds because of its religious messages was in violation of the Establishment Clause of the First Amendment.

816. At issue in this case was whether Congress's attempt to impose gun control through the implementation of the Gun Free School Zones Act went beyond the power of Congress under the Commerce Clause.

817. At issue in this case was whether an employer's fetal-protection policy, implicitly directed only at women, was permissible under the safety exception to the "bona fide occupational qualification" analysis under the Pregnancy Discrimination Act's amendment to Title VII.

818. At issue in this case was whether the Federal Communications Commission's affirmative action policies violated the equal protection clause of the Fifth Amendment.

819. Other attorneys also filing briefs urging reversal included Charles Cooper and Michael Carvin on behalf of the Associated General Contractors of America; William Pendley for Mountain States Legal Foundation; and Daniel Popeo and Paul Kamenar for the Washington Legal Foundation.

820. "National Litigation Fellowships Announcement," www.pacificlegal.org/miscell/fellow.htm (December 6, 2001).

821. "U.S. Supreme Court Puts Tight Lid on Race Discrimination in Public Contracting; Pacific Legal Foundation: A Momentous Victory for Equal Opportunity,"

Business Wire, June 12, 1995.

822. Marcia Coyle, "Justices Tackle Term Limits, Guns, and Beer," *National Law Journal*, October 3, 1994, A1.

823. Anthony T. Caso, letter to California Community College Presidents, American Civil Rights Institute website, www.acri.org/209/plf.htm (March 13, 2002).

824. Anthony T. Caso, "Supreme Court Preview: Compelled Financing of Expressive Activities," *The Federalist Society for Law & Public Policy Free Speech and Election Law Practice Group News*, www.fed-soc.org/Publications/practicegroupnewsletters/ free speech&electionlaw/SupremeCourt-freev3i1.htm (December 1, 2001).

825. Burling is also vice chairman for programs of the Federalist Society's Environmental Law and Property Rights Practice Group (1998–2001) and past vice chairman for pro bono activities (1998).

826. The Lone Mountain Coalition, "The Lone Mountain Compact: Principles for Preserving Freedom and Livability in America's Cities and Suburbs," *Independent Institute*, December 1, 2001.

827. The Lone Mountain Coalition includes members from an impressive array of groups on the Right: the Hoover Institution; the Heritage Foundation; the Acton Institute for the Study of Religion and Liberty; the Foundation for Research on Economics and the Environment; the National Taxpayers Union; the Institute for Justice; the Center for the Study of Public Choice; the Cascade Policy Institute; the Commonwealth Foundation; the Claremont Institute; Malcolm Wallop of the Frontiers of Freedom; Pacific Research Institute; the Manhattan Institute; Cato Institute; the Competitive Enterprise Institute; the Hudson Institute; the Law and Economics Center at George Mason University; and the Reason Public Policy Institute.

828. "PLF Media Resources," www.pacificlegal.organization/miscell/media.htm (December 1, 2001).

829. "Court Invalidates No-Growth Initiative," *Business Wire*, October 25, 1988.

830. 483 U.S. 825 (1987) (must be a close nexus between property burdens and regulatory benefits).

831. See, for example, *Matthews v. Bay Head Improvement Ass'n.,* 95 N.J. 306 (1984), *cert. denied,* 496 U.S. 821 (1984).

832. See website, www.database.townhall.com/heritage/theguide/guide.CFM.

833. Dan Morain, "Oakland Schools Get the Word: Fight Campus Crime," *Los Angeles Times*, December 8, 1986.

834. Ibid.

835. *Hi-Voltage Wire Works, Inc. v. City of San Jose,* 24 Cal. 4th 537 (2000).

836. See www.adversity.net/c13_tbd.htm.

837. Maura Dolan, "Prop. 209 to Face Test in High Court," *Los Angeles Times*, www.usc.eedu/dept/education/CMMR/NEWS/L.A.Times_Sept2_99.html (September 2, 1999).

838. "Race and Sex Preferences Continue Despite Proposition 209," www.pacificlegal.org/press_releases/prendb.htm (May 8, 2001).

839. Ibid.

840. Ibid.

841. Rebecca Trounson, "UC Admissions Plan Would De-Emphasize Grades, Tests; Regents: Panel Endorses Policy, but Critics Call It a Bid to Restore Race-based Preferences," *Los Angeles Times*, November 15, 2001.

842. Rebecca Trounson and Kenneth R. Weiss, "UC Admissions to Weigh 'Personal Achievement'; Education: A Process That Emulates the Ivy League Will Have Greatest Impact at Berkeley and UCLA," *Los Angeles Times*, November 19, 2001.

843. Matthew Tresaugue, "UC Weighs Choices Change—Regents: The Board Votes

Today on a New Way to Select Students for UCLA, Berkeley and San Diego," *Press-Enterprise* (Riverside, CA), November 15, 2001.

844. Howard Mintz, "Suit Claims Gilroy Using Race in Placing Students," *San Jose Mercury News*, November 15, 2001.

845. "Pacific Legal Foundation Says High Court Ruling against 'Racial Gerrymandering' a Victory for Equal Protection," *U.S. Newswire*, June 30, 1995.

846. "About Southeastern Legal Foundation," Southeastern Legal Foundation, www.southeasternlegal.org/document.asp?doc=aboutus (December 21, 2001).

847. Houck, "With Charity for All" (quoting "Message from the President and Chairmen of the Board," *SELF, Third Annual Report 1* [1979]).

848. Carlos Campos, "Legal Group's Action Stirs Concern; Is It Constitutional Watchdog or Right's 'Attack Dog?'" *Atlanta Journal & Constitution*, July 11, 1999, p. 2D.

849. Jonathan Ringel, "Southeastern: Bigger, Meaner Gadfly," *Fulton County Daily Report*, August 15, 1996 (quoting Matthew Glavin at an unidentified Washington news conference).

850. Blodgett, "The Ralph Naders of the Right."

851. Houck, "With Charity for All."

852. Ibid.

853. Blodgett, "The Ralph Naders of the Right."

854. Houck, "With Charity for All" (citing information provided in SLF's tax forms).

855. Houck, "With Charity for All" (note 433), citing SLF's *First Annual Report* (1977), which listed as contributors Alabama Assoc. General Contractors; Alabama Gas; American Business Products; American Cast Iron Pipe; Atlanta Gas Light; Chevron, U.S.; Cooper Industries; Deering-Milliken; Dow Chemical; Duke Power; Eli Lilly; Ethyl Corp.; Exxon; Florida Power & Light; Flowers Industries; General Motors; Georgia Ass'n. of Realtors; Georgia Pac.; Gold Kist, Inc.; Gulf Oil; Irby Construction; J.A. Jones Construction; Kimberly Clark; S.S. Kresge; Mobil; National Bank of Georgia; Pepsi Co.; Redfern Food; R. J. Reynolds; Rohm & Haas; Royal Crown Cola; Sears Roebuck; Shell Oil; Southern Bell; South Carolina Electric & Gas; Southern Co.; Stauffer Chem.; Tenneco; Texas Transmission Gas; Textiles, Inc.; Union Oil; and Winn-Dixie Stores.

856. Ibid., citing SLF, *Fifth Annual Report* (1981).

857. SLF Incorporation Papers, filed with the State of Georgia on January 14, 1976.

858. "History of the SLF," www.southeasternlegal.org/document.asp?doc=history (December 21, 2001).

859. Frank LoMonte, "Foundation Is Answer to ACLU," *Florida Times-Union*, May 6, 1996, A5.

860. "About SLF," *Southeastern Legal Foundation*, www.southeasternlegal.org/document.asp?doc=history (December 21, 2001).

861. See *Tennessee Valley Auth. v. Hill,* 437 U.S. 153 (1978).

862. Campos, "Legal Group's Action Stirs Concern."

863. *Clinton v. Glavin,* 525 U.S. 924 (1998).

864. James Dao, "Census Ruling Reignites a Partisan Battle," *New York Times*, January 27, 1999, A17.

865. See Matthew J. Glavin, "Importance of the Census Debate," *Southeastern Legal Foundation*, www.southeasternlegal.org/p9710061.htm (June 7, 2000).

866. In the most recent term, however, a divided Supreme Court rendered a decision that may moderate somewhat the overall impact of the *Glavin* case. In *Utah v. Evans*, 122 S.Ct. 2191 (2002), the State of Utah challenged the Department of Commerce's use of "hot-deck imputation" to ascertain more precisely the population for purposes of congressional apportionment. This method of population imputation in the 2000 Census led to Utah's loss of a congressional seat, which was gained by North Carolina. The Supreme Court rejected

Utah's challenge, holding that such methodology does not amount to the kind of statistical sampling held prohibited in *Glavin*. Of course, any resulting battles concerning redistricting in light of the loss of a congressional seat could very well lead to additional rounds of litigation over issues including whether minorities are adequately protected from unconstitutional dilutions of their voting power.

867. Steven A. Holmes, "Ideas and Trends; Down about the Count," *New York Times*, April 9, 2000, 5 (quoting the language of the Senate resolution).

868. Rhonda Cook, "Census Bureau Overstepping Purpose, Attorney Contends," *Arkansas Democrat-Gazette*, April 3, 2000, A3.

869. Ibid.

870. Holmes, "Ideas & Trends."

870. *Metro Broad., Inc. v. FCC*, 497 U.S. 547 (1990).

872. *Croson*, 488 U.S. 469.

873. *Northeastern Fla. Chapter of Associated Gen. Contractors v. City of Jacksonville*, 508 U.S. 656, 666 (1993).

874. Patricia Mayes, "Legal Foundation Attempting to Dismantle Affirmative Action," *Southeastern Legal Foundation*, www.southeasternlegal.org/newsdescr.asp?RI=34 (December 21, 2001).

875. See, for example, *Associated Gen. Contractors*, 508 U.S. *at* 666; *Croson*, 488 U.S. 469; *Jan. R. Smith Constr. Co. v. DeKalb County*, 18 F. Supp. 2d 1365 (1998).

876. In which the Supreme Court permitted a voluntary affirmative action plan in a steel company's in-plant craft training program, *United Steelworkers of America v. Weber*, 443 U.S. 193 (1979).

877. Ibid.

878. *Croson*, 488 U.S. 469 (1989). See southeasternlegal.org/document.asp?doc=history.

879. See *Northern Florida Chapter of the Associated Gen. Contractors v. City of Jacksonville*, 508 U.S. 656 (1993); see also Southeastern Legal Foundation, *Affirmative Action Backgrounder* (Dec. 21, 2001), www.southeasternlegal.org/newsdescr.as?RI=33.

880. Ibid.

881. Staci Rosche, "How Conservative Is the Rehnquist Court? Three Issues, One Answer," 65 *Fordham L. Rev.* 2685, 2699 (1997).

882. See Peter H. Schuck, "Affirmative Action: Past, Present and Future," 20 *Yale L. & Pol'y Rev.* 1, 54 n. 267 (2002).

883. See *Regents of University of Cal. v. Bakke*, 438 U.S. 912 (1978).

884. Schuck, *supra* n.267 at 54.

885. Brent E. Simmons, "Reconsidering Strict Scrutiny of Affirmative Action," 2 *Mich. J. Race & L.* 51, 58 (1996).

886. Rosche, *supra* at 2699.

887. Michael Wells, "Naked Politics, Federal Court Law, and the Canon of Acceptable Arguments," 47 *Emory L.J.* 89, 121 n.189 (1998). See also Gene R. Nichol, Jr., *New Challenges in Voting: The Practice of North Carolina Law School*, 72 *U. Colo. L. Rev.* 1029, 1037 (2001). Nichol argues that "the Supreme Court's most generous standing decisions allow white plaintiffs to challenge discriminatory alimony schemes, or affirmative action admissions in professional schools, or racial set-aside programs, or the drawing of legislative districts in ways that seek to increase the representation of Blacks and Latinos," but that, "on the other hand, [the court] has been at its stingiest in denying standing to minority plaintiffs seeking to challenge exclusionary zoning practices, abusive police practices, tax-exempt status for racially discriminatory private schools, or biased child support enforcement schemes."

888. *Lee General Contractors, Inc. v. City of Atlanta, Georgia*, Civil Action No. 1:99-

CV-2194 at 3, 10/22/99.

889. See discussion between Bobbie Battista, Matthew Glavin, and Jabari Simama, spokesman for the City of Atlanta, *CNN Talkback Live*, August 26, 1999, Transcript No. 99082600V14.

890. Ibid.

891. Campos, "Legal Group's Action Stirs Concern."

892. "Citizen's Petition to End Atlanta's Illegal Affirmative Action Program," online version, www.southeasternlegal.org (December 5, 2001).

893. Carlos Campos, "Affirmative Action: Pickets Protest Legal Challenge to Preferences," *Atlanta Journal and Constitution,* September 12, 1999, 2D.

894. Frank J. Murray, "Clinton Resigns from Bar, Bets Deadline for Disbarment by Court," *Washington Times,* November. 10, 2001, A1.

895. Michelle Crouch, "City Agrees to Pay in Minority Suit; Contractor Will Get $300,000 for Being Passed Over on Bid," *Charlotte Observer*, March 1, 2002, 1A.

896. "SLF Declares Final Victory in Legal Challenge to Charlotte Affirmative Action Program," News Release, www.southeasternlegal.org/newsdescr.asp?RI=107 (March 13, 2002).

897. "Benign Busing Plan," *Atlanta Journal and Constitution*, April 15, 1999.

898. Ibid.

899. "DeKalb School Board Votes to Ax Busing Plan," *Atlanta Journal and Constitution*, April 13, 1999.

900. "Benign Busing Plan."

901. "DeKalb School Board Votes to Ax Busing Plan."

902. *Johnson v. Bd. of Regents of the Univ. of Ga.,* 263 F.3d 1234 (11th Cir. 2001).

903. Southeastern Legal Foundation, www.southeasternlegal.org/newsdescr.asp?RI=97 (December 5, 2001).

904. Joseph D'Agostino, "Conservative Spotlight," *Human Events Online,* www.humanevents.org/articles/05-28-01/spotlight.html (December 5, 2001).

905. For listing of SLF's statements related to campaign finance reform, see www.southeasternlegal.org/document.asp?doc=cfr (December 5, 2001).

906. See Seth Lewis, "Georgia to Look at Giving Driver's Licenses to Illegal Immigrants," www.cnsnews.com/Politics/archive/200108/POL20010820a.html (December 5, 2001).

907. "SLF Sends Demand Letter to Charlotte Mayor Challenging City Quota Program," www.southeasternlegal.org (December 8, 2001).

908. "Southeastern Legal Foundation," *Media Transparency.*

909. Sarah Scaife Foundation 1999 IRS Form 990.

910. "Southeastern Legal Foundation," *Media Transparency*, at www.mediatransparency.org/all_in_one_results.asp?Message=Southeastern+Legal+Foundation.

911. John M. Olin Foundation 1999 IRS Form 990.

912. "Southeastern Legal Foundation," *Media Transparency*.

913. Samuel R. Noble Foundation 1997 IRS Form 990.

914. Southeastern Legal Foundation 1999 IRS Form 990.

915. Ibid.

916. Ibid.

917. Ibid.

918. Michael Rowett, "Group Seeking to Disbar President," *Chattanooga Times/Chattanooga Free Press*, May 9, 2000, 2.

919. Southeastern Legal Foundation, www.southeasternlegal.org/newsdescr.asp?RI=75 (January 3, 2002).

920. *McConnell v. FEC*, No.02-cv-582 (D.DC filed Mar. 27, 2002).

921. Southeastern Legal Foundation Press Release, May 7, 2002, http://southeastern-legal.org/newsdescr.asp?RI=127.

922. Southeastern Legal Foundation, 1999 IRS Form 990 (for fiscal year ending June 30, 2000).

923. Don Plummer, "Conservative Foundation's Leader Quits, Denies Charges," *Atlanta Journal and Constitution,* October 5, 2000, 1E.

924. Nancy O. Perry, "Moving Mountains: Kathy Barco and Barco-Duval Engineering," *Harvard Business School Bulletin Online,* February 1999, www.alumni.hbs.edu/bulletin/1999/february/family/barco.html (December 20, 2001).

925. See *Associated General Contractors of Greater Florida, Inc., Northeastern Florida Region,* www.personal.mia.bellsouth.net/jax/a/g/agcne/agcne.htm.

926. 508 U.S. 656 (1993).

927. *Governor's Appointments Office,* September 2001, www.myflorida.com /myflorida/government/bushteam/pdfs/sept2001_vac.pdf. (December 20, 2001).

928. Karen Brune Mathis, "Warehouse Wins JEDC Approval," *Florida Times-Union,* March 10, 2000, C-1.

929. Ann Davis, "Chip Off the Old Block?; Griffin Bell Sr. and Jr.," *National Law Journal,* December 16, 1996, A4.

930. Jonathan Ringel, "Griffin B. Bell Succeeds Proctor as Foundation Chief," *Fulton County Daily Report,* November 23, 1996.

931. Ibid.

932. Davis, "Chip Off the Old Block?"

933. Dick Williams, "Columnist Kent Will Re-energize Southeastern Legal Foundation," www.atlanta.bcentral.com/atlanta/stories/2001/04/16/editorial1.html (December 5, 2001).

934. Ibid.

935. "Phil Kent Biography," www.southeasternlegal.org/document.asp?doc=biokent (December 5, 2001).

936. "Kent Leaves Paper to Lead Foundation," *Augusta Chronicle Online,* www.au-gustachronicle.com/stories/041201/opi_240-5454.000.shtml (December 5, 2001).

937. "Phil Kent Biography," *Southeastern Legal Foundation.*

938. "Florida Farm Bureau Seeks Trade Agreement Exemption for Import-Sensitive Crops," *PR Newswire,* September 7, 2001.

939. Carl Loop, Jr., "On Effective Estate Planning," *Green Beam* website, www.green-beam.com/features/they092799.stm, July 1, 2002.

940. Phil Kent, "Latest Clinton Case Spotlights Fine Record of the SLF," *Augusta Chronicle,* May 10, 2000, A5.

941. "Mack Mattingly: AP Candidate Bios," *Associated Press Political Service.*

942. "Mattingly, Mack Francis, Complete Marquis Who's Who Biographies," *Marquis Who's Who,* July 6, 2000.

943. Ibid.

944. Ibid.

945. "Mack Mattingly: AP Candidate Bios."

946. "Defeated Senator Gets NATO Post," *Washington Dateline, Associated Press,* February 11, 1987.

947. "Prosperity Institute to Form Task Force on Information Exchange and Financial Privacy," *Prosperity Institute,* www.prosperity-institute.org/media/task_force.htm (December 12, 2001).

948. "The Novecon Companies," *Novecon Companies,* www.novecon.com/novcom/ htm (July 6, 2000).

949. "Edwin Meese, III," *Heritage Foundation,* www.heritage.org/staff/meese.htm (June 29, 2000).

950. "Guy W. Millner: AP Candidate Bios," *Associated Press Political Service,* November 30, 1998.

951. Ibid.

952. "Guy Millner: AP Candidate Bios," *Associated Press Political Service*, November 11, 1996.

953. Ibid.

954. "Election '98—Governor's Race: Issues and Answers," *Atlanta Journal and Constitution,* November 1, 1998, 2G.

955. "Guy Millner: AP Candidate Bios," November 30, 1998.

956. Ibid.

957. Ibid.

958. Peter J. Kent, "Ralph Reed to Speak at Crews Fund-Raiser," *Atlanta Journal and Constitution,* December 18, 1997, 17G; George Archibald, "Christian Coalition Settles Workers' Race-Bias Lawsuits," *Washington Times,* January 3, 2002.

959. Edwin J. Feulner, "Welcome," Leadership for America 2000, *Heritage Foundation,* www.heritage.org/leadership/ (December 18, 2001).

960. "In Depth: Atlanta's Wealthiest People," *Atlanta Business Chronicle,* July 10, 1998.

961. Stacy D. Johnson, "Noble Remembered as Man Full of Generosity, Integrity," *Daily Oklahoman,* September 24, 1992, 6.

962. Samuel Roberts Noble Foundation 1998 IRS Form 990 (covering 11/1/98 to 10/31/99).

963. Samuel Roberts Noble Foundation 1999 IRS Form 990 (covering 11/1/99 to 10/31/00).

964. Ibid.

965. "Noble Foundation Aids Think Tank," *Daily Oklahoman,* February 19, 1998, 7.

966. Richard Morin and Claudia Deane, "The Ideas Industry; WTO Remains a Hot Topic for 2000," *Washington Post,* December 21, 1999, A39.

967. Margaret Rankin, "Heritage Foundation Counts Its Blessings," *Washington Times,* December 10, 1999, C12.

968. "Noble, Edward Everett," *Complete Marquis Who's Who,* 1988.

969. Don Plummer, "Conservative Foundation's Leader Quits, Denies Charges; Glavin Says Resignation Would Let Him 'Protect My Family' from the Glare of Public Indecency Case," *Atlanta Journal and Constitution,* October 5, 2000, 1E.

970. Rochelle L. Stanfield, "Synfuels Chief Says He Did It for a Noble Cause," *National Journal,* 18, no. 8 (February 22, 1986): 458.

971. Ibid.

972. Robert E. Rivers, Jr., Clerk of the House, Georgia House of Representatives, 1995/1996 Sessions, HR 1178 – Noble, Edward E.; commend, 01/02/97, *Georgia House of Representatives,* www2.state.ga.us/Legis/1995_96/leg/fulltext/hr1178.htm.

973. Stanfield, "Synfuels Chief Says He Did It for a Noble Cause.".

974. "Edward Everett Noble," *Complete Marquis Who's Who,* 1995.

975. "About Noble Properties," www.nobleprop.com/aboutn.html (July 24, 2000).

976. Foundation of the Holy Apostles Inc., IRS Form 990, 2000; Actor Cordell, "Breakaway Church Faces Opposition to Building," *Atlanta Journal and Constitution,* February 20, 1992, H2.

977. "Tom and Marie Patton Make Landmark Commitment to Faculty Leadership," Georgia Tech Foundation Campaign website, *Campaign Quarterly* (Fall 1999), www.campaign.gatech.edu/html/campaignquarterly/Patton.html.

978. "Richard William Rahn," *Complete Marquis Who's Who,* 1995.

979. "Richard W. Rahn, Ph.D., Senior Fellow," Discovery Institute, www.discovery.org/fellows/rahn/index.html (July 6, 2000).

980. "Officers of the Prosperity Institute," www.prosperity-institute.org/officers/ (December 19, 2001).

981."Mission of the Prosperity Institute," www.prosperity-institute.org/mission/ (December 19, 2001).

982. "Prosperity Institute Press Release 7/16/2001: 'Prosperity Institute to Form Task Force on Information Exchange and Financial Privacy,'" www.prosperity-institute.org/media/task_force.htm (December 19, 2001).

983. "Officers of the Prosperity Institute."

984. "Prosperity Institute Press Release, 7/16/2001."

985. "Speakers Take on Issues of Privacy and Policy," *Pittsburgh Post-Gazette*, March 16, 2000, B3.

986. "Richard W. Rahn, Ph.D., Senior Fellow," Discovery Institute website (July 6, 2000).

987. Ibid.

988. "Mission," American Council for Capital Formation and ACCF Center for Policy Research, www.accf.org/Mission.htm (December 19, 2001).

989. "Richard W. Rahn, Ph.D., Senior Fellow," Discovery Institute Web Site (July 6, 2000).

990. "Mission."

991. Ibid.

992. "Richard W. Rahn, Complete Marquis Who's Who."

993. Fred Barnes, "Inventanegro, Inc.," *New Republic*, Vol. 192, April 15, 1985, 9.

994. Ibid.

995. Ibid.

996. Ibid.

997. Clint Bolick and Susan Nestleroth, *Opportunity 2000: Creative Affirmative Action Strategies for a Changing Workforce,* (Washington, D.C.: U.S. Department of Labor, 1988).

998. Ron Nissimov, "An Evolving Debate: Baylor Professors Concerned That Research Center Is Front for Promoting Creationism in Classrooms," *Houston Chronicle*, July 2, 2000, A1.

999. "Richard W. Rahn, Ph.D., Senior Fellow," Discovery Institute website (July 6, 2000).

1000. "Richard W. Rahn," *Complete Marquis Who's Who*.

1001. "Richard W. Rahn, Ph.D., Senior Fellow," Discovery Institute website (July 6, 2000).

1002. Board membership taken from *Affirmative Action Update* (June 14, 1999), Georgia Black Chamber of Commerce, www.accessatlanta.com/community/groups /gbcc/Affirmative_Action_U.html (December 12, 2001).

1003. "Ben Blackburn Biography, Ben Blackburn Papers," University of Georgia Libraries, www.libs.uga.edu/russell/collections/blackburn.html (December 19, 2001).

1004. Among other notable affiliations, Simon was a Knight of Malta and had served on the boards of the rightist Hoover Institution and the Halliburton Company, of which Vice President Richard Cheney was chairman and chief executive officer. "Biographical Sketch of William E. Simon," Department of the Treasury The Learning Vault, www.ustreas. gov/opc/opc0068.html (December 23, 2001).

1005. Maryon Allen, "Style; Maryon Allen's Washington," *Washington Post,* May 25, 1980, L12.

1006. "Legal Services Foe Is Offered Seat on Board."

1007. Ibid.

1008. "Ben Blackburn Papers," www.libs.uga.edu/russell/collections/blackburn.html (December 17, 2001).

1009. "New Southeastern Legal Foundation President Named," *United Press International*, Regional News, January 2, 1985.

1010. See SLF Incorporation Papers, filed with the State of Georgia on January 14, 1976.

1011. "Flowers, William Howard, Jr.," *Complete Marquis Who's Who*, June 25, 1997.

1012. "Flowers Industries Chairman Emeritus and Baking Industry Leader W. H. Flowers, Jr. Passes Away," Financial News, *PR Newswire*, May 2, 2000.

1013. Thomas Riehle and Deborah Galembo, "People," *National Journal*, May 26, 1984.

1014. DeWayne Wickham, "Atlanta Mayor Punches Back on Affirmative Action," *USA Today*, October 31, 2000, 17A.

1015. Jim Galloway "Columnist Takes Over Foundation; Scandal Repair Task: Indecency Charge against Predecessor a Hurdle for Conservative Group," *Atlanta Journal and Constitution*, April 30, 2001, 1B; Rebecca Schwartzman, "Southeastern Legal Foundations Hogue Catches Media Wave," *Fulton County Daily Report*, December 12, 2000.

1016. Carlos Campos, "Legal Group's Action Stirs Concern," *Atlanta Journal and Constitution*, July 11, 1999, 2D.

1017. Matthew Glavin, "Health Care and a Free Society," *Imprimis*, www.skepticfiles.org/icr/impr9311.htm (December 20, 2001).

1018. "New Rightist Think Tank Roster," *National Journal* 20, no. 40 (October 1, 1988): 2457.

1019. Steve Campbell, "Conservative Ex-Mainer Leads Effort to Disbar President," *Portland Press Herald*, June 4, 2000, 2C.

1020. Ibid.

1021. Joan Vennochi, "Bean Counters; The Private Sector," *Boston Globe,* January 6, 1993, 53.

1022. Nancy Perry, "Gay-Rights Law Magnifies Right-Wing Schism; Carolyn Cosby's Secular Movement Won't Join the Referendum Fray, Leaving It to Religious Coalitions," *Portland Press Herald*, May 25, 1997, 1A.

1023. According to the Center for Responsive Politics "Open Secrets" database, www.opensecrets.org/ (February 27, 2002), Bean and her husband Donald donated $10,000 each to the U.S. Constitution party in 1999. See U.S. Constitution Party, *Constitution Party 2000 National Platform*, www.constitutionparty.com/ustp-99p1.html#taxes (February 27, 2002); see also Kristin Kolb-Angelbeck, "Linda Bean, A Right-Wing Dream," *In These Times,* December 25, 2000, 11.

1024. Campos, "Legal Group's Action Stirs Concern."

1025. "Board of Governors," Georgia Public Policy Foundation, www.gppf.org/about-gppf/boardofgovs.html (December 20, 2001).

1026. "About Us," www.gppf.org/aboutgppf/aboutgppf.html (December 20, 2001).

1027. George Edmonson and David K. Secrest, "On Washington; The Georgia Connection," *Atlanta Journal and Constitution,* November 18, 2001, 17A.

1028. "The Georgia Public Policy Foundation's Tenth Anniversary Dinner and Presentation of the 2001 Freedom Award to Senator Phil Gramm," www.gppf.org/events/fadinfo.htm (December 20, 2001).

1029. Ibid.

1030. Mrs. Deen Day Smith is the widow of Cecil B. Day, founder of the Days Inn motel chain and chairwoman of Cecil B. Day Investment Co., which she founded upon her husband's death. Through the Cecil B. Day Foundation, Smith funds conservative Christian churches and fellowships. Cecil B. Day Foundation's annual grants to conservative Christian causes totaled $1,507,409 in 1998. See Cecil B. Day Foundation IRS Form 990,

1998, 1.

1031. Ringel, "Griffin B. Bell Succeeds Proctor as Foundation Chief."

1032. "Amos R. McMullian of Flowers Industries Elected Chairman of Southeastern Legal Foundation," *PR Newswire*, November 19, 1991.

1033. Carlos Campos, "Affirming His Actions," *Atlanta Journal and Constitution*, October 3, 1999, 6C.

1034. "Amos Ryals McMullian biography," *Standard and Poor's Corporation Register of Directors and Executives*, 2001.

1035. "Barr to Assume Presidency of Southeastern Legal Foundation," *PR Newswire*, January 5, 1990.

1036. Ibid.

1037. "Amos R. McMullian of Flowers Industries Elected Chairman."

1038. Carlos Campos, "City Sued on Affirmative Action; Foundation Follows Through on its Threat to Fight Atlanta Set-Asides," *Atlanta Journal and Constitution*, August 27, 1999, A1.

1039. Carlos Campos, "Racial Rhetoric Escalates over City Contracts," *Atlanta Journal and Constitution*, July 22, 1999, 1A.

1040. Laurie Mansfield, "Plans Halted for Savannah Foods Boycott," *Savannah Morning News*, July 28, 1999.

1041. "Guest of Honor," *Jet*, September 3, 2001, 14.

1042. Carlos Campos, "Adviser Quits Legal Board," *Atlanta Journal and Constitution*, July 23, 1999, 1C.

1043. Tony Mauro, "Silent Justice: The Clarence Thomas Story; Political Book Notes: Jurist's Prudence; Review," *Washington Monthly*, 33, no. 11 (November 1, 2001): 50.

1044. "Representative Robert L. Barr," *Congressional Information Service, Inc.*, 2000.

1045. "Robert L. Barr, Jr.: AP Candidate Bios," *Associated Press Political Service*, November 30, 1998.

1046. "Congressman Bob Barr Biography," House of Representatives, www.house.gov/barr/bio.htm (December 20, 2001).

1047. "Awards Received by Representative Barr," *Bob Barr* website, www.bobbarr.org/document.asp?doc=awardbb (December 20, 2001).

1048. Thomas B. Edsall, "Barr Spoke to White Supremacy Group," *Washington Post*, December 11, 1998, A23; Allen G. Breed, "Organization That Lott, Barr Addressed Defends Positions; Council of Conservative Citizens Says Charges of Racism Are Political Ploy," *Milwaukee Journal Sentinel*, February 7, 1999, 15.

1049. "Robert J. Proctor, Practice Profiles," *Martindale-Hubbell Law Directory*, 2001.

1050. Campos, "Legal Group's Action Stirs Concern."

1051. Ibid.

1052. Ringel, "Southeastern: Bigger, Meaner Gadfly."

1053. R. Robin McDonald, "Not Even Parks Can Help GOP in Map Fight," *Fulton County Daily Report*, August 31, 2001.

1054. Jim Galloway, "Columnist Takes over Foundation; Scandal Repair Task: Indecency Charge against Predecessor a Hurdle for Conservative Group," *Atlanta Journal and Constitution*, April 30, 2001, 1B.

1055. "L. Lynn Hogue, Professor of Law," Georgia State University College of Law, law.gsu.edu/faculty/HogueL/ (December 21, 2001).

1056. "L. Lynn Hogue, Chairman, Legal Advisory Board," www.southeasternlegal.org/document.asp?doc=biohogue (December 21, 2001).

1057. "Conservative Chief Gets Probation for Indecency," *United Press International*, December 15, 2000.

1058. Atlanta Lawyers Chapter, Federalist Society for Law and Public Policy, www.fed-soc.org/Chapters/Atlanta.htm (December 21, 2001).

1059. "Southeastern Legal Foundation Staff, Valle Simms Dutcher," www.southeasternlegal.org/document.asp?doc=staff (December 21, 2001).

1060. "Affirmative Action Backgrounder," Plaintiff's attorneys of record, www.southeasternlegal.org/p99082602.htm (June 2, 2000).

1061. 515 U.S. 900 (1995).

1062. Ibid.

1063. "Affirmative Action Backgrounder."

1064. Rebecca McCarthy, "UGA, Regents Will Not Appeal Admissions Ruling," *Atlanta Journal and Constitution,* November 10, 2001, 1H.

1065. James Salzer, "UGA Admits Student, Ending Bias Litigation," *Atlanta Journal and Constitution,* December 1, 2001, 8H.

1066. Southeastern Legal Foundation, www.southeasternlegal.org, June 16, 2000.

1067. *Webster v. Fulton County,* 235 F.3d 1347 (11th Cir. 2000).

1068. Ibid.

1069. "D. Burke Kibler III: Practice Profiles Section," *Martindale-Hubbell Law Directory,* 2000.

1070. "D. Burke Kibler III," *Holland & Knight,* www.hklaw.com/lawyer 2.asp?id=BKIBLER (March 14, 2002).

1071. Ibid.

1072. Ibid.

1073. Ibid.

1074. As in Christian Right leader Franklin W. Graham's bitter denunciation of Islam as a whole as "a very evil and wicked religion." Ken Garfield, "Graham Stands by Comments on Islam," *Charlotte Observer,* November 19, 2001, 9A. Graham gave the invocation at George W. Bush's inauguration.

1075. Perhaps the most famous instance being Louisiana Republican Congressman Dr. John Cooksey's comment that "if I see someone [who] comes in that's got a diaper on his head and a fan belt wrapped around the diaper on his head, that guy needs to be pulled over." *National Journal's Congress Daily,* November 1, 2001.

1076. Perhaps the most striking instance of this was the report issued by the right-wing American Council of Trustees and Alumni, claiming "college and university faculty have been the weak link in America's response to the attack." Less noticed was the cultural thrust of the report, which called for more of a focus on Western civilization and criticized universities for adding courses on Islam because this "reinforced the mindset that it was America—and America's failure to understand Islam—that were to blame." "Up with Dissent," *Boston Globe,* November 20, 2001, A20.

1077. Michael Greve, formerly of the Center for Individual Rights, the key anti-affirmative action litigating organization, has long advocated just such a tying together across a range of issues of right-wing populism and sophisticated constitutional litigation to turn back the clock on mainstream democratic jurisprudence. See his *Real Federalism: Why It Matters, How It Could Happen* (Washington, D.C.: AEI Press, 1999).

1078. Ann Coulter, "Affirmative Action for Osama," www.townhall.com/columnists/anncoulter/archive.shtml (October 12, 2001).

1079. For instance, Harvard law professor Laurence Tribe, who enjoys a liberal reputation, told the *Los Angeles Times* that he cannot even imagine how law enforcement personnel can be expected to "disregard facts about ethnicity" while performing their jobs. Henry Weinstein, Michael Finnegan, and Teresa Watanabe, "Racial Profiling Gains Support as Search Tactic," *Los Angeles Times,* September 24, 2001, A1.

1080. Eric Lichtblau, "A Surprising Civil Rights About-Face for Ashcroft," *Los Angeles Times,* May 13, 2001, A1.

1081. Horace Cooper, "A Man for All Seasons; History Will Judge John Ashcroft a Statesman," *Washington Times*, October 11, 2001, A25.

1082. Roger Clegg, "Words for the President," *National Review*, June 7, 2001.

1083. Roger Clegg, "Profiling Terrorists," *National Review*, September 18, 2001.

1084. Rove told reporters that capturing a bigger share of Hispanic voters "was our mission and our goal" and warned Republicans that this goal would "require all of us in every way and every day working to get that done." Eric Schmitt, "Hispanic Voter Is Vivid in Parties' Crystal Ball," *New York Times*, April 9, 2001, A 14.

1085. Bolick, *Changing Course*, 122.

1086. Edward Walsh, "Bush Backs Minority Program; High Court Brief Defends DOT Contracting Plan," *Washington Post*, August 11, 2001, A10.

1087. For background on ACRI, see above.

1088. Clint Bolick has said, "the issue of race is radioactive for this administration." Charles Lane, "Affirmative Action Again Facing a Court Test," *Washington Post*, May 21, 2001, A2.

1089. Ward Connerly, "Losing the Soul of the GOP: Republicans Make a Rotten Peace—With Race Preferences," *National Review*, October 1, 2001.

1090. Lichtblau, "A Surprising Civil Rights About-Face for Ashcroft."

1091. Ward Connerly, "Don't Box Me In: An End to Racial Checkoffs," *National Review*, April 16, 2001. The proceedings have been published by the Federalist Society in "Civil Rights: The Use and Misuse of Statistics in Civil Rights Litigation," *Engage*, 2, November 2001, 21–31.

1092. This case was *Adarand Constructors, Inc. v. Mineta*, 534 U.S. 103 (2001) (No. 00-730). Edward Blum, "The Myth of Affirmative Access—Administration's Moment of Truth on Racial Quotas," *Washington Times*, December 5, 2001, A19.

1093. Ibid.

1094. Roger Clegg, "10 Rights Issues Bush Picks Could Topple—Several Standards May Be Rejected as Court Makeup Changes," *Fulton County Daily Report*, March 20, 2001.

1095. Ibid.

1096. Bolick, *The Affirmative Action Fraud*, 113.

1097. *Republican Party v. White*, 2002 U.S. Lexis 4883 (June 27, 2002). See also, Joe Hallett, "Should Ohio Stop Electing Judges?" *Columbus Dispatch*, April 8, 2001, 1G; Tony Mauro, "High Court to Decide if States Can Restrict Judicial Candidates' Speech," *Legal Intelligencer*, December 5, 2001, 4.

1098. Not to be confused with the Gates Millennium education grants sponsored by Microsoft's Bill Gates.

1099. Jones's official biography on the DOE website helpfully notes that he "served as Deputy Legal Affairs Secretary to California Governor Pete Wilson and as Counsel to the United States Senate Judiciary Committee in Washington, D.C, where he worked on nominations, constitutional law and civil rights issues for then-Chairman Orrin Hatch (R-UT)." See www.ed.gov/offices/OGC/jones.html, March 29, 2002.

1100. Brian W. Jones, "The U.S. Department of Education and Two Court Decisions Probe the Limits of 'Disparate Impact' Theory," *Civil Rights News* 3 no. 2. Jones has even criticized efforts to increase the number of Supreme Court clerks drawn from minority groups—ridiculing "the idea that racial identity lends a unique perspective to individuals, and therefore to the work they do." See Brian W. Jones, "A Supreme Fallacy: 'Diversity' and the Supreme Court," *Civil Rights News* 3 no. 1.

1101. *Alexander v. Sandoval*, 532 U.S. 275 (2001).

1102. The words of Washington Legal Foundation Legal Director Richard Samp. Jonathan Groner, "Advocacy Groups' Annual Report: Familiar Friends of the Court Have a Mixed Year—From the ACLU to the Washington Legal Foundation, None of the Groups

That File *Amicus* Briefs Got All They Wanted," *Legal Times,* July 2, 2001, 13.

1103. Julie R. F. Gerchik, "People Are Policy: Timothy Flanigan, Judicial Selection, and the Office of White House Counsel," *IDS Insights* 2, no. 1 (September 2001), available at www.idsonline.org/publications.html.

1104. Federalist Society, www.fed-soc.org/events/lawyersconvention/cheney.htm, March 29, 2002.

1105. The papers can be found at www.fed-soc.org/Publications/White%20Papers/nationalsecurity.htm, March 29, 2002.

1106. Jerry Seper, "Bush Taps Ex-Prosecutor for Civil-Rights Job; Boyd Has Aggressive Record vs. Crime," *Washington Times,* March 7, 2001, A6.

1107. At the Labor Home Page, an issue site of the Heritage Foundation. See "Affirmative Action," www.labor.org/workplace/affirm.html (December 9, 2001).

1108. "That's Amore?" *American Prospect,* February 11, 2002, 6.

1109. Ellen Nakashima and Thomas B. Edsall, "Ashcroft Personnel Moves Irk Career Justice Lawyers," *Washington Post,* March 15, 2002, A5.

1110. R. Robin McDonald, "DOJ Calls Two More from Atlanta—Federalist Society Ranks Depleted," *Fulton County Daily Report,* December 5, 2001. Spakovsky has served on the advisory board of the now-defunct Voting Integrity Project (VIP), which the *Palm Beach Post* reported was part of a nationwide "voter scrub" project designed to identify ineligible voters. VIP's founder is Helen R. Blackwell, wife of Morton Blackwell, head of the Leadership Institute, a key training institute for the right wing. Robert P. King and Joel Engelhardt, "Credibility of Voter Purging Questioned," *Palm Beach Post,* December 6, 2000, 13A. See also letter to the editor by VIP's former chair, Deborah M. Phillips, *Washington Post,* March 24, 2002, B6. Phillips ascribes the demise of VIP to a lack of funds after the 9-11 attacks, and denies that VIP had any role in purging voters in Florida.

1111. Ibid. Wiggins has also served as vice chairman of the Federalist Society Intellectual Property Practice Group.

1112. Jennifer Sergent, "Bitter Critic to Join U.S. Panel on Civil Rights," *Stuart News/Port St. Lucie News* (Stuart, FL), November 24, 2001, B5.

1113. Jackie Calmes, "Washington Wire," *Wall Street Journal,* November 16, 2001.

1114. Jennifer Cabranes Braceras, "Affirmative Action and Gender Equity: New Rules under Title IX?" *Civil Rights News* 3, no. 1.

1115. *United States v. Wilson,* 290 F.3d 347 (DC Cir. 2002).

1116. "An Uncivilized Welcome," *Washington Times,* December 9, 2001, B2.

1117. Charles Toutant, "Civil Rights Lawyers Commiserate over Roadblocks Erected by Court Rulings of Last Term Limited Causes of Action, Fee Applications," *New Jersey L. J.,* 2001.

1118. Leon Friedman, "Overruling the Court; The Supreme Court Has Been Interpreting Civil Rights Laws Narrowly. It's Time for Congress to Intervene," *American Prospect,* August 27, 2001, 12.

1119. Roger Clegg, "Dismissed!" *National Review Online,* November 28, 2001.

1120. Gary Orfield, "Schools More Separate: Consequences of a Decade of Resegregation," Civil Rights Project, Harvard University, July 2001, 3.

Index

About the Author

Lee Cokorinos is research director at the Institute for Democracy Studies (IDS) in New York, where he coordinates the Institute's research programs in law, reproductive rights, and religion. He has edited and contributed to the IDS investigative newsletter, *IDS Insights,* is the author of the IDS report *Antifeminist Organizations: Institutionalizing the Backlash,* and co-authored the IDS briefing papers *The Federalist Society and the Challenge to a Democratic Jurisprudence; Priests for Life: A New Era in Antiabortion Activism; The American Life League Enters Mexico: Recruiting Anti-Choice Activists for U.S. Right-wing Goals;* and *The Global Assault on Reproductive Rights: A Crucial Turning Point,* which was prepared for the 2000 Beijing + 5 United Nations conference. A former research consultant with the Public Policy Institute of Planned Parenthood Federation of America, Cokorinos has published path-breaking research on the Promise Keepers men's movement and edited *PK Watch* for the Nation Institute's Center for Democracy Studies. A graduate of Columbia University's Graduate School of Arts and Sciences, specializing in comparative politics, he has conducted extensive research on Southern African politics and African development issues and directed the Southern African Literature Society in Botswana.

The **Institute for Democracy Studies (IDS)** is a not-for-profit research and educational center founded in 1999 in response to the institutional growth of anti-democratic trends in the United States. Though it is largely recognized that fundamental and once secure centrist concepts of American democracy are under attack, there is little understanding of the forces that are eroding these long-held mainstream values. Through interdisciplinary and educational outreach programs in law, religion, and reproductive rights, IDS has a unique analytical capacity to monitor and report on the complex strategies and shifting patterns that are affecting such key issues as the separation of church and state, gender equality, diversity, and basic civil liberties.

Publications Available from the Institute for Democracy Studies

Priests for Life: A New Era in Antiabortion Activism, April 2001

The Federalist Society and the Challenge to a Democratic Jurisprudence, January 2001

Antifeminist Organizations: Institutionalizing the Backlash, April 2000

A Moment to Decide: The Crisis in Mainstream Presbyterianism, May 2000

The Global Assault on Reproductive Rights: A Crucial Turning Point, May 2000

The Assault on Diversity: Behind the Challenges to Racial and Gender Remedies, December 1999

The American Life League Enters Mexico: Recruiting Anti-Choice Activists for U.S. Right-Wing Goals, July 1999

President
Alfred F. Ross

Board of Directors
Amb. Robin C. Duke
Alfred F. Ross
Alfred R. Stern
Amb. William vanden Heuvel

Institute for Democracy Studies
177 East 87th Street, Suite 501
New York, NY 10128
Tel: 212-423-9237
Fax: 212-423-9352
info@idsonline.org
www.idsonline.org

The Institute for Democracy Studies is supported by generous contributions from foundations and individuals and is a 501(c)(3) tax-exempt organization.